CRUSADER CRIMINALS

CRUSADER CRIMINALS

The Knights Who Went Rogue in the Holy Land

STEVE TIBBLE

YALE UNIVERSITY PRESS
NEW HAVEN AND LONDON

For information about this and other Yale University Press publications, please contact:
U.S. Office: sales.press@yale.edu   yalebooks.com
Europe Office: sales@yaleup.co.uk   yalebooks.co.uk

Set in Adobe Garamond Pro by IDSUK (DataConnection) Ltd
Printed in Great Britain by Clays Ltd, Elcograf S.p.A

Library of Congress Control Number: 2024937313

ISBN 978-0-300-27607-7

A catalogue record for this book is available from the British Library.

10 9 8 7 6 5 4 3 2 1

Contents

CONTENTS

Maps and Plates

Maps

Plates

British Library, London, UK © British Library Board. All Rights Reserved / Bridgeman Images.

3. Scenes of banking and usury, from the Cocharelli Codex, British Library, MS 27695, fol. 8r. British Library, London, UK © British Library Board. All Rights Reserved / Bridgeman Images.

4. The Inner Gate of the citadel of Aleppo. Bernard Gagnon / CC BY-SA 3.0.

5. Mugging and violence with daggers, from the Magnus Erikssons landslag, Östgötalagens kyrkobalk, Uppsala University Library, B 68–., fol. 132v.

6. A gambling scene, illustrating the sin of avarice, from the Cocharelli Codex, British Library, MS 27695, fol. 12r. British Library, London, UK © British Library Board. All Rights Reserved / Bridgeman Images.

7. Scene in a tavern with men drinking, and below a cellarer passing up a drink, illustrating the sin of gluttony, from the Cocharelli Codex, British Library, MS 27695, fol. 14r.

8. Louis IX of France departing Aigues Mortes for Egypt on the Seventh Crusade, Bibliothèque nationale de France, Français 5716, fol. 39v.

9. Crusader leaders playing chess, by William of Tyre, Bibliotheque Municipale de Lyon, France.

10. Northern walls, Cairo. R Prazeres / CC BY-SA 4.0.

11. An assassination, from the Cocharelli Codex, British Library, MS 27695, fol. 9v. British Library, London, UK © British Library Board. All Rights Reserved / Bridgeman Images.

12. The assassination of Turanshah, from Guillaume de Saint-Pathus, *Vie et miracles de saint Louis*, Bibliothèque nationale de France, Français 5716, fol. 127v.

13. A horse thief confronts a camel thief, from *Maqāmāt*, Bodleian Library, MS Marsh 458, fol. 45a. © Bodleian Libraries, University of Oxford, CC-BY-NC 4.0.

14. The sack of Tripoli, from the Cocharelli Codex, British Library, MS 27695, fol. 5r.

Acknowledgements

This book has been the culmination of several years' research and many happy conversations. Dr Nic Morton and Professors Peter Edbury and Malcolm Barber have been extremely kind in sharing their insights and encyclopaedic knowledge of the Latin East. Their input has been greatly appreciated. Similarly, Professor Ronnie Ellenblum, with his uniquely creative and off-centre view of the subject, is greatly missed – his recent death was a sad loss to the academic community.

Many other friends and colleagues in the world of medieval studies have given freely of their time and support, including Professors Jonathan Harris and Jonathan Phillips of Royal Holloway College, University of London; Dr Chris Marshall; Dr James Doherty; Tom Morin; Alessandro Scalone; and Ronan O'Reilly. Other friends, and particularly David Butcher and Charles Masefield, have helped greatly with reading and suggestions.

A new addition to the family was a much loved consultant in the writing of *Crusader Criminals*. Baby Kit's piratical tendencies, finely honed in the soft play centres of north London, can be seen reflected, in sentiment at least, throughout Part VI.

This is my fourth book with Heather McCallum and the team at Yale University Press. They have been unfailingly professional –

ACKNOWLEDGEMENTS

challenging where necessary, but always supportive and a pleasure to work with. The book is much better for their help.

Finally, this book is dedicated to my wife, Dr Faith Tibble, partly for her support as an informal editor of good taste, steering me away from some of my more dangerous errors (generally related to what passes for my sense of humour) – but mostly for her love.

London and Hereford, 2024

Map 1. The Crusader States: The Latin Kingdom of Jerusalem.

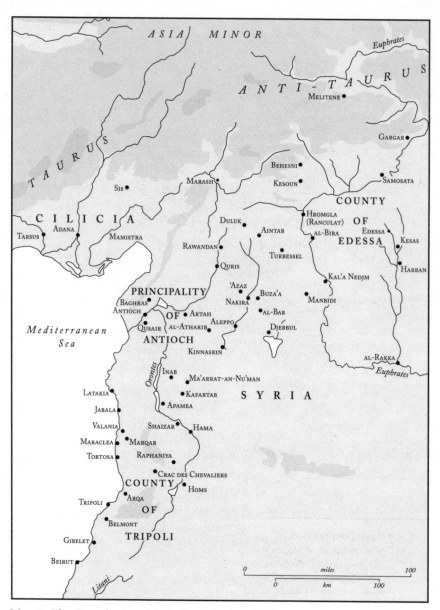

Map 2. The Crusader States: Tripoli, Antioch and Edessa.

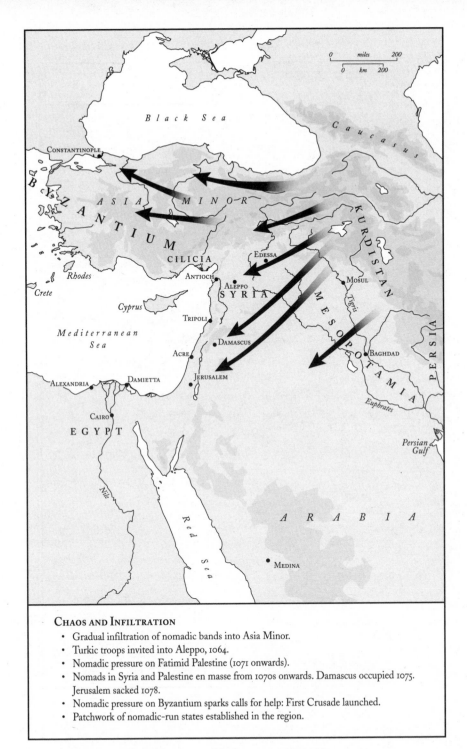

CHAOS AND INFILTRATION

- Gradual infiltration of nomadic bands into Asia Minor.
- Turkic troops invited into Aleppo, 1064.
- Nomadic pressure on Fatimid Palestine (1071 onwards).
- Nomads in Syria and Palestine en masse from 1070s onwards. Damascus occupied 1075. Jerusalem sacked 1078.
- Nomadic pressure on Byzantium sparks calls for help: First Crusade launched.
- Patchwork of nomadic-run states established in the region.

Map 3. Nomadic Activity in the Middle East, c.1064–1100.

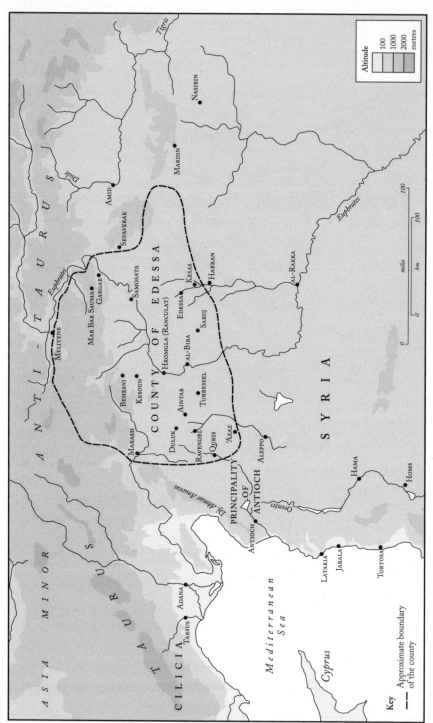

Map 4. The County of Edessa.

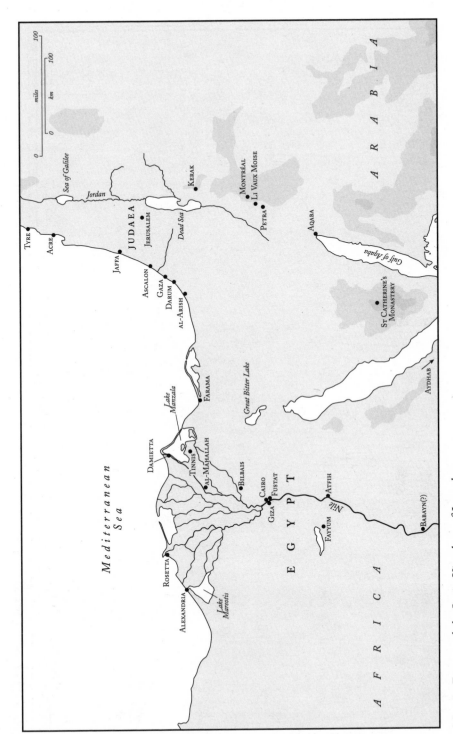

Map 5. Egypt and the Latin Kingdom of Jerusalem.

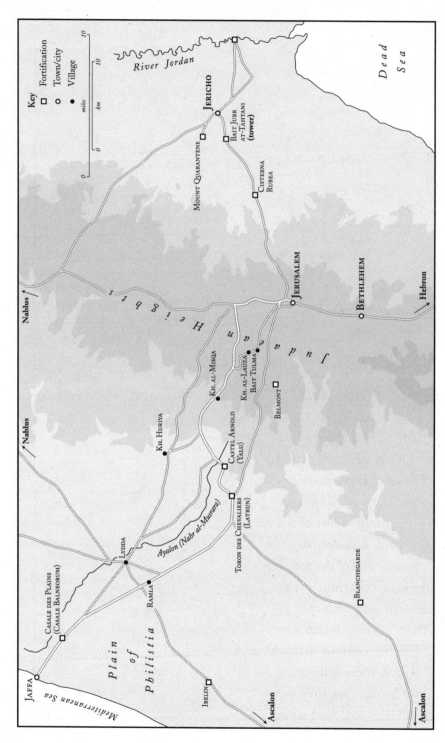

Map 6. A Pilgrim's Journey: Hell on the Road to Heaven.

Foreword

Crusader Criminals explores the dark, but very human, side of a violent time.

In writing three previous books about the crusades (*The Crusader Armies*, 2018; *The Crusader Strategy*, 2020; and *Templars: The knights who made Britain*, 2023), I tried to take a 'macro' view of events. I looked at the bigger issues which influenced the actions of participants, including those of which they were only vaguely aware at the time. I looked at broader anthropological and geographical forces, such as climate change, mass migration and the intuitive development of strategy. These all played a major, but often unacknowledged, part in the tumultuous events of the time.

But I was also conscious that these same forces affected activity at the opposite end of the social spectrum, too. Far smaller, more domestic, patterns of behaviour existed in parallel with these grander determinants of human history.

There is a rich 'micro' history of humanity waiting to be told, alongside the momentous activities of the kings and queens, the sultans and viziers: these individuals have their place and demand our attention, of course; but they are in no way representative of the lives that their subjects led. And while it is vital to rise above the actions of the celebrities to look at the broader forces at play, it is similarly important to duck under the headlines, to examine the impact they had on ordinary people and the ways in which those people responded to the extraordinary conditions of the time.

This book tries to do just that. It looks at the actions of those who are overlooked and underreported, with a particular focus on levels of criminality in this period of unceasing conflict. More importantly, it also tries to place those actions within the context of the bigger events and elemental forces that these people barely understood – forces which nonetheless shaped much of the daily fabric of their lives.

It is based on an academically robust use of the primary sources of the period. The stories are taken from factually based accounts of the crusaders and their opponents, whenever they are available. Where this is not possible, the gaps are filled by contemporaneous examples in comparable societies. The result is often shocking; but at the very least, it is an insight into areas of human activity which the chronicles and history books normally skate over.

We may judge them. We may not approve. But we will never – or hopefully never – be faced with the grim choices that they had to confront.

Part I

THE CRUSADER
CRIME WAVE

1

The Anthropology of Crusader Criminality

Round up the usual suspects.

> Captain Louis Renault, in the film *Casablanca* (1942)

Rounding up the 'usual suspects' is the perennial trope of lazy policing.

It combines the satisfying characteristics of expedience, prejudice and demographic profiling and puts them in one easy and compelling package – and that was just as true in the twelfth century as it is in the twenty-first.

The 'usual suspect' is, in most cases, relatively young; normally male; an outsider, perhaps rootless, without family or connections, or perhaps a foreigner; poor, maybe unemployed or underemployed; and perhaps someone who is accustomed to being armed, or from a group in which the carrying of weapons, such as knives, is overrepresented.

The laziness, then as now, is encouraged by a centrality of truth – the relatively small number of the 'usual suspects' in society are indeed vastly overrepresented in crime statistics. This is particularly the case for violent crime – largely anecdotally in the case of medieval crime in the Levant, as we shall see, but quantitatively and definitively in many other times and places. Crime, and especially serious crime, is massively

5

gendered, for instance – all crimes are far more likely to have been committed by men than by women; and the more serious the crime, the higher the proportion of male offenders.[1]

The big difference between the Holy Land in the time of the crusades and most other periods of history was that the 'usual suspects' did not need to be rounded up.

On the contrary, they rounded themselves up – in huge numbers and over extended periods of time. They threw themselves relentlessly into the political and social maelstrom that was the medieval Middle East. In doing so, they changed history on a grand scale and, at a more granular level, destroyed lives, families and communities.

This book is the strange story of how that happened – and how the forces which propelled such unusual demographic and anthropological surges found their extraordinary expression in the time of the crusades.

Like most aspects of his life, the sexual activities of Zengi, the powerful atabeg of Mosul, were turbulent.

Zengi got married in 1129–1130, but the honeymoon period was short. Within a month, his new wife saw the darker side of his temperament. Turkic politics were bloody, and she was the granddaughter of the man who had killed his father. Zengi began to brood compulsively about something that he must always have been aware of. Eventually, descending into one of his uncontrollable rages, and 'in a drunken stupor on the balcony overlooking Aleppo, Zengi summoned [her], divorced her and ordered her to be taken to the stable where he ordered the grooms to rape her. This they did while he looked on.'[2]

The underlying problem was that Zengi was a psychopath with a strong preference for brutalising and raping young men. From the outset of his rule, it was said that 'when he was unhappy with an amir, he would kill him . . . and leave that individual's children alive but castrate them. Whenever one of his pages pleased him by his beauty he would treat him in the same way so that the characteristics of youth would last longer in him.'[3]

His rule ended as it had begun – at the hands of one of those beautiful, but mutilated, pages.

Zengi's sleeping arrangements were full of pleasures for the great man. 'When Zengi sleeps,' wrote one chronicler,

> a few of his servants sleep around his bed. They attend to his care while awake or asleep. They protect and defend him like lions in battle and almost visit him in his dreams. They are fresh and extremely beautiful, like a morning at sunrise. He loves them as they love him and, despite their loyalty to him, he is sometimes harsh with them. They are the children of the stallions from Turkish, Armenian and Byzantine lords.[4]

But there were dangers. In the unlikely event that any of Zengi's security chiefs had been brave (or foolish) enough to contradict their master, they could have told him that being 'harsh' and surrounding himself at night with abused and mutilated young men was hardly without risk, especially as many of them had been taken from the families of his enemies.

Predictably enough, one of his slaves – a certain Yaranqash (possibly a Turkic nickname, given that he was said to have been of Frankish origin) – eventually knifed him to death. The reasons behind the killing were prosaic and, given Zengi's high-risk lifestyle and temperament, not unexpected.

On the night of 14 September 1146, Zengi, as usual, had been drinking heavily. He slumped into a stupor before he had finished. He woke up to find his servants, led by the unfortunate Yaranqash, finishing off his fine wines without permission. Enraged, Zengi made the mistake of telling his prisoner-lover that he was going to have him killed in the morning. The Frankish eunuch, presumably also drunk, felt that he had little left to lose at this point. He responded by killing his master and, in a final act which speaks to the high emotions involved, beheaded him for good measure.[5]

On one level, this dramatic incident seems lurid, but perhaps not too unusual. Blood and passion are, after all, central components of how many of us envisage the crusades. But it is worth stepping back a little. Who were the people involved in this murder? The answer raises far bigger questions than one might imagine – questions which go to the heart of the crusader crime wave.

First, everyone was male. And, with the exception of Zengi himself (who was in his late fifties), they were all young. Importantly, as far as we can tell, all the actors in this brutal murder were foreigners. Zengi was a Turk of steppe heritage, as were some of his young lovers. His assassin was said to be a Frank, which may literally mean that he was French or, more loosely, that he was of European ethnicity. Others were Byzantine, from the eastern Roman empire, or Armenians, displaced by the Turkic invasions of the preceding decades. None were referred to as being Arab.

Similarly, religion was hardly the dominant factor in anyone's actions or motives. Zengi was (nominally at least) a Sunni Muslim; but his predilection for alcohol and boys speaks to a less than orthodox approach to observance – and many of his young lovers (perhaps the majority) seem to have been from a Christian background.

None of this was what we might expect.

It may seem counterintuitive, but the real problem of the crusades was not religion.

It was young men. Dislocated. Disinhibited. And in disturbingly large numbers. They were the propellant that stoked two centuries of unceasing warfare and, as we shall see, shocking levels of criminality.

The reason they caused such problems was not that they might be over-entitled, over-sexed or over-opinionated about religion – though they were often all of those things. The ultimate cause, and the ultimate reason why these men were the driver of the chaos that engulfed the medieval Middle East, was far more basic – and it was demographic and anthropological, rather than theological.

Criminality was rife in the medieval crusader states and their neighbours. It was fundamentally driven by two interconnected factors. One was the over-abundance of young (and often armed) men in the population. The other was the way in which these men were so strangely disengaged from the societies in which they found themselves.

But why was that? Why was there such a disproportionate level of testosterone in the air? After all, most medieval societies were at war for long periods of time – but very few experienced the levels of violence and criminality seen in the Middle East of the crusades. And why were these men so problematic? Unruly and underemployed soldiers were always disruptive, but rarely on such a scale. Clearly, something was very different. And for this difference to be sustained for two centuries, the reason had to be systemic, rather than anything more coincidental.

Above all, why were there so many young and dislocated men in the region?

Anthropology I – the weather forecast: violence ahead

The Christian historian Matthew of Edessa wrote of a climate catastrophe that slowly ramped up over a seven-year period in the second half of the tenth century. It culminated dramatically in a time when people went 'mad and [started] attacking one another mercilessly and savagely, devouring each other'. Conditions were so bad, he reported, that 'many villages and regions became uninhabited, and nothing else has been built [there]'.[6] But that was just the beginning. Although they were unaware of the full extent of the forces at play, local chroniclers were inadvertently charting the root causes of the crusades.

The fundamental reasons were climate change and its primary human consequences – famine and mass migration. Indirectly, these forces – so powerful and all-pervasive as to be almost invisible to contemporaries – triggered the two hundred years of war that followed.

Food, and the right weather conditions to produce it, are, of course, primary building blocks of human life.

It did not always feel like it, but the eastern Mediterranean was, and is, fortunate in having access to two main weather systems, each with its own implications for food production. Most of the region is subject to the rhythm of cyclones and anticyclones, which are normal for the Mediterranean and western steppes. Importantly, however, alongside these climatic drivers, there is also Egypt, whose rich fertility is driven by the rise and fall of the Nile River. The rising of the Nile depends, in turn, on a non-Mediterranean weather system – the monsoons of eastern Africa.[7]

The distinction may seem like an obscure meteorological footnote, but please bear with me – it is important. This dual weather system and its sustainability (or otherwise) was strangely fundamental to the history of the crusades. It meant that, under normal circumstances, the entire area had the security of a fail-safe device when it came to food production. This built-in insurance policy goes a long way towards explaining why the Middle East has been home to so many of the fundamental advances in human civilisation over the millennia.

Food production in the region is generally adequate, driven by the normal weather conditions of the eastern Mediterranean. But even if this system should fail, the rains from the African Lakes Plateau and the Ethiopian Highlands would cause the Nile to flood. This, in turn, would create huge expanses of newly fertile land, fed by the elaborate irrigation systems of the Nile Valley. There would still be food.

The waters of the Nile rise from mid-June until August or early September, and the crops grown in Egypt, propelled by factors that exist independently of the Mediterranean weather systems, would generally be ample to stave off disaster. Things might be challenging and uncomfortable for a while, but with Egyptian fertility as a fall-back position, complete societal collapse within the region could normally be averted.[8]

Except that in the eleventh century, things were different – nothing happened the way it was supposed to. In the period running up to the crusades, something very unusual, and extraordinarily disruptive, occurred.

First, the weather systems of the eastern Mediterranean and the western steppes failed – and that failure recurred across extended periods of time.

Proof of medieval climate change is necessarily somewhat anecdotal; but in the Middle East at least, it is nonetheless compelling. There is overwhelming evidence that the climate of the eastern Mediterranean and western Eurasian steppes changed substantially for the worse.

This evidence is not theoretical: it was seared in human suffering. There were multiple instances of unusually cold and unusually hot spells in the region. These severe episodes were inevitably accompanied by famines and droughts. Contemporary chronicles told of the dramatic social consequences – food crises in Mesopotamia and Iran, the Jazira region and Baghdad led to localised instances of starvation and civil unrest.

The first signs of long-term trouble emerged in the tenth century. The frequency of periods of punishing cold weather and subsequent famines increased in an unprecedented way. Baghdad in 919–921, for instance, was hit by an extended period of food shortages. The rioting that followed only stopped when the food stores were opened and heavily subsidised supplies were released to the population.[9]

This regional deterioration manifested itself even more profoundly in the eleventh century. The first decade was a disaster. Severe drought and famines in 1007 caused extensive rioting among the population of Mesopotamia – even regular soldiers began to mutiny. Another severe drought in 1009–1010 meant that major rivers such as the Tigris became unnavigable. In 1011–1012 famine in eastern Iran resulted in hundreds of thousands of deaths.[10]

The eleventh century in the eastern Mediterranean may have started badly, but it only got worse. In the period from 1020 through to the 1060s, a series of further climatic disasters pushed Middle Eastern sedentary societies to the brink of collapse. Stability in the region went into freefall.[11]

It was exactly in these circumstances, of course, that the productivity of Egypt could normally be relied upon to take up the slack. But this time, just when it was needed most, the Nile failed. Water levels did not rise when they should have done, and the fertility of the Nile Valley plummeted.

Perhaps surprisingly, in this instance the anecdotal evidence of the chronicles is also supported by a rare, yet powerful set of quantitative data. The water levels of the Nile had been tracked in detail for many centuries, largely because of their fundamental importance for all aspects of life in Egypt: if the river failed, so too did crops, livelihoods and sometimes even governments.

This data shows an astonishing shift in weather patterns over time. In the period AD 300–900 we find only eleven years of drought. This equates to an average of less than two catastrophic incidents every hundred years – bad for those immediately affected, of course, but generally something that societies can survive. In the period running up to the crusades, however, the situation deteriorated markedly.

Between the years 950 and 1072, there was a disastrous drought and crop failure every four or five years – a cumulative total that was ten times the average for the preceding centuries. There was a three-year drought from 1023 to 1026. This was followed by a shocking collapse in 1052–1058 – six years of drought struck Egypt, interrupted by just one normal year. And, to cap it all, an extended famine from 1065 to 1072 made a bad situation even worse.[12]

A cycle of drought, famine and starvation took hold. In its wake, diseases broke out in the weakened population centres of the Middle East. Ominously (and with depressing prescience), some called it 'the great calamity'.[13]

These macro disasters in Egypt were not isolated incidents. As we have seen, they coincided with severe droughts across the eastern Mediterranean and the steppe. Like the Roman empire before them, the sedentary states of the Middle East were about to find out just how destructive dislocated nomadic societies could be.[14]

Anthropology II – the war of migration

In writing of the events in Syria in just one year (the months straddling 1079–1080) one chronicler painted a grim picture of the horrors that had descended on local communities:

> At the beginning of the year . . . a severe famine occurred throughout all the [Christian] lands . . . for the bloodthirsty and ferocious Turkish nation spread over the whole country . . . [There] was a shortage of food, the cultivators and labourers decreased due to the sword and enslavement, and so famine spread throughout the whole land. Many areas became depopulated . . . and the country[side] . . . became desolate . . . An innumerable amount of corpses remained unburied, and the land stank from their putrid-smelling bodies.[15]

Famine caused traumatic disruption to sedentary societies. Cases of starvation, malnutrition and even cannibalism increased, and this inevitably had knock-on effects for social cohesion and internal migration. Settled communities, however, can do something to ameliorate the shock. They have governments with access to economic remedies, however rudimentary or short term they might be. They usually have, for instance, stocks of publicly stored food to fall back on.

For nomadic societies, however, the consequences are far more profound – and far more sudden. On the western Eurasian steppes the Turkic tribes, leading a nomadic rather than settled lifestyle, were hit hard. Unlike sedentary societies, they had few food reserves. Their fragile leadership structures had almost no levers that could be used to deal with the situation.

Quite apart from the lack of food for the humans, if the tribes' animals died, entire communities faced almost immediate catastrophe. These were nomads who traditionally lived a pastoral existence. This lifestyle was hugely dependent on the rhythm of seasonal migration. Flocks needed to be abundant and mobile. Sources of food and water needed to be available over long distances. The regular movement from winter grounds to summer pastures was at the heart of this nomadic existence – but the deteriorating weather conditions of the eleventh century dislocated this primal pattern. The nomads were pushed to breaking point.[16]

As individuals, steppe tribespeople were famously robust. They had a lifestyle that made them tough, hardy and resilient. As societies, however, they were shockingly fragile in the face of climate change. The consequences of environmental destruction were both profound and predictable – the nomadic tribes were inexorably forced to migrate towards areas that were more fertile. Their only chance of survival lay in moving on to less harsh regions further south and further west, and they needed to do so quickly.

In an age that pre-dated the invention of gunpowder, dislocated pastoralists such as these were supremely dangerous – they were among the most powerful forces that humanity could unleash. The great tribal movements off the steppes had triggered the end of the Roman empire in the West; now, once more, the Turkic tribes, hardened by their nomadic existence, were well suited to take what they so desperately needed when they arrived in the Middle East. Destructive and out of options, they were a primal force that could not be ignored.[17]

Among the early entrants to the region were a loose confederation of Seljuk Turkic warbands – recent converts to Sunni Islam, but with only a tenuous grasp of theological matters. They left their tribal lands north of the Caspian and Aral seas and moved south, taking control of much of modern Iran and northern Syria. Baghdad was next. By 1055, the Seljuks had captured the city. Their leader adopted the uncompromising title of 'Power' (*Sultan*).

The settled Christian lands of Anatolia, to the west of this restless 'Seljuk empire', inevitably acted as a magnet for new arrivals to the region. By the 1060s, groups of semi-nomadic warriors began to push into what we now know as Turkey. Local communities were raided and destroyed. The Byzantine authorities were on the defensive, and they struggled to keep the nomads at bay.[18]

Once the Turkic tribes had occupied large parts of Anatolia, other prosperous areas to the south became plausible and attractive targets: Syria, Palestine and perhaps even the riches of Egypt all seemed within reach. In January 1071, the Seljuk Sultan Alp Arslan led the first major expedition south, taking an army across the Euphrates with the intention of heading down through Syria and beyond. This marked, some said, the point at which the 'reign of the Arabs' ended. By the 1080s, nomadic warlords had taken over most of the Syrian city states and much of Palestine.

Moving back onto the offensive in the 1090s, a confident Byzantium called for western 'allies' to help them recover the old Christian lands of Anatolia – and perhaps even to strike further south, to take back the Holy Land. The expedition they had summoned became known as the First Crusade. Thus the second demographic intrusion, the crusading movement, was born.[19]

These new entrants, the shifting alliance of European soldiers who set out on the First Crusade, performed surprisingly well. Much of Anatolia was recovered, and the crusader (or 'Frankish') armies were able to push on down into Palestine. Shockingly, by the summer of 1099, even Jerusalem had been recaptured. Some of the crusaders put down roots and set up colonies and towns. They sent word home to encourage other Europeans to come and join them – to create a new life for themselves, and to defend the newly recovered Holy Land. What later became known as the 'crusader states' were established.[20]

The second major demographic intrusion (the western settlement by the crusaders) had arrived.

Anthropology III – the war without end

The Turkic invasions and the European response transformed a regional conflict into a truly international one. But it was the *length* of the wars, combined with their extraordinary scope, that made the crusading period so unique.

We generally assume that war and peace are two very different states. Our modern experience teaches us that societies may be subjected to short – often relatively unobtrusive – periods of warfare, followed by lengthy spells of peace. This was decidedly not the case during the crusades.

It is no exaggeration to suggest that these interminable conflicts lasted almost unceasingly for two centuries. Most wars end. Even long-standing conflicts are usually interspersed with significant periods of peace. But the crusades were different. This was permanent fighting, raiding or skirmishing, interrupted only by occasional periods of truce. All societies in the region existed on a more or less permanent war footing. Economies and the meagre economic surpluses of these medi-eval societies were all directed towards the demands of the military.[21]

The Byzantine empire, for instance, had a long memory. It never forgot its lost provinces, however long ago they had been overrun, and it was always seeking ways to bring them back into imperial hands. The approach might be diplomatic and indirect (perhaps setting up client states as a buffer between the empire and its enemies), or it might be direct and more brutally military. But there was always a long game to be played.

The crusaders found compromise similarly difficult. The Christian lands of the Middle East had been lost to Muslim invasions in the seventh and eleventh centuries – and now, after so much blood had been spilt, it was hard to envisage a political outcome in which the Christians did not retain control of their newly recovered lands.[22]

The Christian settlers from the West, and the more numerous local Christian communities of the region, were not technically 'crusaders', of course: most had been born there, unlike the men who came on the armed pilgrimage of a crusade. But they had a special religious role to play as defenders of the Christian Holy Land – and they were the ones who would be blamed, however unfairly, for every defeat. Like the

Byzantines, they were necessarily playing a long game and had no easy way to end it without victory.[23]

If the Christians found a lasting compromise difficult to envisage, for their Muslim opponents it was almost impossible. From their perspective, the religious underpinning to the fighting precluded even the possibility of peace. Once jihad was firmly under way, the most that could be contemplated – and even this with mutters of disapproval from the more devout members of the community – was an occasional and strictly time-limited truce with the unbelievers.[24]

The consequences of these almost unique barriers to peace were far-reaching. Everyone operated in a permanent state of war, with all the implications this had for budgeting and the search for new recruits. The crusades were a period of literally unending warfare.[25]

Anthropology IV – the insatiable war

Once war became endemic, another major demographic driver took firm root – the insatiable need for young mercenaries and other long-distance recruits. An unending supply of young men was pulled into this equally unending conflict.

An arms race had begun in earnest. In a pre-industrial age, that race inevitably found its primary expression in the acquisition of warm bodies. Everyone made a dash to attract as many potential out-of-region recruits as possible – and that process ground on for two centuries.

As these were truly international wars, they drew in troops from absurd distances – European troops from as far west as the Atlantic coast of Ireland; slave-soldiers from sub-Saharan Africa; or steppe cavalry from central Asia and the Silk Roads. All were welcome. All were useful. And all were grist to the unremitting mill of blood and violence.

The proportion of young, armed men in the region inevitably shot up – and that was doubly jarring, because the civil population had previously been so largely demilitarised. But these men were not just there in huge numbers: they were generally foreigners, with very different customs, and as such were culturally desensitised. They were often disoriented, and far from the restraints and inhibitions of their homes and families. These were men both simultaneously alienated and yet strangely liberated.

With this new and unstable population in place, levels of violence soared and remained spectacularly high – even by the standards of a region noted for its enduring lawlessness. Disinhibition, testosterone and the potential to exploit male power combined to produce a new level of social upheaval.

A chaotic and supremely dangerous crime wave was coming into its own.

2

◇

Crime and Crusading

There is a medieval syllogism that explains a lot. Not all men were criminals; but the vast majority of criminals were men – and particularly young men with access to arms.

The population shifts experienced during the period of the crusades were not normal – and neither was the effect they had on the societies which tried to absorb them.

Extraordinary demographic movements had a hugely distorting impact on medieval Middle Eastern societies – and the inexorable nature of these shifts became ever more apparent over time. These groups were mainly drawn from the archetypal demographic of criminality – overwhelmingly male, young, unrestrained and heavily armed.

The proportion of these men in the populations of the Middle East as a whole, and the new Christian states in particular, was vastly increased. This had profound consequences – obvious on reflection, but generally overlooked in the history books of the crusades.

Thieving soldiers

One issue was that the boundaries between criminality and soldiering, and between 'civilians' and warriors, were easily blurred.

Lawlessness in the area was already rife. But for many crusaders, and members of other out-of-region armies entering the Holy Land, criminality started long before they had even arrived.

Taking the Second Crusade as an example, one can see that the problem of trying to maintain order grew day by day. King Louis VII of France did his best. He had, quite rightly, made early efforts to impose discipline and a workable code of conduct on his men, as they marched across Europe on their way to the Holy Land. When the crusading contingents had started to congregate, and 'after camp had been pitched outside the city, he waited a few days for the army to arrive; and he enacted laws necessary for securing peace and other requirements on the journey, which the leaders confirmed by solemn oath.'

This was fine in theory. In practice, however, these laws were so thoroughly ignored that we do not even know what they were. As one frustrated royal chronicler bitterly remarked, 'because they did not observe them well, I have not preserved them either'.[1]

Discipline proved increasingly difficult to maintain within an extended army largely made up of scattered and squabbling feudal contingents. At some point along the crusaders' march from Philippopolis (modern-day Plovdiv in Bulgaria) to Constantinople, tensions between the French and German armies boiled over. A French commentator later wrote that trouble broke out when 'some of our men who wished to escape the press of the crowd around the king, and therefore went ahead, lodged near [the Germans]'.[2]

Competition for scarce food supplies was the proximate cause of the fighting that started soon afterwards, but it could have been triggered by any number of reasons. 'Both groups went to market,' wrote a French crusader,

but the Germans did not allow the Franks to buy anything until after they themselves had had all they wanted. From this situation arose a dispute, or rather a brawl for, when one person accuses another in a very loud voice without understanding him, there is a brawl. Thereupon the Franks, after this exchange of blows, returned from market with their supplies.[3]

That was just the beginning of the disorder, however. The Germans, 'scorning the pride of the few Franks, because they themselves were many, took arms against them and fell upon them furiously, and the Franks, likewise armed, resisted spiritedly.' Fighting petered out only as night fell, and after 'wise men among them, falling at the knees of the fools, calmed this rage by humility and reason'.[4]

Even by their own accounts, the French could not pretend to be blameless – discipline was obviously on the verge of breaking down completely. When their army arrived at Constantinople, the trouble only got worse. The Byzantines

closed the city gates to the throng, since it had burned many of their houses and olive trees, either for want of wood or by reason of arrogance and the drunkenness of fools. The king frequently punished offenders by cutting off their ears, hands, and feet, yet he could not thus check the folly of the whole group. Indeed, one of two things was necessary, either to kill many thousands at one time or to put up with their numerous evil deeds.[5]

One particular incident almost led to a small war between the French and their long-suffering Byzantine hosts. As the armies crossed over into Asia Minor, one Frenchman who was on the expedition reported that

food ships, with money changers aboard, followed us. The money changers displayed their treasures along the shore; their tables gleamed with gold and were groaning with the silver vessels which they had bought from us. From the army came people who were bartering for necessities, and they were joined by men who coveted the supplies of others.

The chronicler tried to distance the army as far as possible from what ensued, but it was clear that robbery by members of the Frankish army was the cause. 'One day, therefore, a certain Fleming,' he wrote, 'fit to be scourged and burned in Hell, seeing the great wealth and blinded by immoderate greed, cried, "Havo! havo! [Create havoc!]", seizing what he wished. And by his boldness, as well as by the value of the loot, he incited men like himself to crime.'

They needed little incitement. Once the opportunity for theft presented itself, everyone piled in to fill their boots, and 'those who had money on hand rushed away in all directions'. The market dissolved in a matter of seconds, and as 'the stalls came falling down, the gold was trampled on and seized. In fear of death the despoiled money changers fled, and, as they fled, the ships took them on board; and when the ships left they brought back to the city many of our people who were aboard purchasing food'. The Byzantine authorities were naturally disgruntled. The Franks stranded on board their ships were arrested. Although they were clearly not the guilty parties, they were nonetheless 'beaten and plundered. Also the city plundered her guests as if they were enemies.'[6]

This was a self-inflicted disaster that the crusade did not need. Once more, it was left to King Louis of France to patch things up. 'These circumstances were made known to the king,' wrote the chronicler Odo of Deuil,

> and, hugely angry, he demanded possession of the criminal, who, when surrendered by the count of Flanders, was hanged right on the spot, within full view of the city. Then the king hurried to search for the lost goods, to pardon those who returned them, to threaten those concealing them with punishment like the Flemings; and, so that they might not be frightened or shamed by his presence, he ordered them to return everything to the bishop of Langres. In the morning the money changers who had fled the day before were recalled, and they got back in full what they could swear they had lost.

This violent incident was clearly brought about as a result of ill discipline within the French army. Even then, however, the French chroniclers were quick to assign blame to anyone else – the actions of a Flemish soldier, or the 'over-reaction' of the Byzantine authorities to the attack on their merchants. In the aftermath of the incident, the money changers, who had been robbed and beaten by the crusaders, were accused of fraud by the French. When it came to dispensing compensation, it was said that 'most of them asked [for] more than they ought; but the king preferred to restore the missing articles from his own property rather than to disturb the peace of his army'.[7]

King Richard I of England, who had very firm views about discipline, was similarly compelled to set out a clear and draconian list of punishments for his men during the Third Crusade. In the event of theft, it was decreed that 'a robber . . . shall have his head cropped after the manner of a champion, and boiling pitch shall be poured on it, and then the feathers of a cushion shall be shaken out upon him, so that he may be known'.[8]

This classic instance of 'tarring and feathering' may seem almost comic, but it was far more painful than it sounds. In fact – and this was largely the point of the exercise – it would cause severe scarring to the head: many who experienced this punishment would have had huge areas of scar tissue on which no hair would grow. In an age when there were no criminal records and no identity cards, this was a very visible warning to everybody.

The difference between soldiering and criminality was often wafer thin.

Crusading criminals in the Holy Land

It may seem counterintuitive, but crusaders could be every bit as disruptive once they arrived in the Holy Land. Holy or not, the low-level lawlessness of their marches across Europe and beyond just continued when they reached their destinations. Brawling between soldiers, even of the knightly class, was constant: with so many armed and aggressive young men in the region, keeping a lid on the testosterone was always a challenge.

John of Joinville was involved in one such incident. He later wrote that when he was with the French army at Caesarea in 1250–1251 jostling broke out between some of the king's knights and the Hospitaller warrior monks. The details were mundane (as was often the case), but tempers ran high. The French knights were out hunting and chased a gazelle onto Hospitaller property. Things got a little out of hand, and the local brothers took exception to the knights' over-enthusiastic antics: eventually, 'the brothers of the Hospital charged at them, drove them off and chased them away'.[9]

There were a lot of Hospitaller properties around Caesarea, so the brothers might have viewed the crusaders (with some justification) as trespassers or poachers. Or, given the military monks' status as the 'professionals' of the crusader armies, they might just have been having a bit of fun with newcomers whom they regarded as boisterous and irritating 'amateurs'.[10]

Either way, Joinville 'complained to the master of the hospital' about the brawl. The master doubtless had plenty of far more important things to worry about, but he said 'that he would make amends to [Joinville] in accordance with the custom of the Holy Land, which was such that he would make the brothers who had committed this offence eat sitting on their cloaks until the victims should allow them to get up'.[11]

It is hard for us to see 'sitting on a cloak' as a harsh punishment. But they were knights, men near the top of the social ladder, and embarrassment was a difficult thing for such entitled young men to endure. The punishment worked: the monks looked silly and, perhaps, everyone began to see the funny side of it all. The incident ended quickly. Joinville and his men joined them for dinner, and the Hospitaller knights were forgiven.

The hunting incident with the Hospitallers passed off amicably enough, but largely because it took place between men of the same class and background. Other, more unbalanced situations could become potentially very ugly indeed. In an early and far less romantic precursor to the Three Musketeers, one of King Louis's sergeants, a big bruiser by the name of 'Glutton', got into a scuffle with a knight in Joinville's service and was said to have 'laid hands' on him.

The king counselled forbearance (interestingly, he was more relaxed about social etiquette than some of his nobles). He said that Joinville should overlook the incident as 'the sergeant had only pushed the knight'. And, from a practical perspective, there were good reasons to forget such a trivial incident as quickly as possible: there was heavy demand for experienced soldiers in the crusader states, and good sergeants were hard to come by.

However, Joinville refused to see sense. Unlike his king, he was a snob and a stickler for the social hierarchy. So, 'in accordance with the customs of the country,' wrote the punctilious lord, 'the sergeant came to my lodgings barefoot, wearing his chemise and breeches and nothing else, and with a naked sword in his hand.' The man was obliged to kneel in front of the offended party and 'took the sword by its point and offered the pommel to the knight'. Shockingly, he had to allow the knight to cut off his hand, if he chose to.[12]

Joinville and the knight both declined. The matter was closed – the proprieties had been observed and the sergeant had been humiliated. But the possibility of mutilation for a minor altercation was real – or at least it was, if you did not have the good luck to have been born into the upper classes.

Tensions were always close to the surface when large groups of armed men – particularly from many cultures and of various ethnicities – were brought together. The English crusaders of the Third Crusade, for instance, were shocked at the treatment they received when they arrived at Messina, in north-east Sicily, in September 1190.

As thousands of disinhibited soldiers milled around on the outskirts of the city, there were instances of murder and criminality, doubtless on all sides. 'There were people of all sorts,' wrote one chronicler, 'with tents and pavilions and banners set up all along the shore, for the city was forbidden to them. They stayed near the shore until the kings arrived, because the townsfolk . . . ill-treated us, murdering our pilgrims and throwing them into the latrines. Their activities were well attested.' Grievances quickly escalated.[13]

Many of these grievances were about women. Sexual jealousies were a natural source of conflict. The newcomers, hardened foreign men, were viewed with deep suspicion – and often with good reason. The English complained a lot, but it is clear that, even by their own accounts, they were hardly blameless. 'When the two kings had arrived,' wrote one chronicler, 'the [Sicilians] kept the peace, but the "Longebards" would quarrel and threaten our pilgrims with the destruction of their tents and the taking of their goods, for they feared for their wives, to whom the [English] pilgrims spoke.' The English later admitted that they had, in the fashion of football supporters at an international away match, been doing this just to antagonise their foreign rivals – they had been chatting up their women 'to annoy those who would not have thought of doing anything'.[14]

Tempers among the bored and excitable soldiery ran so high that something as mundane as trying to get a bargain could quickly turn to violence. 'It happened one day,' according to the Norman poet Ambroise,

> that a woman who was called, it is said, Ame, brought her bread for sale among the army. A pilgrim saw the bread, that it was soft and warm and he haggled with her over it. That woman was indignant at the price he offered for it, so that she nearly struck him, so angry and so beside herself was she. Such a commotion arose that the townspeople joined in. They then took the pilgrim, beat him, tore his hair and badly ill-treated him.[15]

This was just a low-level trade dispute that got out of hand. It is interesting to see, however, that even with an everyday incident such as this, it was a woman and her perceived mistreatment by a foreign male that featured at the epicentre of the problem. Tensions ran very close to the surface. Within a few days, Richard I had had enough – he and his men attacked and captured Messina itself (4 October 1190). Concerns about the safety and chastity of the women had not been unfounded. The English crusaders later boasted that 'the town was soon pillaged and . . . they acquired women, fair, noble and wise women'.[16]

Boredom and xenophobia were natural drivers for criminality among soldiers; but theft and petty lawlessness in time of war could often be propelled by even more basic forces – poverty and hunger. One chronicler at the siege of Acre in the summer of 1191 wrote that

necessity leads to many actions that are to be blamed and criticised. In the army were many men from many lands ashamed to beg for bread; they would steal bread from the bakers, coming right up and grabbing it. One day a prisoner was taken for such a misdeed. He who had captured him took him away to his lodging place and tied him as best he could, with his hands behind his back, there being no support [to which he could be tied]. Those who were there, busy loading the oven, went up and down paying no attention to the prisoner.

Eventually the thief

broke the bonds tying his hands. He was sitting on a heap of bread, so while the men-at-arms were idly looking elsewhere, he ate the bread and, hidden in the shadow of the seat, put one under his arm . . . he fled at speed, back to the army, where he related what had happened to his companion men-at-arms, who were dying from lack of bread. They ate and shared the bread that he brought them, which strengthened them for a while but not for long.[17]

Once again, this petty incident highlights the problems of administering punishment in an era with precious little infrastructure. Keeping a prisoner restrained was difficult. There were no prisons, and few quick ways to administer justice, other than those involving swift violence. The thief seems to have been tied to a chair or tent post, as the only remotely 'secure' way of restraining him, but the situation was entirely inadequate. Even the chronicler had some sympathy for the starving soldier and his comrades, despite making the customary comments about how such behaviour was 'to be blamed and criticised'. Expectations were low and delivering justice in moderation was difficult.[18]

Petty criminality was never going to go away. The best one could hope for were better ways to handle the consequences.

Monastic miscreants

Even when dealing with the monks of the military orders, supposedly fanatical upholders of Christian morality in the crusader states, criminal behaviour was an ever-present possibility.

The pervasive nature of larceny within small communities is apparent from the strict and wide-ranging definitions of the crime that were set out in the Rule of the Templars. Theft was broadly defined as being 'when a brother steals things from the house'; or even more circumstantially, 'when a brother leaves a castle or other fortified house at night except by the gate'. It was specifically stipulated that 'if the master or commander asks a brother who is under his command to show him the things of the house that are under his command and authority, the brother should show them all; and if he keeps anything back and does not show it, he will be considered a thief'.[19]

In an age without many keys or locks, keeping hold of one's own possessions was a delicate and important matter: trust was the real lock, and every effort had to be made to keep that trust intact. This, too, was reflected in the ordinances of the Templars. If, it was written, 'a brother puts his hands in another's bags and the brother to whom they belong says that he has lost what was inside, and he can have him convicted of having put his hand inside the bags and can prove that he has lost what he says from the bags, he will be convicted a thief'. Proof of guilt was inevitably hard to find, but if caught in the act, there had to be penalties.[20]

Most of this was hardly major criminality. It was just theft of the most petty kind – the perennial combination of human weakness, temptation and opportunity. At Château Blanc (a Templar castle in the county of Tripoli), for instance, a brother was suspected of fraud. He was confronted about the matter. The accused knight was the man 'in charge of the sheepfold' – unglamorous work, but presumably someone had to do it. His superior 'told him to show him all the things that he had under his command, and the brother showed him everything except a jar of butter and said that he had nothing else. And his commander knew that the jar was there and accused the brother . . . so he was expelled from the house because of it.'[21]

The outcome may seem a little harsh to us, perhaps, but presumably this was felt to be indicative of broader issues surrounding his behaviour which had sparked the original suspicions. The order did not seem to be too sad to lose him, so there were perhaps other, unspoken, reasons for his dismissal.

We also know that several Templar knights in Cyprus were expelled because of theft. The rot started at the very top: one of the accused knights was the Templar commander of Paphos, a certain Brother John Harelip, who was found guilty of embezzlement. He had been given 600 silver besants, 400 of which were for the building of a house for the order, while 200 were to be held in reserve for later contingencies. After a while, his senior officer 'sent a brother who asked him for the [reserve fund of] 200 besants, and Brother John said that he had put them towards the expenses of the house. And the commander sent for them and ordered the besants to be given to him.' When finally confronted, Brother John was forced to confess the fraud – he 'told him that he had spent them, and he could not [or would not] say on what'.[22]

Theft in the form of 'wastage' (as modern businesses describe shoplifting by their own staff), was also rife, even in religious orders. 'Losing' equipment – either accidentally or, as was suspected, stealing it to pay for illicit pleasures such as gambling or prostitutes – was explicitly recognised as a problem. Many sections in the Rule of the Templars were devoted to defining which items it was acceptable to 'take away' from barracks, and which must not be removed.

Even if the items themselves could legitimately be taken out, there was a continual battle to stop the more wayward knights selling (or otherwise 'losing') them.

Templar case law, for instance, mentioned that a certain Brother Marli

> left the house at Château Blanc, and went to [the Hospitaller fortress of] Crac [des Chevaliers] and on his way he lost a longbow that he was carrying, and his sergeant found it and returned it to his commander; and the brother said that when he left he had left a sword in his place, and the commander did not find it; then the brother returned and pleaded for mercy . . . And the brothers decided that because of the sword which was lost to the house and because of the longbow which was lost – for the house had not recovered it through him – for each of these he was sentenced to be expelled from the house.

Swords, in particular, were very valuable items. The fate of the weapon was never fully established, but it must have been assumed that it had been sold or traded by the errant brother.[23]

Monks, and particularly the aristocratic, war-hardened and proud monks of the military orders, were also as prone as any other men to petty quarrels – and the violent disorders that frequently ensued. At one point, the Rule of the Templars states that if 'a brother strikes any Christian in anger a blow from anything which could kill or maim, he should not keep his habit [i.e. he would be expelled from the order] and should be put in irons'. Multiple admonitions for the brothers not to attack other Christians in the course of resolving arguments occur throughout the Rule of the Templars – and the way they are repeated reflects the recurring nature of the offences.[24]

But although the theory was clear-cut, in practice the brothers were all too prone to weakness. An example of the order's case law explained how one particular fracas had come about. The Rule stated that it 'happened in Acre that Brother Hermant was commander of the livestock, and two clerks took some *doriez* doves which belonged to the dovecote of the house. And the commander told them to do it no more, [but] they did not wish to stop it.'[25]

Up to this point, the Templar brothers were clearly in the right. But they took matters too far. The clerks foolishly came back to steal some more. The incensed Templar commander

had a brother who watched them when they took the doves, and the commander with the brothers beat them hard and wounded one on the head. And the clerks appealed to the legate, and the legate informed the master ... [The brothers'] habits were taken from them and they were put in irons and sent to Cyprus, because the blow was very serious.

The severity of the punishment meted out to the brothers was not because the clerks were innocent – indeed, they were clearly guilty – but because of the disproportionate severity of the wounds that the Templars had inflicted on the thieves.[26]

Another example of case law in the Rule is just as telling. It recounted how a fist fight had broken out between two Templar knights (for reasons that are now not entirely clear). Perhaps tempers were just frayed, as the brothers were exhausted and had been instructed to carry on working at night. 'It happened,' we are told, 'that the convent was in Jaffa, and they were ordered to load their baggage at midnight; and some brothers who were in lodgings together heard the words, and one brother laid hands on the other by the hair and threw him to the ground, and there were brothers who saw it.'[27]

The fight itself was relatively minor; but the breakdown in discipline was more serious – and for that reason, the consequences of the brawl needed to be addressed. The next day

> the convent came by day to Arsuf, and they heard mass and the hours. And Brother Hugue de Monlo was Marshal, and had heard this news . . . The brother rose and said that he was struck and that there were brothers who had seen it, and the Marshal thought that they should come forward . . . And the brother who had done the deed rose and pleaded for mercy . . . he was sentenced to lose his habit and be put in irons. And so there was a great debate among the old men of the house, because the blow was not apparent, nor was there any blood; and others maintained, since he had laid hands on the brother in anger and the matter had come to chapter, that it could indeed be done.[28]

In the event, the offender was sent to the dungeons of Château Pèlerin, but presumably not for a long period of incarceration: discipline was important (and had to be administered very visibly), but every able-bodied knight was needed on the front line.[29]

White-collar crime

Many crimes in the crusader states were very visible – often shockingly so. But there were other crimes that were far more discreet – and far more insidious. These were the kind of crimes that thrived on things unsaid, and on the exploitation of unspoken social norms.

Bribery, tax evasion and fraud were the pervasive forms of 'white-collar crime' – they were easy to commit, hard to prevent and very profitable, if you got away with it. Relatively small-scale fraud and profiteering such as this was impossible ever to eradicate fully.

A lack of centralised resources made medieval bureaucracies particularly vulnerable to abuse by those who sought advantage through corruption. Capital and corporal punishment was there as a form of high-profile deterrence; but the rewards for such crimes were high – there is little evidence that the punishments were ever entirely successful.

A Venetian report of 1243, for example, talks of bribery being used as a means of helping tax evasion. Government officials who took bribes laid themselves open to the possibility of extreme punishment, including execution by hanging; but the practice was so lucrative that it could not be stopped.[30]

In such desperate times, even the military orders could not always be trusted. The Hospitallers certainly had their share of fraudsters. For instance, one of the brothers – a man named John of Isca – was based at the order's house in Paris in the 1280s. John ran off with 11,000 livres tournois, a huge sum of money that had been gathered from the tithes of the region to help defend the Holy Land. This scandal was a major embarrassment for the order, diverting resources from the front line at a time when the Latin East needed all the help it could get.[31]

Despite (or perhaps because of) their roles as auditors and invest-ment bankers, the Templars could also be untrustworthy. Two of the Templar masters in Ireland were fraudsters, and were punished for their crimes.

The first was a Londoner named Brother Ralph, who came from the appropriately rough and seedy area of Southwark. In 1234, he went rogue, absconded and abandoned his habit. Henry III ordered that the corrupt Templar should be arrested if he ever again showed his face in Ireland. The behaviour of one of Ralph's successors in Ireland was even more scandalous, however. Walter the Bachelor was the master of Ireland at the turn of the fourteenth century, and he too succumbed to temptation. It emerged that he had been stealing from the order, and he was also found guilty of fraud. He was arrested, shipped back to London and died soon afterwards, possibly at the hands of his angry fellow brothers.[32]

Even the preparations for the Third Crusade, launched to bring help to the Holy Land in the wake of Saladin's invasions in 1187–1188, were hindered by the white-collar crimes of a senior Templar. In 1188, Gilbert of Hogestan, one of the British brothers, was caught embezzling funds that had been earmarked to help the Latin East. Overcome by his own greed, Gilbert had stolen so much money from the tax receipts that cash levels were steadily going down, rather than up, and his fraud was uncovered. The magnitude of the crime and the sums involved were such that even the king got involved. King Henry II did not exact punishment himself – probably out of respect for the jurisdiction of the Templars – but he handed the thief over to the order for punishment. Roger of Howden, one of the leading contemporary chroniclers, was suitably outraged and judgemental: in his *Gesta*, he wrote that Gilbert deserved to be hanged for the outrage, and roundly castigated him.[33]

But what was true of the Templars in the West could also be true in the East. In 1250, John of Joinville was given some money by King Louis IX of France on his release from captivity in Egypt. He had been reduced to abject poverty by his imprisonment, and was forced to dine with the king 'wearing the garment that had been made for me out of scraps of my blanket when I was a prisoner'. This was also an obvious and ostentatious way of signalling his poverty to the king, of course – and very important for a man looking for handouts.[34]

King Louis, who usually tried to do the right thing, responded accordingly. He gave John 400 livres as wages for his service. Very sensibly, John put 10 per cent of the money aside for immediate expenses and gave the rest to the Templars for safekeeping. The trouble began, however, when he wanted to start drawing down on his reserves. The fraud was not even subtle: the local Templar commander denied that Joinville was a customer and told him 'that he did not have any of my money and that he did not know me'.[35]

Entirely understandably, Joinville kicked up a fuss. He complained to the master of the Templars. The master was a friend of John's (or so he thought), but even he told him that if he did not withdraw his complaint, there would be consequences: his actions were causing reputational damage to the Templar 'brand'.

John held firm to his complaint, however – he was so impoverished that he had little choice. He had the king's ear, and he refused to let things drop. The Templars were forced to reconsider – suspiciously quickly, wrote John, 'the Master came to me, all smiles, and told me he had found my money. They were able to trace these funds because it transpired that the former [Templar] commander of the palace had been replaced. He had been sent to a village called Le Saffran, from where he returned the money.'[36]

Culprits were clearly just transferred from one location to another, rather than being brought to justice. Defrauding newly released prisoners of war was clearly unimpressive, and threatened to harm the Templars' image. Ironically, and unbeknownst to all concerned, within a few decades they would need all the help they could get: the order was suppressed for arrogance and, just as importantly, for having run out of corporate objectives and friends.

Fraud upon fraud was the norm, however. Having regained access to his money, John of Joinville then found that his servant was stealing from him. He later wrote that 'I asked my new servant, Guillemin, to show me his accounts, which he did. I found that he had cheated me out of a good ten livres or more . . . When I asked him for the money he said he would repay me when he could. I dismissed him and told him I would give him what he owed me, since he had certainly earned it.'[37]

It later transpired that dear Guillemin already had an extensive criminal record and was a well-known crook. Once the Burgundian knights, his previous employers, had returned from their captivity as prisoners of war in Egypt, John had an opportunity to question them about Guillemin. He 'learned from them that they had brought Guillemin overseas in their company, and that he was the most obliging thief that there ever was'. Interestingly, even the knights were complicit in his theft, and he often stole things to order for them: 'whenever a knight was in need of gloves or spurs or anything else, Guillemin would go and steal it and then give it to him'.[38]

Everyone associated with the Burgundian servant seemed to have been party to fraud and theft. This suggests a possible answer to the strange and unresolved question as to why Joinville did not ask Guillemin to return the money he had stolen. Perhaps John, too, had been party to some of his activities; or perhaps Guillemin knew things about John that were best left untold – we know, for instance, that it was Guillemin who had ensured, perhaps at his master's request, that they had taken lodgings conveniently (perhaps suspiciously) close to the prostitutes and bath-houses of Acre.

Much the same happened in the early years of King Edward II's reign, at some point before 1315. One of the royal household, a certain John of Bosham, was sent out to Palestine to act for the king in an undisclosed mission. The task was both secret and sensitive – perhaps John was a spy, or possibly he was sent on a humanitarian mission to free some of the many English prisoners of war still in the region. Whatever the objective, Edward's agent was given the large sum of 150 gold florins to take with him, perhaps for bribes or possibly for ransoms.

To ensure that he had the benefit of local knowledge on his mission, John was accompanied by a Hospitaller brother, a man stationed in Rhodes. But the Hospitaller knight, far from helping John, stole his money and did a runner. Much embarrassed, the Hospitallers in England were forced to pay their erstwhile comrade's debts to the king in full.[39]

But not all experiences of dealing with the authorities were bad – corruption was common, but not entirely inevitable. Ibn Jubayr, the twelfth-century Spanish traveller and merchant, started his journey to Mecca (1183–1185) with uniformly low expectations of officialdom in general, and of port tax collectors in particular – coastal duty offices were a traditional place where merchants might be stung for 'irregular fees' by the local officials. He left a vivid account of his dealings with the tax officials at Acre, the main port of the Latin Kingdom of Jerusalem; as those officials were crusaders (and he was not), Ibn Jubayr was expecting even worse treatment. 'We were taken to the custom-house,' he later wrote,

which is a khan [that is, an inn or caravanserai] prepared to accommodate the caravan. Before the doors are stone benches, spread with
carpets, where are the Christian clerks of the Customs, with their
ebony ink-stands decorated with gold . . . All the dues collected go
to the contractor for the customs, who pays a vast sum [to the
government, for the privilege of doing so].

The potential for corruption and coercion in this situation was
obvious. The tone of Ibn Jubayr's account shows that it was something
he was fully expecting: from his perspective, it was all very depressing,
but just part of the cost of doing business. In the event, however, he
was pleasantly surprised at how well everything went. The merchants
were charged the correct dues. Those who claimed to have 'nothing
to declare' had their baggage searched. But again, contrary to his
expectations, 'all this was done with civility and respect, and without
harshness and unfairness'. In fact, commercial relations between the
Franks of the crusader states and their Muslim subjects were so good
that Ibn Jubayr found it altogether rather troubling – this kind of thing
might encourage Muslims to live far too comfortably alongside unbelievers.

He worried that his co-religionists

have been seduced, for they observe how unlike them in ease and
comfort are their brethren in the Muslim regions under their
[Muslim] governors. This is one of the misfortunes afflicting the
Muslims. The Muslim community bewails the injustice of a landlord
of its own faith, and applauds the conduct of its opponent and
enemy, the Frankish landlord, and is accustomed to justice from
him.

Ibn Jubayr's comments may have been exaggerated to make a point; but
they clearly say as much about the endemic corruption in Muslim territories as they do about the Franks.[40]

Beyond this, however, the anecdote speaks volumes about the prevalence of criminality as a whole. *Not* to be defrauded by corrupt officials was so surprising that it was felt to be noteworthy and exceptional.

Crime rates were high and expectations were, entirely correctly, low.

3

The Demographic Crime Wave

Everybody wanted military help – but when it actually arrived, it was often in a form that was scruffy, rough and dangerous. For the Franks of the Latin East, crusader armies were the most obvious source of such men. More to the point, the numbers involved were huge, particularly in relation to the relatively small populations of the time.

The interpretation of numbers in a medieval context is always problematic. Chronicles often use suspiciously large and strangely rounded numbers. But the magnitude they try to express in doing so reflects (at certain times) the intense popular enthusiasm in Europe for crusading.

Even before anyone set foot in the East, the numbers were astounding. In 1074, Pope Gregory VII had suggested that he would personally lead a force of 50,000 men out to aid the defence of fellow Christians in the Holy Land. Within a year of Pope Urban II's call to arms at the Council of Clermont in 1095, it is estimated that up to 75,000 Europeans may have headed off to the crusader states.[1]

A century later, the human (and primarily young male) traffic remained just as intense. There were probably 50,000 or more men in total fighting on the battlefield of Hattin in 1187. Some estimated that just the German contingent of the Third Crusade (1189–1192) was

100,000 strong; and the Fourth Crusade of 1204 had shipping capable of carrying some 20,000 men on a single trip.[2]

Population surges such as this led to a pronounced, albeit usually temporary, demographic distortion: when a crusade or a fleet arrived in the region, the proportion of young, heavily armed men in the Christian East inevitably spiked. Most of these crusaders either died on campaign or returned to Europe once they had fulfilled their vows. Many stayed, however. And it is clear that in some cases (when people put their affairs in order all too carefully before they departed) they had had no intention of ever returning.

A get-out-of-jail card . . .

These men were not a representative sample of the male population. Perhaps ironically for societies with a heavily religious tinge to their foundation, a disproportionate number of those who came to the crusader states were criminals.

As is so often the case, the link between semi-professional soldiery and criminality was a close one, and not always in the ways one might suspect. Most obviously, there was the increased predisposition of young armed men to take advantage of civilian populations when the opportunity presented itself. (One only has to look at the newspaper headlines of any modern war zone, any narco-controlled area in South America, or any long-running uprising in Africa to see the depressingly consistent nature of that male exploitation.) But, even beyond that sad and basic anthropology, there were institutional factors that increased the criminality. The crusader states, desperate as they were for armed men, were often used literally as penal colonies.

This was partly a reflection of life in the Middle Ages as a whole. This was an era when central control was loose or non-existent. States generally existed without an adequate police force, and prison facilities were limited in the extreme. As we shall see, it was a 'golden age' of crime.[3]

The situation in the crusader states was even worse, however.

As with many colonial enterprises, the need to encourage settlers was paramount – and, given the risks involved, this was not always easy. Traditionally, one partial solution to this problem has been to ship out convicts from the motherland, as an alternative to offering them other, even less attractive, forms of justice.

Taking medieval England as an example, it is clear that the penal system was a ready source of new recruits for the crusades: many people (normally men) were prepared to face an uncertain future in the Holy Land, if only because the options available to them at home were clearer, but also bleaker. For some, this was a way of atoning for their sins, as well as of conveniently evading the harsh hand of medieval justice – and there was a long (not entirely glorious) tradition of shipping criminals off to places where they might do something more useful with their testosterone.[4]

It was an established practice in twelfth-century England for convicted murderers to be sent to the Latin East as penance: this was an elegant way of turning the problem of punishment into a solution for colonial settlement and recruitment into the armies of the crusader states. The crusades were Holy Wars – redemption was on offer for many of those who were bold enough, or unlucky enough, to be participants. To make things even clearer for men who might be wavering, going on crusade was specifically enforced as a punishment by certain judges – something which, in itself, shows how difficult it was to attract willing settlers.

Many local criminals were indeed sent out to the East. A number of serious offenders from Usk (unenticingly described as 'the most notorious criminals of these parts . . . robbers, highwaymen and murderers') were dispatched to fight in the East, for instance. So, too, were a number of murderers from St Clears.[5]

English 'volunteers' for service in the crusader states were sought throughout the legal system. No one was too sinful to be rejected for military service. On 29 December 1170, four of King Henry II's knights had brutally hacked Thomas Becket, the archbishop of Canterbury, to death in front of many witnesses. The murderers tried to make their penitence more tangible by giving lands to the Templars. Two of them went on pilgrimage to the East, and there were even suggestions that they joined the order, so that their violent inclinations could be put to better use.[6]

Richard Siward was another high-profile and upmarket reprobate. He was an inveterate rebel and political nuisance; but luckily for him, he was also a skilled military enthusiast. In 1236, not for the first time, he found himself in custody. By a fortunate coincidence, preparations were in hand for a crusade. Richard was offered the chance to have his prison sentence commuted, if he instead went to fight in the East. Perhaps not surprisingly, given his warlike temperament, he found the offer far more congenial than remaining incarcerated in Gloucester prison. He took his crusading oath and went with Richard of Cornwall on his crusade of 1240–1241.[7]

In another particularly notorious case, Peter de la Mare, the constable of Bristol, was found unambiguously guilty of murder. He had seized a certain William of Lay from a church sanctuary (bad enough in itself) and had then proceeded to behead him. Peter and his cronies were excommunicated – but they were also told that they would be forgiven if at least one of them went out to fight in the East. This tempting offer was seemingly accepted. Peter presumably paid one of his men to go in his stead, stayed in post and, in a telling aside which perhaps explains his relatively lenient treatment, continued to serve the king faithfully.[8]

Similarly, according to the Worcester chronicle, William of Forz, the third earl of Albemarle, rebelled against King Henry III in 1221. He was duly excommunicated, and not for the first time. When he was finally defeated, he was sentenced to serve in the Latin East for six years as a socially acceptable (and extremely useful) punishment for his sins. And when Faulkes of Bréauté went into revolt in 1224, three of his men were treated the same way: they were besieged in Bedford castle; having surrendered, they were sentenced to become Templars and to perform active service in the Holy Land.[9]

Even after the loss of the Latin East, prisoners continued to be sent to the East to bolster the Christian forces. An aristocratic Frenchman, Amanieu of Astarac, was famous for his activities as an upmarket bandit and dissolute. His activities became more serious over time, and in 1318 he was involved in a fight in which several men were killed. Helped by his influential connections, Amanieu seems to have been able to talk his way out of this debacle, but quickly returned to his antisocial behaviour.

By 1323, we find him in trouble with the law again, this time languishing in a Parisian prison awaiting trial for a series of unspecified offences. The following year he was found guilty and sentenced to serve in the Latin East (either on the frontiers of Cilician Armenia or in Cyprus) with six of his men-at-arms, for a period of two years. Amanieu seems to have died while in the East, some time before his service was due to finish (in 1326). His body was shipped back to France and buried in the Cistercian abbey of Berdoues, in Gascony. Leading an army unit in the East was clearly felt to be a better use of the troublesome nobleman than leaving him languishing in a royal dungeon.[10]

Getting rid of men who were a nuisance or dangerous (or both) by sending them abroad to do God's work was a well-established ploy – but it obviously did little to help levels of criminality in the East.

The 'other' crusaders – settlers and *pulani*

Quite apart from the human detritus of individual crusades, however, there was a continuous flow of men, criminal or otherwise, from the West. Particularly in the twelfth century, when Christians still dominated much of the rural hinterland, there were far more colonists than one might perhaps imagine: at the peak, there were possibly 150,000 or more Frankish settlers in Palestine, alongside thousands of others elsewhere in the East.

This was no coincidence: the armies of the crusader states were almost invariably outnumbered, and the Frankish societies of the Middle East needed all the help they could get, particularly in the form of men with the skills and enthusiasm for a fight. They sent out endless embassies and recruiting parties to attract settlers, mercenaries, merchants and temporary volunteers (men we now tend to call independent 'crusaders'). Recruits duly trickled in over the years, filling the ranks that became all too quickly depleted by war and disease.[11]

The scale of the manpower requirement was huge and, inevitably, highly gendered. When King Baldwin I of Jerusalem collected his men and set out on an expedition down to the desert regions of the Egyptian border at the end of 1100, for instance, we are told that his entire field army consisted of just 'one hundred and fifty knights and fifty infantry'. Without an adequate pool of European men to call upon for military service, the crusader states would have been quickly snuffed out.[12]

The obvious solution was to grow the Frankish population by increasing the number of settled European families in the region. The crusaders very astutely put an immediate and substantial colonisation programme in place. This started in the earliest years of the Latin Kingdom of Jerusalem and grew in intensity as the borders became more stable and the threat posed by the Egyptian army to the interior of the Latin Kingdom of Jerusalem diminished.[13]

In fact, colonisation by the crusaders was widespread and extremely sophisticated – a programme organised and executed on a surprisingly large scale. Within the Kingdom of Jerusalem alone, we now know of no fewer than 235 Frankish rural sites. The nature of this colonisation process meant close social ties and much intermarriage with the local Arab-Christian communities. These were extensive settlements of new mixed-race and multi-cultural 'Frankish' settlers (*pulani*) – men with nowhere else to go, prepared to fight for their land and their new families.[14]

As well as a growing number of armed colonial settlements inland, there was also an increasingly large, and disproportionately male, European population in each of the main coastal cities. As borders stabilised and city walls grew in size and sophistication, so it became easier to attract new urban settlers. The coastal cities of the eastern Mediterranean became the new commercial hubs between East and West.

By medieval standards, the larger cities, such as Acre or Tyre, were major conurbations: their suburbs were sometimes so substantial that additional fortifications had to be built to protect the newly overflowing civil population. Importantly, each of these urban communities was a rich source of money and manpower. They contained a significantly larger proportion of young males than one would normally expect to find. Most specifically, they had the capacity to attract and retain tough mercenaries from other parts of the Middle East and Europe. The crusader states were the one place in Christendom when any man, at almost any time, could find well-paid employment as a mercenary.[15]

Not surprisingly under these circumstances, the crusader states had many of the more dangerous cultural characteristics that we associate with large numbers of volatile young men – habitual criminals, sailors in a foreign port, edgy militia and rough mercenaries rarely make relaxing companions.

As a result, generations of Christian moralists complained about what they saw as the iniquities of the crusader cities of the Levant. Their invective was often naïve and misguided, given the underlying need to attract men who could defend the area. But the accusations were not entirely without a basis in truth. The European cities of the East had the levels of danger and criminality that one would associate with a war zone, a penal colony or a frontier region awash with young armed men – for the very good reason that they were, indeed, all of those things.[16]

Members of the western clergy, such as James of Vitry, might moan about the lack of manners and general lawlessness that they found in crusader cities such as Acre; but the very existence of the Latin East depended on the actions of the same tough and restless men that he was castigating. God's armies found some of their best recruits in the strangest, and not necessarily most genteel, places.[17]

It is in this context that we need to see the crusaders' rogues gallery as it unfolds around us. Appalling acts of criminality took place on all sides – things were done for which there can be no excuse. But it is also far too easy to rush to quick judgements.

These were harsh times. Communities lived in the permanent shadow of violence, rape and the threat of ethnic cleansing, and such circumstances inevitably produced generations of hardened, desensitised men and women. Violent criminals do not make for ideal neighbours under normal circumstances; but when faced with waves of ferocious Turkic nomads, a lot of otherwise unpleasant habits could easily be overlooked.

Elite and entitled

Criminality was not confined to rough mercenaries and prisoners on parole, however.

We might imagine, for instance, that the concept of 'chivalry' as a (theoretical) code of conduct might help ameliorate the lawless tendencies of the more upmarket male population.

As fighting dies down, ruling elites generally settle into ways that allow them to better exploit the new arrangements. This creates an opportunity to establish social norms that promote stability, reduce levels of violence and minimise the repercussions of criminality among the 'civilian' population (however loosely one defines such a status in the medieval context). And so it was in the Latin East.

This was not altruism. It was in the interests of rulers and their nobles to create more stable and productive societies, if only to allow them to capture a greater share of the fruits of that productivity. The most obvious manifestation of this logic in a western context was the concept of chivalry (which became increasingly formalised towards the end of the period under consideration), but there were cultural equivalents elsewhere, and one finds parallels in the Muslim concept of *furusiyya*.

What was promised in theory was far more limited in practice, however. These codes tried to reduce the inherent problems of entitled violence in a medieval society, but often caused as many problems as they solved.

At the core of the idea of chivalry, for instance, lay recognition of a social tension. All medieval states – and particularly the crusader states and their neighbours – needed lots of armed and highly skilled fighting men. But those states were also acutely aware of the dangers that these individuals posed to social order.[18]

Then, as now, leaders had a duty to establish tolerable conditions of safety and security for their subjects. As a result, almost all elite groups had informal rules that sought to dictate (or more realistically, 'encourage') better behaviour, particularly among their armed men. The lower classes would be protected from the more predatory inclinations of the wilder elite males; productivity and economic surplus would increase; the poor would survive and the rich would get richer. In theory, everybody won.[19]

Practice, however, was very different. On the one hand, chivalry was certainly a code of conduct for the appropriate restraint of armed men and their violent tendencies. The semi-religious underpinning of the code stressed (rather optimistically) the role of knightly powers as a positive force in the permanent struggle against sin and the forces of evil.[20]

But the reality of medieval warfare as a whole, and of crusading warfare in particular, told a very different story – one of murder, rape, destruction and the systematic exploitation of the weak. For knights and other upmarket soldiery, settling problems by violence was often a first, rather than a last, resort. This was precisely the opposite of what chivalry ostensibly intended. Alongside this, even more paradoxically, almost all the literature of chivalry praised, and often idealised, the use of arms. Violence and violent men were understood to be constantly in need of control – but even the code of chivalry itself was perverted to help glorify that violence.[21]

From the very outset, the issue of chivalry was beset by the tensions in that fundamental dichotomy. The crusades gave a further twist to these troubling dynamics. The spirit of crusading permeated the fighting nobility – where the emphasis was firmly on 'fighting', rather than on 'nobility'. Knights liked to fight, and they liked the spiritual rewards offered by fighting on crusade: the two things went together very naturally.

It is no coincidence, for instance, that of the seventeen English barons and earls whom King Henry III explicitly banned from participating in the massively brutal tournaments in Northampton and Cambridge in 1234, no fewer than fourteen 'took the cross' as crusaders. Similarly, in July 1278 his son Edward I ('Hammer of the Scots' and, as the nickname suggests, himself no stranger to violence) held a tournament at Windsor: of the thirty-eight knights listed as having received equipment for the games, fifteen had been with him on the English crusade of 1270.[22]

Chivalry thus played a highly ambivalent role in the crusades and in medieval society as a whole. Its very existence was a tacit recognition that there needed to be a means of channelling violence into more socially positive or religiously approved areas of activity. But proficiency in the arts of violence ('prowess') was simultaneously held in high esteem, as the ultimate justification for the entitlement of an elite. The skills of war and murder were, perversely, admired and set up as standards against which the achievements of young armed men might be measured.[23]

Ironically, one of the easiest ways of squaring this intellectual circle was to restrict the protections offered by chivalry to those who were already most entitled. This helped limit any negative consequences to those who were least able to protect themselves or to complain about their treatment. Chivalry was thus twisted to extend its greatest benefits to those who were already strong, while simultaneously allowing the continued exploitation of the weak.

Upmarket male violence, whether on crusade or elsewhere, continued in spite (or perhaps even because) of the strictures of a chivalric code.

Part II

CRIME AND PUNISHMENT

4

❖

Crusader Crime: Prevalence, Poverty and Productivity

Instances of criminality and civilian violence appear time after time in the contemporary sources of the crusades.

This is no coincidence. Tales of the wild days of the crusading era were not just a literary trope – they were a depressingly accurate reflection of people's everyday experiences. The crusader criminal underworld was a genuine, and deeply troubling, phenomenon.

Murders and other violent crimes grab the headlines – and that was true of medieval chronicles, just as much as tabloid newspapers. But in the crusader states, as in our own time, they constituted only a relatively small proportion of the ambient criminality.

The geography of fear

Much of the problem centred around the legal system as a whole. Poor resourcing brought with it consequences – and not just in terms of punishment. Criminal activity, without any prospect of redress, had a cumulative and hugely destructive impact on the fabric of society. In extreme cases, lack of access to a respected system of justice could cause complete social breakdown.

This was an issue in Europe, as well as in the East. In the 1250s, for instance, getting access to honest justice in the king of France's lands was so difficult that it even began to affect royal revenues – people literally voted with their feet and moved elsewhere, to places where they felt their property rights, among other things, would be better respected.

John of Joinville, the French crusading biographer, later wrote that 'there were so many criminals and thieves in Paris and beyond that the whole country was full of them'. King Louis IX, for reasons of good kingship and morality, did everything he could to improve matters. But he also understood that a strong moral stance went hand in hand with good business and sound finances. After the system of justice had been reformed, 'the king's territories began to improve, and people came to them because of the sound justice done there. There was such population growth and regeneration that the king's revenues from land sales, legal proceedings, trade and other sources doubled in value compared with earlier times.' Doing good could sometimes be its own, very tangible, reward.[1]

These problems in France seem to have been – and were – extremely serious. But the scale of the problem in the Latin East was of an entirely different order. So serious, in fact, that even the maps of the region were sometimes a direct reflection of the levels of lawlessness.

The density of population in parts of the Latin Kingdom of Jerusalem, for instance, was in directly inverse proportion to the presence of Bedouin nomads in the region. This was a situation that significantly pre-dated the crusades and was fundamentally anthropological, rather than a religious 'clash of civilisations' – it was a reflection of the ancient tensions between sedentary and nomadic lifestyles, rather than the more obvious theological cliché of 'Muslims versus Christians'.

Most Bedouin had become Muslim over time (though some remained Christian or pagan). Religion was rarely the guiding principle for their behaviour, however. They had been raiding the provinces of Syria since the sixth century, before Islam even existed. As Romano-Byzantine power in the region faded, they used the chaos of the early

Arab invasions as an opportunity to raid again in earnest. By the late tenth and early eleventh centuries they dominated some parts of Syria. Rural life in adjacent unfortified settlements became extremely difficult under these circumstances – and for travellers, the situation was hazardous in the extreme.

Eastern Galilee, for example, had a large bandit presence and a significant Bedouin population. The insecurity this created directly impacted levels of sedentary occupation in the area. The entire region had gone into catastrophic decline in the early period of Islamic invasions, centuries before the crusaders arrived. At least half of the settlements occupied by sedentary groups during Roman and Byzantine times were abandoned in the face of nomadic incursions. These rural populations were forced off their land, either finding safety by migrating to quieter, more defensible areas, or else joining the nomadic tribes that had destroyed their way of life.[2]

This was a negative and self-perpetuating cycle of decay, rather than a one-off event. Limited sedentary occupation meant lower levels of policing – and poor security increased the opportunities for further debilitating lawlessness.

The crusaders tried hard to reverse this process, mainly by building large castles, which were impervious to nomadic pressures, such as the Templar fortress at Safad. Their efforts to protect rural communities were partially successful. But it was a constant struggle – it was always tough to counter primal anthropological forces. In the crusader period, some Arab farmers were able to repopulate parts of eastern Galilee (albeit precariously), but there were no Frankish settlements at all beyond the suburbs of castles.[3]

Criminality was so destructive that it made large areas of the Middle East literally uninhabitable. Even as late as 1263, when the Franks had been forced back into tiny protective zones, the need for security was pressing. A truce with the Mamluk Sultan Baybars was painfully negotiated, but then nearly fell apart as the crusaders were forced to carry out unauthorised building works to repair the outer walls of Arsuf.

Hugh Revel, the Hospitaller master at the time, explained that they had no choice, and that 'we built this simply to guard the destitute from Muslim brigands'. The 'crusades' might nowadays be synonymous with the horrors of war, but they were also a time of far more prosaic banditry.[4]

The architecture of fear

It was not just military architecture that had to adjust to a climate of fear, however. Western Europe in the period of the crusades generally used domestic construction techniques that produced homes which were relatively insubstantial, even where there was ready access to stone as a building material – wattle and daub was easier to work with, and far cheaper. Ordinary houses were so flimsy that burglars would often break in through the walls – it was easier than smashing the door down. Similarly, when a fire broke out in a western medieval town, houses could be pulled down using just hooks and ropes to make a firebreak. More expensive materials, such as stone, were reserved for those with bigger budgets and more moveable property to protect – merchants, moneychangers and other middle-class residents.[5]

Things were different in the crusader states, however. The need for security was greater, and wood was far less plentiful – stone was therefore the building material of choice for almost all domestic residences.

For Europeans adjusting to a different climate, having thicker stone walls had certain advantages. They retained the relatively cooler temperatures of the Mediterranean evenings into the following day; and in winter they were also better at retaining the heat generated by fires or (more aromatically) by domestic animals. But one of the main reasons for using stone seems to have been for protection. The security measures used in Frankish houses were hardly hi-tech, but they were the best that could be provided with the available materials – and, given the dangers from bandits, nomads and criminals (on top of the more obvious threat of enemy armies), this was hardly surprising.[6]

Less was sometimes more. Protection was partly achieved by not having staircases. The normal layout for a Frankish house was to have the main living (and certainly sleeping) areas on the upper floor. In most instances, access to these rooms would have been by a ladder, which could be pulled up by the residents when they went to sleep at night. There may, of course, also have been some examples of wooden staircases; but as wood is such a fragile material, these do not appear in the archaeological records. For larger properties, there were also stone vaults, which gave more protection for goods in storage, and enclosed courtyards, which provided still greater defence against criminals or bandit attacks.[7]

Smaller, more obvious, security measures were also used in the crusaders' houses. Locking mechanisms on doors were substantial, often supplemented by a solid beam bolt – these generally stretched down to fit into a slot made in a stone slab on the threshold. The wooden beams could be drawn quickly in the event of attack, or more routinely put in place at night. For those with more sophisticated tastes, we know from manuscript illustrations that there were metal keyholes, but we have few surviving examples of keys or locks.

Windows, the other main point of access to a residence, were protected by iron bars or shutters, though there were a few with glass. When James of Vitry referred to the opening of windows, for instance, he almost certainly meant 'pulling back the shutters'. If occupants had sufficient warning of danger, windows might even be blocked up with stones, as seems to have been the case at Arsuf in 1265.[8]

Criminality and danger left their own sad imprint on the domestic architecture of the Holy Land.

The economics of justice: poverty and productivity

As if endemic criminality were not bad enough, there were two fundamental economic forces that made matters still worse – and they turned what were always going to be bad problems of criminality into something even more severe and systemic.

The first of these was the behavioural propellant of poverty. Productivity in medieval societies was depressingly low. Most of the population were living close to basic subsistence – and opportunities for crime, then as now, were more attractive to those mired in poverty, with minimal prospects for social mobility and little to lose. Desperation stretches moral theory to the brink and almost inevitably helps breeds crime – and this was just as true of the crusader states as it was in other parts of the medieval world.

Poverty also encouraged the overrepresentation of an underclass in what passed for the crime statistics of the time – the perennial and convenient 'usual suspects'. Social and economic status was a strong indicator of potential criminality. This was not a guaranteed correlation, of course: being a criminal did not mean that you had inevitably started life in poverty; and being poor did not mean that you had to turn to lawlessness. But it did help.

There were many people in the crusades who had no obvious career path, other than soldiering. These individuals (invariably men, of course) might find themselves in a situation when they had no soldiering work to do, or when other short-term opportunities appeared more lucrative. Having steppe tribesmen flooding into the region, for instance, placed the local Muslim states in a dangerously binary position. If a military position (and sufficient money) were available, the tribesmen could fulfil a useful role by attacking the Franks or rival Muslim states. But if nothing could be found for them, they would almost certainly become a profound nuisance extremely quickly: unemployed and impoverished, they would inevitably turn to destruction and criminality within a matter of weeks.[9]

But unemployed mercenaries were not the only ones to whom crime came naturally. Other people might be dedicated career criminals, carrying on a family tradition. There were large numbers of men who knew no other way to make a living. Opportunity and need were often the overriding drivers of such activity. High levels of unemployment or underemployment, coupled with almost non-existent social safety systems, encouraged desperate behaviour.

Crime, for large parts of society, was a first (and only) option. The trope of the criminal underclass – the thieving vagrant or the untrustworthy vagabond – had a grounding in the day-to-day experience of medieval justice, just as much as it does in our own courts.[10]

Weapons and consequences

Efforts to control criminality were also hindered by the widespread availability of weapons. The problem was not entirely unique, and still has echoes today. There were regular attempts across the whole of Christendom to ban the carrying of arms. Having access to weapons inevitably played a major role in the escalation of violent crime. The crusaders and their contemporaries did not have guns; but then as now, proximity to and familiarity with arms meant that these were more likely to be used in instances of 'civilian' violence. Weapons encouraged quarrelling and an upsurge in other criminal activity. More importantly, they generated much higher fatality rates – greater access to weapons, particularly among men, led to more frequent fighting, as well as more serious outcomes.[11]

There is a debate among medieval criminologists as to how much of the population actually carried weapons. Women generally did not. And even among men, not all violent crime involved bladed weapons: in thirteenth-century England, for instance, only a third of murders involved knives. But there is also the obvious argument that the widespread – albeit not ubiquitous – practice of carrying a weapon contributed to the seriousness of fights, and particularly to the seriousness of the wounds that were inflicted during them.[12]

The Latin East was, yet again, different – and worse. Attempts might be made to reduce weapon-carrying in the West, but no one even tried to do that in the crusader states. Cities were full of mercenaries and other soldiers. Towns had large-scale militias for self-defence. And the villages were full of armed peasantry, who knew that they might need to pick up their weapons to defend their communities. Perhaps not surprisingly, metal knives have been found in many Frankish sites – not just at castles like Belvoir and Chastellet, but also in rural locations such as the village at al-Kurum and a farmhouse at Har Hozevim.[13]

The example of the crusader settlement at Magna Mahomeria is a telling one. The settlement itself was relatively small, certainly by modern standards. It had been established as a Frankish colony at some point before 1124, by which time it was described as being a small village (or *viculus*).

It is only by a sad accident of fate that we know of something extraordinary which happened to the male population of this colony. At the end of 1170, Saladin, the newly installed ruler of Egypt, led his armies across the southern frontiers and invaded the Latin Kingdom of Jerusalem. He besieged the crusader castle of Darum and quickly pinned down the Frankish army through sheer weight of numbers.

With no crusader field army to trouble him, Saladin abruptly switched his attention to the bigger prize of the Templar castle at Gaza. The garrison had been depleted, as many of the men had joined the field army. His troops broke through into the walled town relatively quickly, surprising and killing many of the defenders as they went. Among these men, we are told, was 'a company of sixty-five light-armed youths, valiant fighters, natives of a town called [Mahomeria], near Jerusalem. They had arrived that very night at Gaza on their way to join the army and . . . had been assigned to the gate of the outer city.'[14]

These young men had joined the army too late for the initial muster, presumably because they were militia infantry and hence travelled on foot. The better armed and more seasoned fighting men of Magna Mahomeria had apparently gone on before them, and were with the king and the rest of the army. It is only because of the accident of their destruction that we know the settlement made any military contribution at all to the defence of the kingdom. Shockingly, it is clear that almost all males in the village – everyone from young teenagers to elderly men – had arms to hand and were expected to play their part by joining the army at a moment's notice.[15]

Manpower in the Christian East was in such short supply that even the clergy were often armed. This was extremely unusual: priests in Europe were strictly forbidden to carry weapons or commit violence of any kind. In the Latin East, however, such restrictions were quickly identified as a luxury that the heavily outnumbered settlers could ill afford.

Priests were often the default leaders of the small and isolated Frankish rural communities scattered throughout the Holy Land. Inevitably under the circumstances, leading their flocks often involved a very practical intervention in the more violent aspects of the secular world. The laws drawn up at the Council of Nablus in 1120 specifically stated – in a matter-of-fact way that speaks volumes for practice on the ground – that if 'a cleric bears arms in the cause of defence, he is not to be held culpable'. The clergy were involved in leading their parishioners into battle; or, more likely, in helping with the defence of their settlements against criminals, bandits or nomadic raiders.[16]

Some senior religious leaders relished such martial opportunities. Frederick, bishop of Acre and later archbishop of Tyre, was disapprovingly described as being someone who 'possessed little education but was inordinately devoted to the art of war'. Similarly, Ralph, bishop of Bethlehem, was an English cleric who was all too fully immersed in worldly matters. He carried the True Cross (the cross upon which Jesus was believed to have been crucified) into action and was wounded in the course of campaigning in Egypt in the 1160s. One friend wrote of him, in an otherwise fulsome description, that the genial old bishop was perhaps in this regard 'too worldly' (nimis secularem).[17]

Among Frankish men, the ownership of arms was almost universal – and with good reason. But it also had a profoundly negative effect on the prevalence and seriousness of criminality in the crusader states. Life might be hard in medieval Europe, but it was even harder on the fractured and fluid frontiers of the crusader colonies. This was a time of unremitting danger, hard decisions and difficult compromises.

Above all, the most significant difference in criminality in the Latin East, certainly when compared to modern western states, was not the *existence* of violence, but rather its *scale*. Levels of violence tend to increase the further one goes back in time; but the crusades were a spectacular up-tick, sadly impressive even by medieval standards.[18]

Expectations about criminal behaviour were extremely low. But perhaps we should leave the last word on the subject to King Louis IX, the French king who dominated much of the crusading movement in the thirteenth century.

The prevalence of crime in an age of poverty was perhaps not unsurprising. But Louis's experiences on crusade left him consistently disappointed in human nature, even as it went about fulfilling what he regarded as a supremely noble and spiritual enterprise. When he returned home to France in 1254, he had time to reflect on such things. He poured his heart out to John of Joinville, and told him just how disillusioned he had become with his subjects' behaviour.

Joinville wrote the king's sad thoughts down, perhaps almost verbatim:

> 'And I tell you these things,' said the king, 'since this world is so grasping that there are few people who consider the salvation of their souls or the honour of their persons if they have the chance to seize other people's property, either justly or unjustly.'[19]

Whether you were a commoner or a disillusioned king, you could only avoid disappointment by setting your expectations for criminal behaviour at the very lowest possible level.

5

Frontier Justice

Money, or rather the lack of it, was not just a major cause of crime – it was also the fundamental brake on the provision of justice. The absence of infrastructure had a profound impact on the form which justice and punishment had to take.

The quality and sophistication of justice was inevitably closely related to economic productivity. The low productivity of medieval societies was exacerbated in the Middle East by the demands of endemic warfare – the needs of the military soaked up most of what extra money was produced. The siphoning of that (generally very meagre) economic surplus away from the needs of civil society was hugely limiting.

Even in Europe, warfare was a constant backdrop for almost all political activity. It was the main preoccupation of kings and princes. Relatively peaceful medieval states produced precious little economic surplus, but states at war produced almost none.

In the medieval Middle East, the military absorbed most of the budget, in most states, most of the time. Punishment, crime prevention and policing were always expensive, and resourcing for them was consequently in chronically short supply. Frankish legal treatises sometimes refer to a 'lord's prison', but the context makes it clear that these were merely secure rooms or dungeons in which recalcitrant knights and other senior vassals could be punished. This was not the infrastructure of broader law enforcement. Most states had almost nothing left over for dealing with minor crimes – there were few courts, even fewer prisons and (at best) embryonic police forces.[1]

In 1169, for instance, Saladin took over Egypt. He now had the wealth of the region's most prosperous state at his command – a country whose relatively rich economy was powered by the fertility of the Nile. That wealth could be harnessed to any number of projects, but its distribution was, in fact, disappointingly predictable. The chronicler al-Fadil wrote that the money spent on the army was five times what the government spent on everything else put together. Even the relatively small sums left over from the army's budget mostly went on other military expenditure, including Egypt's major refortification programme and the hugely expensive attempts to revive its navy.[2]

The effect of diverting resources away from civil projects was far-reaching. At the same time as the need for law enforcement was increasing, the resources needed to fund it were being taken away. Egypt, the most cash-rich society in the area, had some prisons and a police force – but even these were rudimentary and inadequate. In the crusader states and some of their smaller neighbours, the infrastructure of justice was almost non-existent.

The Franks had a tiny police force and only a very basic system of courts, primarily aimed at dealing with civil cases – and even that tiny infrastructure was largely outsourced and decentralised because of the costs involved. Luckily, this necessarily low-key approach seems to have worked well enough under most circumstances. There is evidence that even local Muslim communities living under Frankish jurisdictions felt well treated in this respect. They were left to their own devices as far as possible, if only because it was too expensive to do otherwise.[3]

But this was nonetheless a world with only very limited capacity for incarceration and, by modern standards, a relatively rudimentary money economy. Importantly, this meant that many criminals could not be punished with a fine. The consequence, as we shall see, was that penalties for transgression tended to be highly polarised: they either had to be severe and very visible (combining finality and deterrence) or handed out with a light touch. Longer-term and more measured punishments were expensive and required a level of central resourcing that simply did not exist.[4]

There were a few Frankish castle dungeons and holding facilities. The tower was an obvious architectural design which lent itself well to operating as a small prison. We know of a tower belonging to the Venetians in Acre, for instance, where the upper floors were rented out to travellers and merchants, while the basements (which were presumably less economically attractive) were, far less cheerily, given over for use as dungeons. The Genoese, not to be outdone, had two towers in Acre, rather unimaginatively called the 'Old Tower' and the 'New Tower' – both of these seem to have operated as prisons from time to time. Similarly, at the end of the twelfth century there is a reference to King Amaury giving a prison tower (or *turris carceris*) to a certain William of Petra.[5]

For archaeologists, toilets sometimes indicate the existence of a prison. Few people had access to their own facilities, and most presumably used the surrounding countryside or public lavatories. Captives, however, whether criminals or prisoners of war, did not have such flexibility, and had to be given toilets of their own. This could lead to security, as well as sanitation, problems. A latrine in Acre, for instance, probably in a prison near the city walls, is mentioned during the Third Crusade: one of Saladin's emirs escaped through its window in 1191, presumably to the great chagrin of his captors, who had been expecting a large sum for his release.[6]

Apart from these fairly rudimentary holding facilities, often designed to hold prisoners awaiting ransom, rather than criminals, prisons were rare in the Latin East, however.

In the face of such limited assets, imprisonment was often part of a 'blended' punishment. It could, for example, be combined with exile, a fine (one small enough to be paid) or time spent in the pillories. Perhaps not surprisingly, given the lack of centralised resources, prisoners generally had to pay for their own imprisonment. This had entirely predictable consequences: the rich were able to buy relatively comfortable conditions for themselves, while the poor were often left in a state of borderline starvation.[7]

A penal code for settlers

There were many strange quirks associated with the justice systems of the crusader states. They were, after all, on the frontiers of Christendom, and many aspects of their law books were arcane in the extreme.

Assaults, for instance, were so frequent that there were well-established and suitably gruesome procedures in place for dealing with them. Fines had to be paid if someone had been struck by '[the] hand or [the] foot or with a stick'. If the attack was more serious, however, the punishment could be more severe and fashioned to fit the crime: if the assailant had used a weapon and inflicted a blow – say 'from a sharpened weapon or an iron mace' – then the penalty was to have a hand cut off. In such an instance, because the penalty was so severe, it was possible for the accused to demand trial by combat, in order to determine his guilt (see the next chapter).[8]

Similarly (and with a gruesome sense of the literal), the penalty for biting someone was a substantial fine – or, if that could not be paid, to have the two top front teeth knocked out. If the bite wound became severely infected, all four top front teeth were to be removed. And if the bite victim died, the perpetrator was to be hanged. There was an established hierarchy of pain and punishment, mirroring the impact on the victim.[9]

Animals also had their own special place in this legal backwater. The entire region was dominated by cavalry armies and controlled by social elites who fought as mounted warriors, so good horseflesh was in high demand. Stealing animals was the medieval equivalent of car theft; and stealing horses, the most valuable animals, was akin to grand theft auto.

As always, if you were caught, the penalties were harsh: someone found guilty of stealing a horse, a donkey or a mule would have a foot cut off for a first offence. In the unlikely event that anyone with one foot was still capable of stealing such a large animal, hanging was the penalty for a second (and final!) offence. Even stealing smaller animals, such as pigs, was often punishable by hanging.[10]

Some of these animal laws were endearingly peculiar to the crusader states. One piece of Frankish legislation, for instance, contained rules about the financial liabilities of camel drivers for the animals left in their charge. In an interesting aside that is sadly indicative of the fragile conditions of frontier life in the Latin East, there were also specific statutes to legislate for livestock raids; and particularly for cattle stolen and then taken abroad into Muslim territory. Animals that were transported across the frontier but subsequently recaptured by Christians could not automatically be reclaimed by their original owners – instead, they needed to pay appropriate compensation to the new owners, in order to recover their beasts.[11]

Rustling or theft was not always easy to prove, of course. There was a fascinating sliding scale of penalties in the case of animals that had been 'lost', but then subsequently found to have been illegally held by another man. These show the cultural and economic value placed on different kinds of animals: fines ranged from 300 besants for a horse and 100 besants for a hawk or a mature falcon, down to 25 besants for a mule or donkey and, very unsentimentally, a single mark of silver for a dog.[12]

Justice in the crusader states was certainly unusual, but there was one form of trial that was spectacularly idiosyncratic: trial by combat.

6

❖

Deus Vult: Trial by Combat

Trial by combat was, in many ways, the epitome of Frankish justice. Throughout the twelfth and thirteenth centuries, there was a gradual shift in western Europe towards the establishment of guilt by (shockingly enough) the presentation of arguments and evidence in court.[1]

Ironically, the innate ferocity of 'exemplary' punishment had an ameliorating impact on the administration of justice, particularly where juries were concerned. As a result, conviction rates – especially in countries with a strong jury system, such as England – tended to be relatively low by modern standards. Verdicts were tempered (usually downwards), by the severity of the punishments that were on offer: the consequences were so drastic that jurors needed to be absolutely sure before they found someone guilty.

Proven thieves and career criminals with long track records were often found guilty. But beyond that (and perhaps contrary to our modern expectations of the Middle Ages), juries tended to take a commonsense view of what was fair and just, rather than being driven purely by the letter of the law. English jurors, for instance, were very likely to acquit, because the process of evidence gathering was so rudimentary: the lack of certainty was generally enough to get a suspect off.[2]

The job of a medieval jury was a difficult one. Verdicts were often based on hearsay, relying on assertion and reputation in the absence of much hard evidence. But there was little alternative: jurors often had to form their judgement on stories and stereotypes. In this context, caution was the only fair way of approaching sentencing.[3]

As we have seen, resources (or rather the lack of them) were the major pinch point in the justice system. The infrastructure of law enforcement was tiny, despite the fact that the scale of the underlying problem, in both Muslim and Christian states, was enormous. The polarising effect of a lack of resources for the judicial process was even more exaggerated in the war-torn Latin East. Longer-term remedies were expensive (and hence rare), and there was a natural social desire to stop arguments developing into interminable and debilitating family feuds. As a result, many – perhaps most – cases were settled out of court.[4]

At the other end of the spectrum, however – and despite a trend across Europe for justice to move away from the use of ordeal as a way of identifying the guilty party – trial by combat remained a satisfying judicial option in the crusader states.

Communities in the Latin East operated in a harsh external environment. They were also legally more conservative in many ways. Culturally, it is perhaps not surprising that trial by combat was an attractive proposition to them. As vulnerable societies, they placed an understandable emphasis on personal bravery and weapons skills, combined with a profound trust in God's ability to intervene in the affairs of humanity. Trial by combat was necessarily brutal and savage – it seems arbitrary and irrational from our perspective. But it was also strangely appropriate for people who lived in a semi-permanent state of war and were believed to be fighting for 'God's frontiers'.

Trial by combat or ordeal presented a particularly stark difference between the judicial system of the crusader states and our own legal systems: everyone from lords down to peasants could be made to fight for their justice, in the most literal and visceral sense. The process may seem barbaric to us, but, as we shall see, such summary justice could sometimes, strangely enough, produce the correct result, particularly when all parties believed in the methodology of the process. More to the point, letting God's will express itself through the martial prowess of suspects and accusers (or their nominees) was cheap, quick and definitive.[5]

The process of trial by combat was deliberately designed to be intimidating and potentially highly destructive for all parties, and was part of a broader process of encouraging settlements out of court. Once again, justice was to be extreme and binary in its outcomes, in order to compensate for the absence of infrastructure.

If a witness came forward to make an accusation, the defendant was encouraged to rush towards him (it was usually a him) in court, just as he knelt to swear to the truth of the evidence. In a classic act of courtroom drama, the defendant would then seize the witness and lift him up from the kneeling position, saying: 'Stand up, for I raise you as false and perjured; for there is no question that you are perjuring yourself, and I am ready to show you and prove by my body against yours just as and when the court shall determine . . .'[6]

The court would then set the date of the battle. Not everyone was expected to defend his rights by combat in person – such a failsafe was obviously essential if justice was to be available to those who were less physically able. All parties (accusers, witnesses and defendants) could choose to nominate a champion to act on their behalf if they were, say, female, disabled or over the age of sixty. Similarly, if a crusader or pilgrim was murdered whilst in the Holy Land, anyone who was on the same boat, or who was from the same part of Europe, could appeal and pursue justice by combat for their dead comrade.[7]

Social standing also had a part to play in determining how the combat was to be played out. If the parties involved were of knightly status, they were expected to fight each other mounted. If they were both deemed to be of lower status, they would fight as 'sergeants' on foot. In the case of a knight being accused by a sergeant, the knight was forced to swallow his pride and fight in the potentially demeaning fashion of an infantryman.[8]

Despite some Hollywood suggestions to the contrary, there were, as far as we know, no professional champions in the Latin East. There were clearly, however, some people who were better suited to the task (by temperament, physique and training) than others – and there were suitably intimidating lists of the equipment which the well-dressed champion of the day should expect to carry with him.[9]

Trial by combat was legislated for as a legitimate recourse, but in practice it seems to have been relatively uncommon. One Frankish lawyer was blunt in saying that even once the process for a trial by combat had been set in train, 'many times I have seen the court say that there is no battle'.[10]

This was policy rather than accident. Choosing a 'battle-date' was often just a way of getting litigants to focus their minds. Most people would choose to avoid the possibility of physical harm if at all possible; and even if matters went so far as the selection of champions, the court generally set the date for the 'battle' forty days in the future – in order to ensure that all parties had an opportunity to resolve matters, either by agreement or by compensation, before more blood was spilt.[11]

Justice, however limited in scope, was to be made as widely available as possible. Lords were expected to do everything they could to make it accessible. They were advised that they

> should always have champions and arms for battle. If it happens that any man or woman who is entitled to appeal by champion wishes to appeal and does not have the ability to do so, the lord, for his honour and because he is bound to do justice and aid the needy, should provide for him from what he has put by. If any accuser who is not a vassal of the lord wishes to accuse any needy man or woman of the sort who can employ a champion, and the lord believes that the person accused is not to blame, he ought well to aid the accused just as much the accuser.

Having a store of arms and armour to hand was one way of helping the poor gain access to judicial combat, however eccentric that process may seem to us.[12]

Not everyone was allowed to be a witness. The law displayed a robust self-confidence in precluding testimony from 'all convicts, all perjurers, all those who are faith breakers, all defeated champions, all those who have renounced God and gone to another "law" [i.e. apostates] and all those who have served the Saracens and other unbelieving peoples against Christians in arms for more than a year and a day'. Also excluded were 'all those who are not born in legal marriage' and priests who had left Holy Orders. The aim of the law was clearly to stop people with a bad reputation bringing false accusations into court – but it also meant that you needed to be very careful who was around when you were murdered.[13]

Even arguments about money between relatives could end up in combat. At one point a financial dispute over fiefs in the Latin Kingdom of Jerusalem between a certain lord Daniel de Malenbec and his nephew, Thomas of St Bertin, got out of hand and a judicial 'battle' was only narrowly avoided.[14]

The ultimate trial by combat – an almost endless series of 'battles' – was reserved for those who were angry enough (or foolish enough) to question the probity of the High Court. In the event of such a situation arising, statutes laid down that everyone in court should challenge the offender to personal combat, one at a time. This extraordinary series of 'battles' was expected to 'start from the day [of the offence] . . . and it should be completed within forty days after'.[15]

The unlucky litigant faced severe penalties if he failed in combat:

if he [was] defeated, he should have his head cut off; his tongue should be pulled out from the back [through a hole cut in the nape of the neck] and attached behind his head, and his head placed on a lance, and [a] man on a horse should carry it the length of the town where the lord shall be, and the crier should call out ahead: 'Protect yourselves from saying such an outrage as this man did; he called the High Court of my lord false, when it is good and true.'

Outrageous and overly dramatic though this may appear, however, the true aim was probably deterrence, rather than punishment. The objective was to maintain the authority and integrity of the court. There is no evidence to suggest that the penalty was ever invoked.[16]

Trial by combat was rare, but extremely memorable. As well as having a couple of instances of case law, and the theory of the law books, we are also lucky to have surviving evidence of how a trial by combat actually took place from an extremely unlikely source – Usama ibn Munqidh, the itinerant Shaizari prince and diplomat, was 'an eyewitness one day in Nablus when two men came forward to fight a duel.'[17]

The story he told shows that dealing with banditry was a recurring element in rural life – and the socially corrosive nature of such criminality meant that harsh justice was often meted out to those taking part.

Bandits had raided one of the villages in the vicinity of Nablus, taking it by surprise. One of the local Muslim peasants was suspected of being complicit in the attack – and, for reasons that are now unclear but are probably related to the fact that he went on the run soon afterwards, it was widely suspected that he had acted as the bandits' 'inside man'.

The man's children were arrested and, in effect, held as hostages. The suspect was eventually forced to return. He still claimed that he had had nothing to do with the bandits, however, and demanded trial by duel as a way of proving his innocence. The local lord needed to find a hefty tenant who could take on this role on his behalf. The job was given to the strongest man in the village who was, perhaps not surprisingly, the local blacksmith.[18]

The blacksmith's physique was well suited for the task, but he was not a natural fighter – he lacked the killer instinct, and was less than enthusiastic about the judicial combat that had been foisted upon him. Usama was present at the trial, and it clearly made a big impression on him. 'I saw this blacksmith. He was a physically strong young man,' he later wrote, 'but his [nerves] failed him. He would walk a few steps and then sit down and ask for a drink.'

The peasant, on the other hand, with his children under arrest and a death sentence hanging over him, was highly motivated:

> The one who had made the challenge was an old man, but he was strong in spirit and he would rub the nail of his thumb against that of the forefinger in defiance, as if he was not worrying over the duel. Then [in] came the viscount, that is, the lord of the town, and he gave each one of the two contestants a staff and a shield and arranged the people in a circle around them.

The two men squared up to each other and 'the old man would press the blacksmith backward until they looked like pillars smeared with blood'. The peasant's desperation gave him the upper hand in the first half of the contest, and indeed it looked at one point as though he would win. But the longer the combat continued, the more it started to ebb away from the older man. He began to tire 'and the blacksmith gave him a blow which made him fall'.

The contest became increasingly bloody, a visceral fight that could have only one ending for the exhausted older man. Eventually his 'staff fell under his back. The blacksmith knelt down over him and tried to stick his fingers into the eyes of his adversary, but could not do it because of the great quantity of blood flowing out. Then he rose up and hit his head with the staff until he killed him.' It was over. Guilt had, in some strange but public way, been established.

Even now, the ordeal of the guilty party was not quite over. The men of Nablus 'fastened a rope around the neck of the dead person, dragged him away and hanged him'. The corpse was strung up as a high-profile warning to others who might want to follow his example. This is a disturbing and bloodthirsty tale. But whether the peasant was innocent or guilty, it certainly shows that banditry was a perennial problem, and that the sanctions of justice in such cases were severe.[19]

Usama, the source for this story and ostensibly himself an eyewitness, was a strange and vainglorious figure – a murderer and braggart who was regarded as self-serving and untrustworthy by many of his Muslim co-religionists. Not surprisingly, it is often said by academics that Usama needs to be treated with great caution. This is certainly true in some cases, but it also, in part, does him a disservice.

We cannot treat Usama's work as an unadulterated history book, but it is important to remember that he never intended it to be used as such. In composing his main surviving work – the *Kitab al-i'tibar*, written in the 1180s, towards the end of an exceptionally long life – Usama was not writing a chronicle. In fact, this was not even a memoir or an autobiography. It can be incredibly frustrating: the text jumps around, and there is no chronological consistency or logic. It often appears to be just a series of disjointed anecdotes or jokes – stories usually told, with his unerring blend of smugness and childishness, at the expense of other races or his Muslim rivals.

We certainly need to treat the material with care and to bear in mind how and why it was written. But within these limitations, it has value and, on occasion, unique insight. Usama's account of the trial at Nablus was written down over forty years after the event, and was the recollection of somebody who was relatively unfamiliar with Frankish justice. But interestingly, where we can check his narrative, it bears many remarkable similarities to what we know of crusader justice in this period.[20]

The description of the part played by the viscount, for instance, is entirely consistent with the role of the office in Frankish society. Coincidentally, we know that the viscount of Nablus at this time was a Frankish knight named Ulric, who held the position from 1115 to 1152 – a remarkably long tenure at a time when office holders came and went with a remorseless regularity, largely dictated by disease and the accuracy of Turkic archery. He was a frequent member of King Fulk's retinue, and his presence at Nablus with the king is entirely feasible.

Usama wrote that he was 'visconte' (which he endearingly transliter-ated as 'biskund'); but he also equated the role (again very accurately) with that of the Muslim office of the *shihna* – often translated as 'chief of police'. The responsibilities of this office-holder would, for example, include maintaining public order, keeping the roads safe and clearing out bandits and robbers. He would be in charge of the court where local criminals were arraigned and judged.[21]

It is also the case that under Frankish law, anybody who associated with bandits, thieves or other similar criminals could be held equally responsible for their crimes. As such, the old peasant man would indeed have been held responsible in law for the actions of those he was suspected of having abetted.

Bizarrely, many of the other, more minor, details of Usama's account of the trial by combat are also broadly true. We know from slightly later law books, for instance, that the Frankish courts would indeed provide the participants in challenges or judicial combats with refresh-ments and equipment. This equipment would include the parapher-nalia used for the fight itself – traditionally a staff and a shield and, strangely specifically, red clothing and footwear. But again – and very accurately, given what Usama said about the blacksmith stopping for drinks – the court would also provide food and drink for each of the combatants.

Duels would usually take place at midday, so that neither participant could benefit from the position of the sun; and local people would be arranged around them to act as witnesses and to prevent the combat-ants from running away. The undue length of time which the duel in Nablus seemed to be taking was doubtless particularly irritating, because the longer it went on, the more the position of the sun would have changed. Interestingly (and again confirming the veracity of Usama's memory), Frankish law at the time also demanded that the loser, whether alive or dead, should be taken away and hanged, just as the elderly peasant was treated at the end of the anecdote.[22]

Usama's literary style might look idiosyncratic now, but it contained much that was true: unlike us, he had witnessed at first hand the most characteristic expression of Frankish justice, with all its eccentricities and flaws.

7

Women and Justice

We may think of the crusades, however crudely, as fanatical wars of religion or as a clash of cultures. But they were also a clash of identities and genders.

Patterns of crime inevitably adapt to the society in which those crimes are committed – and that is as true of gender and social environment as it is of poverty and economic status. Crime is what academics call a 'gender-associated activity' – put more simply, the vast majority of criminals were, and are, men. Ideas of what constituted 'manly' behaviour in the medieval world reinforced the idea that violence was far more acceptable for men than it was for women – and that violence found outlets in criminality, just as much as in warfare.

Gender disparities in criminality are obvious, but often unspoken. The clearest similarity between twenty-first-century crime and the crusader underworld is that in both eras the overwhelming majority of criminals were (are) men. The UK's prison population is currently 96 per cent male, and the equivalent figure for the US is very similar (93 per cent). This is true across all crimes – fraud, theft and so on – but it is particularly the case with violent crime. Women certainly feature in violent incidents, but mainly as victims. Only rarely are they the instigators of such activity.

These disparities also existed in medieval Europe; but they were even more pronounced in the Latin East. The social and demographic groups most likely to be serious criminals, particularly young men, were also those most likely to be attracted to the medieval Holy Land. They were thus the most likely to be artificially overrepresented in the crusader states and their warring neighbours.

Not surprisingly under the circumstances, women were overwhelmingly victims rather than perpetrators; and even when they were criminals, they tended to commit different, less serious crimes. Female crime tended not to encompass murder or other major acts of violence, for instance, being far more centred around theft and petty fraud.[1]

Different crimes were reflected in different trials and punishments. Female criminals tended to receive greater leniency: they were less likely to receive capital or corporal punishment – female offenders were rarely given a whipping, for instance. They were also more likely than men to receive pardons.[2]

Patterns of criminal behaviour were very different, too. This was particularly true with violent crime, where women played a relatively minor role. Crime data is always problematic: we have no quantitative figures for the crusader states, for instance, but contemporary case studies in European societies shed light on the gender patterns underlying violent offences.

In mid-thirteenth-century England, less than 10 per cent of the people accused of murder were female. Similarly, in France, the court records for the period 1389–1422 show that women represented only 4 per cent of petitioners seeking a pardon for serious crimes. And, even when women were the perpetrators, they were far less likely to be prosecuted, as their crimes were often less serious than those associated with men. The lack of severe consequences was not just a function of biology and physiology: they were also far less likely than their male counterparts to be fighting with weapons. Hence, violent crimes committed by women were much less likely to escalate into outright murder.[3]

There was a similar pattern of behaviour associated with theft: female offenders tended to be involved less often and, even when they were guilty, their transgressions were largely at the less serious end of the spectrum. Women were usually involved in petty crime, and when they were 'professional' or habitual criminals, they tended to be operating in particular roles, such as fences for stolen goods. The typical medieval female criminals were nurses or servants or pub landladies who stole from their clients, rather than cold-blooded bandits or violent muggers. Petty theft involving deception was the classic female crime.[4]

Victims of crime

Being underrepresented in the criminal perpetrator statistics should, of course, be a source of satisfaction for women. Far less positive, however, was the way in which women were forced into the role of victim, and how, as victims, they were treated by the legal system. Even in clear-cut cases of domestic violence, the odds were invariably stacked against them. In fact, any abuse that stopped short of murder was unlikely ever to get to court.

When a wife was murdered, for instance, the punishment for the killing involved a far smaller sum of money than the penalties for killings outside the family. In the case of northern France, it was generally less than 20 per cent of the sum involved if someone beyond the (highly male-dominated) family hierarchy was killed. The death was, the law implicitly implied, a far less important incident.[5]

Domestic violence was an issue, as always, but was even harder to define in the Middle Ages than it is today. Then, as now, it was often learned behaviour: children who grew up in a household where violence was accepted as normal were more likely to become perpetrators themselves in later life. This phenomenon may well have been even more exaggerated in the crusader states, where military and other violence – or at least the permanent and imminent threat of violence – was so ingrained in the common social experience. But we do not have the evidence to be definitive about this.[6]

There was also the issue of what was 'unacceptable' domestic violence, and what was somehow deemed to be acceptable 'correction' or 'discipline' within the confines of a marriage. The concept has gradually become alien in western society, but in the time of the crusades a man was, in many instances, actively encouraged – or even expected – to punish his wife for her perceived transgressions. Husbands might be criticised (and very occasionally prosecuted) for 'excessive' punishment, but the issue of what constituted 'excessive' was hard to define: the point where supposedly legitimate discipline strayed from 'correction' into 'abuse' was never clear cut. But as a broad rule, beatings administered by hand were rarely considered abusive, whereas more savage beatings or violence – particularly involving weapons – were far less acceptable.

An incident in 1325 – in this case from Saint-Germain-en-Laye, just to the west of Paris – shows the kind of escalation that could occur once matters were pushed too far by either party. A married couple was known to have been arguing incessantly. The husband, a man with the deceptively harmless name of Colin the Barber, said that his wife habitually threw many 'villainous and injurious' insults at him. This had been done publicly enough for many in the local community to believe what he later said in mitigation, or at least to understand his side of the case.

One evening, Colin had had enough. He left the marital home to get away from it all, and went – again, endearingly and incongruously – to play billiards with his friends down the pub. His wife, Eustache, had not finished the argument, however. She followed him to the tavern, and continued berating him in front of his friends. Goaded on by his comrades, and doubtless much disinhibited by alcohol, Colin tried to punish her for what he claimed were her harsh words. Matters escalated quickly. The 'correction' soon came to include the use of a billiard cue. The evening ended with Eustache being beaten ferociously in the pub. She lay bloodied and severely injured on the floor, the culmination of the most savage kind of domestic abuse. She died shortly afterwards of the wounds she had received.

Even by the low standards of medieval society, the case was so serious that it could not be ignored. But Colin's evidence in mitigation was cleverly constructed to exploit social prejudices. He claimed that the death of his wife was an accident; that he had not used a bladed or sharp weapon (though it could clearly be argued that a billiard cue is, in itself, a weapon); and that he had 'only' been seeking to frighten and chastise her.

Strangely to our eyes, this elaborate and fundamentally flawed attempt at mitigation was enough to get him acquitted. Coupled with the character references provided by his friends and his previous lack of convictions for violent behaviour, the defence was sufficient for the court (which was, not coincidentally, all male) to give him the benefit of the doubt.

To add insult to her very real injury, the court even tried, with the extraordinarily perverse logic for which the Middle Ages has become famous, to imply that Eustache was largely responsible for her own death. If only she had treated her wounds with greater care, the court opined, she could have saved herself. It was decided that if she had been more assiduous in her wifely duty of wound-care, she might have been able to save her husband from the embarrassment of appearing in court at all. The bizarre implication, of course, was that it was all her fault, and that Colin had not actually delivered a truly fatal blow, even though she had subsequently died of it.[7]

Fortunately enough for Colin, the murder of a spouse (the spouse usually, of course, being the wife) was most generally achieved through stabbings; the use of a billiard cue was sufficiently unusual to allow him to argue that it was 'not really' a weapon.

Stabbing one's wife to death clearly involved the explicit use of a weapon, however, and was thus unequivocally 'illicit behaviour', even in the eyes of the most patriarchal medieval judge. The widespread carrying of daggers did not help in this regard, but at least it drew a clear line, beyond which it became easier to get the police and the community at large involved.

A certain Jehan Duquesne, for instance, stabbed his ex-wife to death in the street. Rather than being given a rap over the knuckles, he found himself being pursued by the entire local community. After a dramatic candlelit hue and cry, he was cornered and held captive until he could be taken into custody.[8]

Another instance of domestic violence escalating into murder occurred at the end of the crusading era. By the early fourteenth century, the Kingdom of Cyprus was the last main Frankish outpost in the East. Much had been lost as the Latin East collapsed, but echoes of the crusaders' legal procedures were kept alive through the treatises that governed best practice and case law in the High Court of Cyprus. Luckily, one of the examples of case law cited in these treatises gives us an insight into an extraordinary murder plot, and the even more eccentric way in which justice was eventually served.

On 12 May 1314, the wife of a knight named James Artude was killed in her home. The marriage seems not to have been a happy one, and suspicion naturally fell upon her husband. His motives were, from this distance, unclear. But this was an age when divorce was difficult and many marriages were arranged for convenience: land ownership and the transfer of rights between families could assume greater importance than love. There was plenty of scope for marital discord.

James denied that he had killed her, but the dead woman's mother (who was a widow) went to the High Court to formally accuse him. She demanded justice for her daughter by means of combat and, in the legal jargon of the court, 'she offered a champion for proof'. The king was obliged to extend his protection to widows and orphans, so the matter was swiftly escalated.

The king put forward one of his own men for the job of 'widow's champion', a squire named John Pansan. The archaic nature of the law – extremely conservative, even by the standards of the fourteenth century – meant that the judicial combat was conducted on horseback. The two men met to fight a month later, on 12 June. The stakes were high and the combat was closely contested. The king's champion was wounded in the shoulder, but in the end it was adjudicated that he had won. James was judged to have been 'driven from the field' and *conoissance* (judgement) was given that he had been defeated.

This seems, to our eyes, to be a wildly eccentric, almost barbaric, method of determining guilt. And yet strangely, when all parties bought into it, trial by combat could still deliver the truth. So it proved in this case: James was taken away to be hanged for the crime of murder. Like the rest of those in court, he believed that God had delivered justice to him, albeit through the rough medium of a heavily armoured squire. As he stood below the gallows, he finally confessed.

James admitted that he had wanted his wife killed, and had commissioned her murder. He had not committed the act himself, as he wanted to be able to swear that he had not touched her. But he had hired someone else to do it for him. The grieving mother-in-law was entirely vindicated in her efforts to bring a prosecution and avenge her daughter's death. Bizarrely, justice really was done.[9]

Ultimately, however, the cases of Jehan Duquesne and James Artude were exceptional. Women were usually the victims – of crime in general and of sexual violence and domestic abuse in particular. For most women, justice was hard to come by.

Sexual abuse

The age of the crusades was disproportionately skewed towards the needs and interests of men.

This sad generalisation is even more spectacularly true of sexually based criminality. Conditions were perfect for exploitation and abuse: men were generally at the top of the social hierarchies and exploited the power this gave them. Even in the lower reaches of society, this was an era when armies of mercenaries and other irregular soldiers were often uncontrolled and uncontrollable. In these male-dominated war zones, violence and rape were commonplace, as was – particularly in the Muslim world – the longer-term mistreatment of women as sex slaves.

Perhaps not surprisingly, male entitlement dominated much of the geography of sexual relations at the time of the crusades. Disappointingly, there was a very well-established spectrum of predatory behaviour across the upper echelons of medieval society, regardless of conventions such as chivalry or *furusiyya*.

Inequality in sexual relations was rife in society, but it was exponentially heightened when there were major differences between the participants in terms of power or social status. As always – in our century just as much as in any other – being successful, rich and at the top of the social hierarchy brought serious sexual privileges along with it; and many opportunities to abuse those privileges.

A knight, for instance, not only had the chance to have affairs with the wives of his peers, but he could also play the field (often literally, in these largely rural societies) much more widely. His resources gave him the opportunity to keep mistresses. And his social position made it far easier for him to have sexual access to women of lower status.

If there was a significant social distance between the two parties, the distinction between adultery – illicit extramarital sex – and rape could be a fine one. With sex between a knight and a peasant woman, for instance, issues of consent are often hard to judge: the boundaries between a coercive and a consensual liaison are almost impossible to determine from this distance.

The line between coercion and consent was further blurred by the issue of definition. Rape in medieval Europe was never an easy crime to classify. Religious law (that is, canon law) said that extramarital sex was wrong; secular law said that violence was wrong. But rape, and sexual violence, fell uneasily between the two – it was often seen as trivial for the man, but deeply shameful for the woman. And, from a practical point of view – then as now – the lack of consent was extremely difficult to prove in a court of law.

Regardless of ties of affection, women were generally seen as male property. Perhaps not surprisingly, given the gender of those who were running the judiciary, the law and its consequences were framed to reflect that underlying attitude. This inevitably had ramifications for the way in which sexual violence was treated. Thus, perversely, even something as devastating as rape was seen as just as much an affront to the men – the male partner or the male relatives of the female victim – as to the woman herself. 'Honour' was the elite status symbol *par excellence*, and anything which diminished that honour reflected on the male 'victim', as much as on the female.

In many instances, chivalry was a sadly shallow form of entertainment – little more than 'virtue signalling' for the male elite. Even the knights of the Round Table allegedly had to swear – on an annual basis – that they would not rape 'ladyes, damesils, and jantilwomen'. This is encouraging on one level; but what does it say for a society in which such annual oath taking is necessary? And what does it imply for the protection which might – or might not – be extended to ordinary females, those who did not have the protected status of 'jantilwomen'?[10]

'Saving' women was certainly a common theme of chivalric tales, but what happened after they had been saved is more commonly overlooked. There were many coercive – or certainly less than entirely consensual – ways of interacting with women outside marriage. The tales of chivalry, largely written by men for the entertainment of a male audience, idealised behaviour that would result in a lengthy prison sentence in a modern court (in the – still unlikely – event that such a case could be brought and proved, of course). Male superiority was a common theme, and such thinking drifted easily into ideas of sexual entitlement, particularly among the already vastly entitled upper classes.

Although chivalric literature was squarely aimed at the elite, even women in the highest echelons of society could find themselves at risk if events moved too quickly beyond their control. In the *Story of Merlin*, for instance, King Leodigan rapes the wife of one of his officials. While he is doing so, she is threatened that 'if she shouted a single word, he would kill her with his sharp sword, or if she thrashed about in the least'. Perhaps unsurprisingly, 'the lady defended herself with words as much as she could, but she did not dare speak out loud'.[11]

Although there was no unified or mandatory rule of 'chivalry', the code, such as it was, did not often apply to lower-class women. Even the normally gallant King Arthur was said to have fathered bastard children – at least one of them by an attractive young woman, whom he encountered while hunting. The ensuing 'romance' took a minute or two and was clearly less than fully consensual. The young woman, it was said, 'still knew nothing of such matters . . . she began to cry out while he was lying with her but it did her no good'.[12]

Romantic love and chivalry was fine (as far as it went), but only if it was not too inconvenient. It was a natural assumption in northern Italian courts, for instance, that the upper classes would exercise their power in a sexual way, and that any nobleman was entirely capable of acting as a 'rapacious wolf' among the women of his peasantry.[13]

Even priests and monks got in on the act, and often in the most brazen way. The Templars were accused of many crazy things at their trial. One of the more plausible charges, however, was that some of the monks occasionally indulged in homosexual acts. Ironically, faced with such charges, the defence of many brothers was to suggest – again, all too credibly – that this could not possibly apply to them: not because they were celibate (the obvious riposte), but because they were very actively heterosexual and had ready access to the local peasant women.[14]

In Cyprus, similar boasts were circulated with typical Templar braggadocio: no girl could claim to be a real woman, they said, until she had had the pleasure of sex with one of the brother knights. One Templar was even more specific when questioned about his sex life. He protested that the charges of homosexuality levelled against him were outrageous:

he was insulted on the grounds that he could get as many women as he wanted, and often did just that.

And although this was clearly forbidden by the religious authorities (and indeed by the Rule of the Templars), it does not seem to have been too frowned upon by the rest of society. Ironically, despite the charges of same-sex activity that were thrown at the Templars in the process of their dissolution, they had, until then, faced very little criticism in that regard – far less, in fact, than most other monastic orders. On the contrary, the Templars had, over time, become closely associated with courtly, romantic and very aggressively heterosexual love.[15]

The underlying rationale for that part of the Templars' image lay in the unhealthy expectation that adrenaline-filled elite troops were bound to need such outlets – after all, 'knights will be knights'. Men of their class had a profound sense of entitlement and were known to be entirely capable of indulging in sexual activity with women, should the opportunity arise. This was understood – and implicitly condoned – by others of their class. Chivalry was fine as far as it went; but it was not all it was cracked up to be – or at least not from a female perspective.[16]

Rape, sexual slavery and the exploitation of women were far more pronounced than they are now. Shockingly, rape, like the murder of a wife, was often treated as a 'lesser crime'. Partly this just reflected the gender bias and nature of the criminality: women were the primary victims, and men the primary perpetrators. Even when girls and women were recognised as victims, however, the 'offended' parties were often assumed to be their menfolk: women were male property, and the presumption was that their fathers or husbands were those who had been 'dishonoured' by the brutality inflicted upon 'their' females. This was a man's world, with a male-dominated judiciary. Expectations of male sexual behaviour were low and, sadly, often with good reason.

On the war-torn frontiers of the crusader states, sexual abuse at the hands of the enemy was so much the norm, so casual and habitual, that it was entirely expected. For female prisoners *not* to be raped was deemed so unusual as to be implausible: women released from captivity, whatever the circumstances and however much they might protest, were seen by all sides as 'damaged goods'.[17]

Perhaps surprisingly, this is the last time we will look at sexual violence in this book. It was so prevalent and so unremittingly depressing to write about that I have not included it further. For our current purposes, however, it is important to remember that its absence from the text in no way suggests that it was absent from society. On the contrary, the reality – or very real threat – of sexual violence was everywhere.[18]

8

Police and Thieves

When writing about the trial by combat that he had witnessed, Usama was broadly correct in pointing out the role of the viscount or 'chief of police'. It should come as no great surprise, however, to find that these police chiefs had only extremely limited resources at their disposal. There were very few dedicated law-enforcement officials in the crusader states, and we have only a handful of recorded instances of how they operated.

Viscounts in the Latin East, who were local court officers and administrative officials, were generally responsible for policing. We know that they were often supported in this role by another official known as a *muhtasib* (or *mathesep*). The exact duties of the latter are unclear; but more importantly, they were both backed up by a rudimentary police force in the form of a group of sergeants. Together, they were expected to enforce the law in their local area, arrest known criminals and check for instances of commercial fraud or breaches of trading standards.

The sergeants were tasked with enforcing court verdicts and punishing criminality, using violence when necessary. Some of these sergeants were known as *placiers* – nightwatchmen who had responsibility for a particular district within a town, overseeing property rights and acting as muscle for the local viscount on his evening patrols.[1]

But this was all very basic. Police officers, or their medieval equivalent, were hard to find. And on the rare occasions when they were available, the way they operated in Europe would not have filled one with optimism.

The police were often experts at bribery and extortion, having both the law on their side and ready access to violence (or the threat of violence) at their disposal. There are few examples from the Latin East, but the contemporary French police records show what might be expected.

Police corruption was disappointing, but perhaps inevitable. These were societies in which there were few distinct boundaries between the interests of the state, the dictates of the feud and the needs (however corrupt they might be) of the individual. As a consequence, some of the most outrageous instances of medieval muggings were actually perpetrated by the police, rather than the criminals they were employed to catch.

The French royal sergeants had a particularly poor reputation. They enforced the law with great brutality, and often exploited their position of authority for their own interests. Many were known rapists, and some were even murderers. In one particularly notorious case in Merck in 1288, a police officer killed one of his personal enemies. He then doctored the evidence to make it look like suicide. This was clearly a case of murder, but it was also a more intricate example of premeditated fraud. Anyone who committed suicide automatically lost the right to pass their possessions on to their heirs – the officer had, not very subtly, hoped to keep his victim's goods for himself.[2]

But criminality was a dangerous business in such a violent time, even when the police were committing the crimes. In 1248, in the midst of King Louis IX's preparations for what became known as the Seventh Crusade, John of Joinville came across a bloodbath perpetrated against the police force. Counterintuitively, it was also a massacre carried out by a civilian bystander.

'As I was on my way to Paris', wrote John,

> I came across three dead men on a cart whom a clerk had killed, and I was told that they were being taken to the king. When I heard this, I sent one of my squires after them to find out what had happened. The squire told me that the king, when he came out of his chapel, stood on the steps to look at the dead men and asked of the *prévôt* of Paris [that is, the local administrator of royal justice] what had happened. The *prévôt* told him that the men were three of his sergeants from the Châtelet, and that they had gone into the back streets in order to rob people.

Ironically, the Châtelet was the foremost law court in Paris, and the 'sergeants' referred to were the nearest thing the state had to what we might now term 'police officers'.[3]

The *prévôt* had an extraordinary story to tell. He said that the policemen 'came across this clerk you see here and stripped him of all his clothes. The clerk, wearing only his chemise, went to his lodgings and took up his crossbow.' Ominously for his assailants, he also sent a boy to fetch his falchion (a short, hefty sword with a broad, curved blade, similar to a large machete): the robbed man was determined to be better prepared when he next encountered the police.

The clerk was an unlikely vigilante: the word 'clerk' in this context denoted someone who was preparing to enter religious orders. But the police had picked on the wrong man this time. He ran after his assailants and 'shouted to them and said that they would die on the spot. The clerk drew his crossbow, fired and struck one of them in the heart. The other two took flight, while the clerk took up the falchion the boy had been carrying and chased them by the light of the moon, which was bright and clear.'

The intrepid clerk, who, as a trainee for the priesthood, was not encouraged to draw blood, even when confronting criminals, could not contain himself:

'One of the robbers decided he would cut through a hedge and [escape] into a garden, but the clerk struck him with that sword,' said the *prévôt*, 'and cut right through his leg so that only the boot is holding it on, as you see. The clerk resumed his chase of the other robber, who had decided to enter a stranger's house where people were still awake. The clerk struck him in the head with the falchion, splitting it down to the teeth, as you can see,' said the *prévôt* to the king [and pointing at the bodies in the cart]. 'My Lord,' he said, 'the clerk showed what he had done to the householders in the street and then he went to give himself up to your custody.'[4]

The king, who was mustering an army for crusade, knew a useful man when he saw one. With ecclesiastical employment now extremely unlikely, Louis gave him the opportunity to make a profound career change:

'My lord clerk,' said the king, 'your bravery has lost you the chance of priesthood, but because of it I will retain you in my pay and you will come with me overseas. I would have you know that this is because I strongly desire my people to see that I will not uphold them in any of their wrongdoings.'[5]

The Church's loss was the Seventh Crusade's gain.

Sadly, there were many other examples of law-enforcement officers being similarly corrupt. The bailli, or chief of police, of Arras in the late thirteenth century, for instance, was an infamous individual by the name of Jehan de Beauquesne. He was so notoriously corrupt that he was eventually arraigned by the count of Artois for his offences. The scale of his wrongdoing was impressive – no fewer than fifty criminal cases with which he had been involved were retrospectively investigated for possible bribery, extortion and other illegal practices. Almost everything he touched was corrupt.

One example of his activities was the murder of a certain Jehan de Feuchi in 1294. On an otherwise quiet night in Arras, Jehan de Beauquesne and his sidekicks were summoned to the scene of a violent crime. A corpse – that of the late M de Feuchi – lay on the ground. The fight that had culminated in his murder had been watched by many bystanders, eight of whom were still there when the police arrived. Ostensibly, this was an open-and-shut case.

Except that it wasn't. The murderer, a man named Robert de Cans, was allowed to leave the scene, and the police decided not to press charges, even though the crime was of the most serious kind. It was later established that the murderer had paid them off. Presumably the witnesses were Robert's friends, who could be relied upon to give false testimony – or perhaps they, too, had been bribed to stay quiet. Most said, entirely implausibly given the presence of a dead body, that the alleged crime had never taken place.

Another example was just as shocking. Two men – Wauteron Li Buriers and Sousse Soumillons – raped a woman just outside the city walls of Arras. The incident had occurred in broad daylight and in front of witnesses. Again, one might imagine, this was an open-and-shut case. But no. Bailli Beauquesne opened up discussions with the rapists' friends and dropped all charges, in return for a suitable cash payment.

Sometimes, when the case was less serious, or when he knew that there was less money to extort, the bailli would not even charge much to pervert the course of justice: he had his own sliding scale of corruption. In the aftermath of a drunken fight in 1294, for example, which ended in what we might today call 'wounding with intent', Beauquesne asked the assailants' friends to pay for it all to go away. However, when no money was forthcoming, he said he was prepared to drop the matter altogether in return for some wine. 'Justice' could come cheap.

The count of Arras did his best to root out the problem, and his investigators found that Beauquesne had a crude, and consistently corrupt, business model. His standard approach was to draw up charges verbally, put the consequences to the guilty men and their friends, and then offer to drop all charges in return for a cash sum or, where that was not possible, for goods or services in lieu.

The bailli was found guilty of taking massive bribes, over a period of several years, in order to pervert the course of justice. He was dismissed from office. So far, so good it would seem: medieval justice might have been slow to stop his corrupt ways, but at least it had eventually brought him to justice.

But it was not such a clear-cut, happy ending. Within three years, we find the irrepressible Beauquesne back working in the senior ranks of law enforcement, this time as bailli of nearby St Omer. Money and contacts had presumably allowed him to jump back into the upper echelons of the money-making scam that passed for policing in thirteenth-century France.[6]

The crusader states' Muslim neighbours had their own equivalent experiences and anecdotes – the role of 'chief of police' was closely associated with criminality, but not always in the way one might expect.

Taking a single Muslim city as an example – in this case Aleppo at the turn of the twelfth century – we get a sense of the complex and infinitely corrupt world of the medieval police chiefs of Syria. In 1097, the chief of police in Aleppo was a man named Boukat. Boukat was, by the standards of the time, almost overqualified for his post. His nickname was 'the Madman' and, as if that were not enough, Kemal ed-Din, a local chronicler, described him as one who was used to associating with 'good-for-nothings, rogues, highway robbers and debauched people'. Ironically, of course, it was this intimate knowledge of the local underworld that had helped him get the job in the first place.

Boukat served under three of the lords of Aleppo, during which time he created a one-man crime wave of his own – at one point he even had the vizier, Abou Nasr, strangled to death because of a trivial dispute over the price of some rugs. Foolishly, he finally overreached himself: he felt strong enough to start a rebellion of his own against Ridwan, the ruler of Aleppo (r. 1095–1113), and hoped to use the urban militia as his own army. His successor as police chief, however – a man named Ibn-Bedi – was still in control of the local military forces, and he persuaded the militia to desert their old boss. 'The Madman' was captured by Ridwan's troops, placed in one of his old prisons and, inevitably, 'condemned to the most appalling cruelties'.[7]

In 1118, Ibn-Bedi, the police chief who had arrested Boukat, came to an equally bloodthirsty end. While on his duties, he and his sons boarded a small boat so that they could cross the river just outside their castle. While they were thus distracted and confined, two Assassins 'attacked him and rained many blows upon him'.[8] The assailants were killed by Ibn-Bedi's sons, who started to carry their father back to the castle, so that he could receive medical attention. While they did so, however, they were attacked by yet another Assassin, who was determined to complete the job: he finished off the old chief of police and killed one of his sons for good measure. This last Assassin escaped by jumping into the river, but seems to have drowned while attempting to evade arrest.[9]

Soon after, in 1121, yet another Aleppan police chief, this time a man called Rais Mekki, suffered a similarly violent end to his term of office. The new ruler, Il-Ghazi of Mardin, decided to depose Mekki, ostensibly (and entirely plausibly, given the context) because 'the people had made great complaints against him'. Il-Ghazi had Mekki's eyes burned out, his tongue cut off and (probably more to the point) confiscated all his goods. Mekki's brother, who also seems to have benefited corruptly from his relationship with the chief of police, was tortured and had all his property confiscated.

Holding high office in the Aleppan police force was a potentially lucrative, but extremely high-risk career option.[10]

9

Criminal Competitors: Muslim Neighbours

Criminality in the era of the crusades was a highly competitive environment. As with the crusader states, thieves were a permanent feature of the Muslim societies that were the Franks' neighbours, enemies and, occasionally, allies.

The casual, almost homely, nature of low-level criminality speaks volumes about its prevalence. The headman of the village of Araja, in the area of Kafartab, in north-western Syria, for instance, reported an incident to Usama Ibn-Munqidh, the itinerant author and diplomat. According to the headman: 'I once went on a hot day to the well at Araja to drink, and I saw a man wearing a woman's get up [probably a woman's wrap, used as a common disguise by bandits] and on his shoulders was a sack of clothes. A desire for this sack came over me, and so I said to him "Hand over the sack".'

The headman fought with the bandit, but was eventually outdone when his opponent pulled out a knife. The bandit did not kill him, however. He just gave him a shirt from the sack and walked off, saying that he had recently got the clothes 'from Ma'arrat [a town to the north of Kafartab]. Yesterday I knocked over a dyer's shop and took everything in it.' It is interesting to see that the thief was himself a potential victim of crime, and that the headman – presumably the main upholder of the law in the village – was also an armed criminal who slipped seam-lessly into the role of mugger. Even more strikingly, it is apparent that no one seemed to take a mugging (or even an armed robbery) too personally – it was so ingrained in the social norms of the time that it was almost to be expected.[1]

Fatimids and slave-soldiers

No one would suggest that Palestine and Syria were a rural idyll before the arrival of the crusaders. Criminality was already rife. But the distorted demographic surges from the 1070s onwards (which massively overrepre-sented the 'usual suspects' of medieval criminality) made a bad situation far worse.

It was not just the Franks who encouraged large numbers of foreign men to enter the region and take up military service. Their Egyptian enemies (and occasional allies) had a similar interest in boosting the number of testosterone-fuelled soldiers in the area.

The Fatimids were a rich Shi'ite Muslim regime that controlled Egypt and, until shortly before the crusaders arrived, Palestine. Their army lacked the glamour of the Turks or the crusaders, and as a result is relatively little known today, but for much of the period it was the largest, best-equipped force in the region. It was also, for most purposes, the only one which might approximate to our modern definition of a 'regular' army. Significantly, this army, like most others, consisted largely of foreigners. These mercenaries were drawn into the army from far afield, both from the south (Africa) and from the north-east (Armenia). Like many of their enemies, the recruits were young men driven to the region by desperation or money, opportunity or piety.[2]

Militarised slave-soldiers were to be found in sub-Saharan Africa, and the Fatimids used their money and diplomatic connections to buy as many of these as they could. The main sources of these troops were the two Nubian kingdoms to the south of Egypt, Alwa and Makuria, both of which were largely Christian. They provided good infantry and gave additional access to manpower from the lands beyond, further into the heart of Africa.[3]

These men were available in very large numbers and were organised into ungainly brigades of perhaps some 5,000 men each. It has been estimated that there were approximately 30,000 men in these 'Black' (*Sudani*) units by the 1160s and early 1170s. Their martial qualities were often unappreciated, however, and there seems to have been an element of institutionalised racial prejudice against the sub-Saharan regiments. Usama, himself an officer in the Egyptian military in the early 1150s, writing for a primarily Arab or Turkic audience, contemptuously described them as 'defenceless, useless fools'.[4]

The Fatimids also sought the service of Armenian mercenaries. The Armenians formed the core of the Egyptian army's cavalry in the first half of the twelfth century. They were mainly Christians, famed for their skills as archers, both mounted and on foot. There were so many of these foreign troops that they had to build their own churches in Cairo.[5]

Steppe warriors were also sought after, but were never consistently available. This was partly because of religious, racial and cultural tensions between the Shi'ite Fatimid state and the rival Turkic-dominated Sunni regimes in northern Palestine and Syria. Scarcity was also compounded by geography: warriors coming off the steppes would generally find more culturally compatible employment long before they reached Egypt. The lack of good pasture in Egypt did not help either, as Turkic cavalry traditionally needed to support large strings of ponies.

Efforts to keep attracting steppe mercenaries into the region continued until the end of the Fatimid regime. In 1150, for instance, Usama was sent on a recruitment drive to Syria. Significantly, although he was only given access to the poor-quality nomadic mercenaries in the vicinity, who had already been rejected for service in the local armies, Usama had recruited no fewer than 860 cavalrymen within a relatively short period of time.

This anecdote, mentioned as a casual aside, reveals a shocking and fundamental truth. In just this area, at this particular time, there were almost a thousand nomadic warriors readily available for hire, even after the vast majority of their compatriots had already been absorbed into the armies of Nur al-Din, the Zengid ruler of Syria (1146–1174), and his competitors. It is not clear what would have happened had they not been hired by the Fatimids. Rejected by local employers, they would probably have been quickly reduced to criminality. The entire region was clearly awash with armed, but dangerously underemployed, foreign men.[6]

As if this influx was not dangerous enough, the other main option for the Fatimid government in its efforts to improve its light-cavalry arm was to recruit large numbers of Bedouin tribesmen – and in doing so, they had no choice but to acquiesce to nomadic Arab tribes operating in what would normally have been areas of primarily sedentary occupation.

After a battle, the Bedouin would generally look to exploit the weakness of the losing side, regardless of whether or not that was their employer. They were also notoriously 'neutral' when dealing with stragglers, civilians or villagers, being just as likely to rob and kill their own side as the enemy. But once invited in and given official status, they could maintain a semi-independent existence within Egypt, if only because the Fatimid administration lacked the light mounted troops to police them effectively.[7]

Criminality and social disruption were thus inevitable, if unwanted, corollaries of the unending search for new recruits. As always, demographic influx had an unintended impact.

Mercenaries from the steppes

Egyptian recruitment did not help. But the heart of the massive influx of restless groups of armed men (a far more disruptive force than either the crusaders or the Fatimids) was the inward migration of Turkic tribesmen from the western steppes.

Crusaders visiting the area might have been unruly; but the situation was, if anything, even worse with the Turks called in to help their Muslim neighbours. At best, these were men to be tolerated and treated with suspicion, rather than wholeheartedly welcomed. At worst, the local Arab population saw them as little better than the enemies they were brought in to fight.

The effect they had on civil society in the towns ruled by their employers was often disruptive. When steppe tribesmen reported for duty, they were sometimes refused entry into the towns they were supposed to be protecting. Instead, they were forced to camp outside the walls. This suspicion was often well founded. The newcomers spoke a very different language and looked very different as well – sporting dreadlocks or plaits, and with the swagger of tough young mercenaries, these men cut a deliberately intimidating figure.[8]

Their continued presence was inevitable, however. The original Turkic warlords and their Sunni Muslim states had gradually gone native: as local victors, they slowly left their hard nomadic lifestyle behind and adopted a more comfortable, but increasingly sedentary, culture. As a consequence, and in the face of the unending warfare, they also needed a constant flow of tough new recruits from the steppes to fill their ranks, create new armies and prop up their dynasties.

Steppe mercenaries were, in many ways, a general's dream. Granted, discipline might be a problem; but these were hard men and, with the right leadership, they could be almost seamlessly turned into a voracious and formidable military machine. In nomadic societies, the boundaries between warriors and civilians were even more blurred than in their sedentary equivalents, and this flexibility could be quickly exploited.[9]

Many Turkic bands (particularly the smaller ones) lacked neat ethnic labels. What the vast majority had in common, however, was that they, like so many of the soldiers fighting in the period of the crusades, were young foreigners. Even when fully employed, they were hard to handle. But they were always borderline criminals – men who were armed, drifting and looking for any opportunity they could grasp.

This influx, whether by invasion or recruitment, and whether from Europe, Africa or the steppes, would bring with it severe consequences.

Mugging and banditry in rural Palestine and Syria was, as we shall see, endemic. But what was true of village life was even more apparent in large cities. There was always something about an impersonal and anonymous urban environment – whether in Paris or Damascus, London or Cairo – that encouraged criminality.

Even Egypt, with all its riches, had major problems in resourcing law enforcement in the face of widespread criminality. Ibn al-Furat, an Egyptian historian writing in the fourteenth century, provides good examples of the scale of the problem. In the space of just one month, and in one location (in this case Mamluk Cairo in late summer 1281), he mentions several high-profile acts of criminal violence, all of which took place, no doubt, alongside a vastly higher number of unreported, unrecorded or lesser crimes:

During [this month] one of the water-sellers in . . . Cairo passed by a fellow, crowding up on him with his beast of burden, which excreted upon him. The two of them had words, grabbed each other, whereupon that fellow stabbed the water-seller with a knife and killed him. This was the story, so he was ordered to be hanged.

During [the same month] one of those troops under arms in Cairo passed by a tailor who asked from him if he would hand over some-thing to be tailored by him, so the two of them had words, whereupon the soldier struck him, then killed him. He was ordered to be hung.

During [the same month], a fellow known as al-Kuraydī in . . . Old Cairo was detained. It was said about him that he would strip [his victims], and that he was known for his thievery and bawdiness. An order was given to nail him up, so he was nailed upon a camel. He lingered for days, being paraded around through Old Cairo and Cairo. One of the most amazing things told about him was that the trustee [jailer?] responsible for him deprived him of food and drink, not in order to increase his suffering, but to shorten his life. However he said, 'Don't do it, because bad life is better than death', so he fed him and gave him drink. Then some interceded for him, so they let him go, and he was let go while still alive, but put in prison, where he died after a few short days.[10]

Regardless of whether it was sparked by a stream of camel urine or an over-enthusiastic tailor's sales pitch, the casual nature of criminality on the street is striking. The presence of so many weapons allowed disputes to escalate far too quickly – and those same weapons ensured that the consequences were more likely to be irreversible.

In a time with little infrastructure for moderate responses, the authorities needed other approaches to stopping crime. Hanging was the most common punishment for major crimes, but the use of a 'mobile crucifixion' – which involved fixing the guilty party to the side of a camel – allowed the maximum number of people to see the consequences of criminality.

Despite the risks, however, a stream of gang leaders emerged. The more high-profile among them had an established, albeit disreputable, place in their society. They had reputations. They were men of substance, at least within their own milieu. And their activities were often hugely disruptive.

According to Ibn al-Furat, in 1280 'a fellow appeared known as al-Jāmūs'. This was a redolent nickname, meaning 'Water Buffalo', which doubtless says much about his physical presence and robust character. Water Buffalo was known as

a trickster and a bawdy fellow. He would wield a sword, a scimitar [simanṭāra], alone, and try to duel with those who opposed him outside of protected Cairo, then take whatever he wanted from them. People were afraid of him, and he stayed with a number of people in their homes, as he overawed them and they gave him what he wanted.

The Water Buffalo became increasingly bold and violent. He 'killed a number [of people and] another fellow appeared together with him called al-Maḥwajab, and the both of them were active for a while'.

A dangerous reputation was helpful for a gangster like the Water Buffalo: he was a man who traded in intimidation – 'people were afraid of him, used him as a by-word, and began to talk about him a lot. Proverbs were even made about him.' But having a high profile was only useful up to a point. He began to believe his own propaganda, and his personal reputation eventually, inevitably, became his downfall.

The Water Buffalo's antics became an embarrassment for the authorities. Finally, one of the Mamluks of the governor of Cairo 'saw a fellow, who he didn't like, but then became aware that he was al-Jāmūs. So he shot him with an arrow, whereupon the latter fled, entering one of the orchards where he was detained.'

High-profile criminality demanded high-profile justice. The Water Buffalo and his henchman were 'brought before the governor . . . so the Sultan ordered them to be nailed up, so they were, at Zuwayla Gate, one of the gates of protected Cairo. There they stayed for days until they both died.' People entering the city had to pass the two men as they were slowly crucified.[11]

Everyone could see the message: crime doesn't pay and no one can evade justice indefinitely. But more specifically, no one can embarrass the authorities without facing the consequences.

Urban conmen, violent burglars and petty thieves were so commonplace, and so much part of everyday life, that amusing manuals were even written about them as a form of entertainment, ostensibly to warn people of their activities. One such book was composed by a certain al-Jawbari, a self-confessed dodgy character from the Damascene suburb of Jawbar. He wrote a treatise entitled 'The Book of Charlatans' (or, less catchily, 'The Book Containing a Selection Concerning the Exposure of Secrets').

Al-Jawbari conducts us on an eccentric and vivid tour around the darkest corners of the Muslim underworld. In it, he describes the different types of criminal one might encounter, and gives advice on how to avoid them. But the stories of murderers and thieves are told in an almost affectionate way – crime was so familiar that it had become a form of entertainment. Al-Jawbari speaks knowledgeably (and admiringly) of the skills involved in becoming a successful criminal: it seems likely that the author himself had been a conman, or worse, in an earlier life.[12]

The idea of 'honour among thieves' was a tangible one. Criminal groups existed, with their own codes of conduct and with specific social or religious agendas. In addition to better-known groups such as the *futuwwa* (of which more later), there was, for instance, a mysterious 'tribe of charlatans known as the Bahriyyah', who are thought to have been a sub-cult of the Haydari dervishes. These men had their own 'rules' which, according to al-Jawbari, led them to 'believe they shouldn't enter this or any other place unless they take something with them on the way out . . . They are a kind of sneak thief.'[13]

Other types of criminal were more familiar to our eyes, although no more attractive. Some, for instance, were described as 'thieves who enter houses unlawfully . . . [they] are the lowest of the low and they are craftier and more violent than the thieves who commit murders . . . Their modus operandi is to enter a place without permission and quickly snatch anything they can lay their hands on.'[14]

In an interesting indictment of the construction techniques used in medieval Muslim homes, there was also a particular sub-set of criminals who 'enter houses by making holes in walls and committing murder'; they used a toolkit which included specialist items such as 'a crowbar, an iron spike, a metal plate, a lock breaker, and an iron hand with iron fingers'. If they were caught in the process of a robbery, the consequences could be severe. According to al-Jawbari, 'if they enter a place and its owner hears them and opens his mouth, they will kill him and that's an end of it. They will take property and life alike.'[15]

Fraud and corruption

There were also less blatant, but potentially even more profitable, forms of crime. As we have seen, the practised traveller Ibn Jubayr had an extremely cynical view of the corruptibility of Muslim officials. This jaundiced view was not without foundation.

In April 1288, even the emir Alam al-Din, the state administrator of Egypt and one of the leading Mamluk ministers, was arrested for fraud on a massive scale. His corruption had been so astonishingly blatant that it was almost endearing.

The emir had used his high status to gain access to the state-run arsenals of Egypt. He then sent his men into the storerooms to gather the stocks of weapons together and shipped them up north for sale to the regime's arch-enemies, the Franks. When caught, he came up with an ingenious, albeit transparently bogus, explanation for his bold money-making scheme.

He admitted that he had indeed 'sold a number of spears and weapons from the sultanic storehouses to the Franks'. But that was, he suggested, just a ruse:

> Yes, I sold them for a hefty profit and a clear advantage. The profit was that I sold those spears and weapons which were old and falling apart, and were of little benefit. I also sold them at twice their value, and worth, just so the Franks would know that we are selling them weapons out of contempt for them, and taking them lightly, and because we do not care about them.

This was a highly imaginative effort on the part of Alam al-Din, but the sultan's agents were unimpressed. Their riposte was to the point and had the advantage of being far more plausible. The Franks, they said, 'do not allow weapons to be sold to them in the manner at which you have hinted. What is common knowledge among them, passed back and forth by the enemies, is that they say that the ruler of the Egyptian homelands and Syrian lands is in such need that he sells his weapons to his enemies. That is about what they say!'

The sultan issued orders for Alam al-Din's 'belongings to be confiscated, and fined him a large amount of gold. He was not allowed

to sell any of his horses, his weapons or the provisions or saddles of
the emirate. The sum to be paid had to be delivered in cash. He did
this after they had fallen upon him.' Just for good measure, and
presumably to ensure that he was not hiding any further treasure, he
was also subjected to torture. Bankrupted and disgraced, the emir's
other misdemeanours quickly came to light, among which were
kidnapping and human trafficking. Police raided his private prison
and freed various individuals from whom he had been extracting
money.[16]

Occasionally, there were even heart-warming stories of multi-cultural
fraud. One day a Muslim, a Christian and a Jew decided to steal some
agricultural produce belonging to the Mamluk Sultan Qalawun – it
sounds like a bad joke, but they very nearly failed to see the funny side
of it.

In 1285, a senior Arab cavalryman from Damascus, a certain
al-Shihab b. al-Dubaysi, had come up with a clever 'get rich quick'
scheme. Together with his two partners, a local Christian and a 'Jewish
Samaritan', he made elaborate forgeries of letters purporting to be from
the sultan. These they used to divert some of the harvests from the
Sueth region (which had, many years previously, been farmed as a
condominium with the Franks) for their own use.

Their scam was discovered, however, and reports of their crimes were
sent to the sultan himself. He was furious and decided to sentence them
to punishments that were significantly in excess of the legal guidelines
– probably because of the seriousness involved in the *lèse-majesté* of
forging documents in his name. The Muslim perpetrator was sentenced
to have his tongue cut out and then be 'publicly exposed' (presumably
tied and left as a high-profile warning to others). His colleagues were to
be crucified ('nailed up') as a similarly visible deterrent.

Qalawun was subsequently advised by a brave judge that his
sentencing had been unduly – perhaps illegally – harsh, and the punishments were scaled down. Instead, the sultan's men were instructed 'to
beat them and imprison them, as a warning to prevent anyone from

doing this'. Hardly a happy ending for the fraudsters; but although they perhaps did not realise it at the time, it could have been far worse.[17]

Furusiyya ~ another restricted promise

As in the crusader states, criminality was not confined to an underclass.

Muslim societies had codes of conduct which, while not being strict equivalents of chivalry, had some clear parallels. The practice of *furusiyya*, for instance, started out as a guide to looking after horses, but gradually became more generally associated with mounted combat skills. Eventually the word *faris* (literally 'horseman') became broadly equivalent to that of the European word *knight*, and the philosophy became more generally applicable to standards of elite warrior behaviour as a whole. There were also some parallels within the *futuwwa* ('young-manliness') societies, which had their own semi-chivalric moral codes.[18]

Regardless of moral codes, however, the Muslim elite were just as prone to self-indulgence and tantrums as their Christian counterparts. The irritability of the entitled classes could very quickly bring with it violent consequences, and workplace incidents might morph into murder or grievous bodily harm. Lords could exercise the power of life or death over those who served them – and, for the more enthusiastic, murder could start young.

In 1105, Usama, the Shaizari princeling, was only ten years old. But even as a child, he murdered one of his family's irritating servants, and was proud enough of the incident to recount a story about it – one in which he boasted of his precocious bravery in killing an unarmed man, whom he had taken by surprise.

One day, wrote Usama, 'an attendant belonging to my father . . . slapped one of the young servants of the house. The latter ran away from him and came and clung to my clothes. The attendant . . . caught up with him and slapped him again, even as he clutched at my clothes. So I . . . then pulled out a knife from my waist and stabbed him with it.' Taken by surprise, and hardly expecting a young boy to stab him, the dagger 'struck his left breast and he fell down'. The wound was deep and deadly. By the end of the day 'the injured attendant was dead and buried'.[19]

We know, from the clues he left within his memoirs, that Usama was extremely unpopular in Shaizar, his hometown, and was treated with deep suspicion even within his own extended family. He was forced to leave Shaizar and subsequently spent most of his life on the move, relying on self-promotion, intrigues and storytelling to make a sometimes precarious living, as he sought employment among the other ruling houses within the region.

He is never explicit about the reasons for his unpopularity, but the story of his first major act of violence provides a solid clue: this shocking tale of a proud ten-year-old murderer, coupled with (as we shall see) his father's own bloodthirsty temper, goes some way towards explaining why he was not trusted by those who knew him best. An arrogant psychopath could be a liability, even in the twelfth century. In fact, Usama was forced into exile in 1138 by his uncle, the lord of Shaizar. Other sources confirm that the uncle feared, not unreasonably, that Usama and his brothers might murder his sons in order to take control.[20]

Usama's nonchalance about using deadly violence against an unarmed co-religionist was largely learnt behaviour. The petulant abuse of domestic servants was something of a family tradition: life was cheap, and the lives of retainers were very cheap indeed.

'My father,' Usama later wrote in a different anecdote, 'had a groom called Jami. Once, the Franks made a raid on us, so my father put on his *kazaghand*-armour [that is, a padded mail shirt] and left his house to mount up. But he could not find his horse, so he stood there for a while, waiting. Eventually Jami the groom, who had been delayed, arrived with the horse.'

Usama's father lashed out and struck him with his sword. The weapon was still partially in its scabbard, but even so it was sharp enough to cut the unfortunate man's arm off. Usama glowingly recalled his father's virtuousness in regretting his temper. He commented approvingly that his father generously 'supported this groom and his children after him on account of this wound'. The views of the injured man and his family are not recorded: their opinions have no voice in history, but were probably far less fulsome.[21]

Life as a servant in the Munqidh household was a high-risk occupation. More broadly, the incidents recounted above were also indicative of the prevalence of violent behaviour in this era. As with chivalry, *furusiyya* was meant to be a force for good, in curbing the violent instincts of the overly entitled Middle Eastern elite groups. But in practice, both moral codes were often the exception, rather than the rule.

Part III
VICE AND VICTIMS

10

Gamblers

The crusaders had an ambiguous relationship with vice: like most people at that time, they lived in a deeply religious society; but they also loved a bit of low life. Their priests, not surprisingly, disagreed: for them, vice was a fundamentally bad thing. The Christian settlers were defending the Holy Land. They were, in a loose kind of way, expected to be on an extended, life-long pilgrimage. The potency of any pilgrimage was thought to be seriously undermined by lax behaviour; and immorality meant that God's favour would be diminished. With the very existence of the crusader states teetering on a permanent knife edge, spiritual support was always desperately needed.

But crusader lives were hard, occasionally brutal and frequently short. Temptation was ever present. Perhaps inevitably, the local Franks and the exhausted, battle-weary crusaders on campaign in the East grabbed their pleasures where they could. The bath-houses and brothels (which were often one and the same thing) were kept constantly busy. The many taverns were likewise well patronised and were associated with such vices as brawling and knife fights. As well, of course, as with their other, more obvious areas of business – drinking and gambling.

Monks as medieval high rollers

Bernard of Clairvaux wrote his famous and massively sycophantic treatise on the Templars, *In Praise of the New Knighthood*, in the 1130s. In it, he wrote, approvingly and smugly, that 'if they are caught speaking in an insolent way, or doing something unnecessary, or laughing excessively, or grumbling under their breath, or whispering, none of this goes unpunished'. They also, he claimed, 'hate chess and dice, abhor hunting, and get no pleasure from the common and stupid practice of hawking. They reject and abominate actors, magicians, storytellers, lewd songs and plays as being vanities and pure madness.'[1]

Bernard clearly did not get out much. In this view of things he was being not just over-optimistic, but in fact plain wrong.

Ironically, given the relatively rigid views of the Church, a disproportionate amount of the archaeological finds associated with gaming in the Holy Land (including boards, dice, tokens and gaming counters) comes from religious houses and the castles of the warrior monks, the military orders. The Templars, and their comrades in the Hospitallers, are vastly overrepresented in the surviving evidence. Far from sharing Bernard's prudishness about such things, they were among the most enthusiastic gamblers of the Latin East.[2]

However, Bernard of Clairvaux was right up to a point – at least in theory. The Templars' predilection for gambling was certainly discouraged: they were forbidden from playing board games such as *eschaçons* (which used counters or tokens), backgammon or chess. They were, however, allowed to play *marelles* (or nine men's morris), so long as there was no gambling associated with the game.

They were also allowed to play a game called *forbot* – provided the counters, usually made of wood, belonged to one of the brothers. The implication is that if anything of intrinsic value was involved, even the counters, the brother knights would not be able to resist the temptation to gamble with them. This highlighted the underlying issue. The problem was not with the game (whatever that might be), but rather with the gambling that would inevitably accompany it.[3]

Given the consistent disapproval and the inclusion of anti-gambling statutes in the rules of the military orders, it is amusing to see how often they were honoured in the breach rather than the observance. Evidence of these games being played by the knightly classes is pervasive and, perversely of course, is most prevalent in religious institutions. Multiple *marelles* boards, carved in stone, have been found in Templar castles at Jacob's Ford (Chastellet) and Château Pèlerin ('Atlit). At 'Atlit, one board was even etched out on the plaster of a stable roof, so perhaps the brothers played while they enjoyed a little fresh air and sunbathing, relaxing in the evening air. Or perhaps they just went onto the roof because they were gaming in secret.

Two *marelles* boards have also been found at the Hospitaller castle of Belvoir – where, strangely, the board bears an uncanny resemblance to the building plan of the advanced, new design for concentric castles, of which Belvoir was a leading example. Interestingly, one of the boards was found in the kitchen, where it may have been used for whiling away the time during the short gaps in the unremitting rhythm of preparing food in bulk for the large and hungry garrison.

At one point, the Hospitaller order even tried to impose a blanket ban on dice, clearly aimed at stopping gambling, specifically 'on Christmas Eve or any other time': strangely to our eyes, and contrary to the self-deluding rhetoric of Bernard of Clairvaux, the implication must be that major religious holidays and festivals were an acknowledged peak time for gambling among the warrior monks.[4]

Some religious establishments seem to have taken the instruction not to gamble more seriously than others – or at least they made more active attempts to stop it. One gaming board found at a Hospitaller castle, for instance, was attached to the underside of a stone mortar, which could presumably have been turned over quickly if someone in authority – someone who took the statute seriously – approached.[5]

Most seem to have been in plain sight, however, so perhaps many of the senior monks turned a blind eye to the statutes. In the refectory (or dining room) of the Hospitaller garrison at Bethgibelin, for instance, a gaming board was even scratched onto one of the tables: there was nothing remotely secretive about this garrison's gambling habits. Maybe, after a hard day's patrolling and skirmishing with the nearby Egyptian garrison at Ascalon, it was felt that the knights deserved a bit of rest and recreation.

The fact that the statutes of the Templars and Hospitallers both felt it necessary to explicitly ban gambling is, of course, an indirect acknowledgement of its prevalence. We know that the Templars placed wagers while gaming, because their regulations specifically tried to limit them to bets for items of no intrinsic value: an attempt to stop all gambling was implicitly recognised as an ultimately quixotic project.[6]

Even in the infirmary, while they were sick or convalescing, the brother knights were forbidden from playing games such as chess or, even more shockingly, from reading romantic novels. The mind boggles at the thought of these hardened, battle-scarred knights reading such books, but entertainment was clearly scarce.[7]

Gambling was so popular that it crossed all the obvious cultural boundaries. Monks did it, as did people of different ages, religions, genders and degrees of social status. This was not usually a problem – on the contrary, in an age without many material sources of diversion, it was often, in practice, seen as a harmless pastime for people who had precious little else to give them pleasure in their short, dangerous lives.[8]

The problem (for those in authority who saw it as such) was similar to that of prostitution: in theory, one could ignore it; but it could become an issue if it started to interfere with military matters. For the crusader states, living on the permanent brink of disaster, anything that interfered with the war effort was extremely dangerous. And, like alcohol, gaming could be seen – quite correctly – as a 'gateway drug'. Once you had a gaming problem, you were in a milieu where you could readily acquire other vice-related habits, such as sex, drugs and alcohol.[9]

Weakness and strength

The words 'game', 'gaming' and 'gambling' are obviously all closely related, and this was even more apparent in the twelfth and thirteenth centuries than it is today. We might play a game – say, of Monopoly or Jenga – just to pass the time; but in the Latin East, playing a game was almost entirely synonymous with gambling.[10]

Gambling was popular in Europe, but there were major differences with gaming in the Holy Land. Crusader gambling is unusual in that there is a disproportionately large number of references to gaming in the context of sieges. This is perhaps understandable. Sieges were binary, highly polarised affairs: apart from the gut-wrenching terrors of a short and bloodthirsty assault, they could be long and interminably dull. Horror and tedium were the finely balanced extremes of the crusaders' everyday experience.

The men naturally sought entertainment when they were away from the trenches and siege lines. From the perspective of many frustrated Frankish commanders, however, it was an extremely unhelpful distraction for their troops. And for the chroniclers, far from being just a harmless pastime, it was something to blame if everything went wrong.

Gaming was a social activity that Christians and Muslims had in common, and this had negative implications for the way in which westerners viewed the Latin East: these sorts of habits allowed local European settlers to be characterised as having 'gone native', and hence, in the simultaneously homophobic and xenophobic parlance of the time, having become 'soft and effeminate'.

It did not help that crusaders and Frankish settlers were, once again, seen as doing the work of the Lord: inevitably, this created unrealistically high expectations. Whether participating in the armed pilgrimage of a formal crusade or, as settlers doing the good work of defending the Holy Land, their behaviour was expected to be better than normal. And that expectation extended to gambling. Gambling was firmly characterised as a vice by the clergy, and thus undermined the sanctity of the role that crusaders – perhaps somewhat unfairly, and certainly unrealistically – were required to play.[11]

In this context, gambling was inevitably viewed as a weakness of character. Some – the more addictive personalities – had enduring problems with such habits. In the spring of 1260, Julian Grenier, lord of Sidon, got into serious trouble. Julian had inherited many of his family's larger-than-life and eccentric characteristics – one of his ances-tors, as we shall see, was a famous pirate and renegade. The difference with Julian was that he had the misfortune not only to have bad habits, but also to live in a time of impending and unavoidable disaster. Almost unstoppable waves of Mongol warriors had entered the Middle East, sweeping all aside as they progressed. The tiny armies of the crusader states wisely hunkered down and tried to avoid them wherever possible. But Julian chose not to take that option.[12]

According to one Christian source, Julian, as volatile and intem-perate as his buccaneer ancestor, had raided lands held by the Mongols and attacked Muslim civilians who were under their protection. In retaliation, a Mongol army set up camp around Sidon, the centre of his lordship, and started preparations for an assault: the fortified city had two strong castles within it, but only undermanned and vulnerable town walls to protect the civilian population. The invaders deliberately tried to intimidate and provoke a response. Julian duly obliged and organised a defiant defence.[13]

He made sure the Mongols did not have everything their own way. As they launched their assaults, the chronicler now called 'the Templar of Tyre' wrote that they were 'resisted in [their] attack by the lord of Sidon, Sir Julian [Grenier], who was on his horse at the entrance to the gate, defending the entrance so vigorously with the few men that he had that two horses were killed under him'. Julian's fierce resistance was brave and, up to a point, calculated: he was trying to defend his vassals and the civilians of the town, and help them to escape. He made sure that he 'held the entrance so long that the common people had a great deal of time to retire together to a pair of castles, one inland and the other on the sea'. A complete massacre was averted, but the loss of life was still considerable.

When the Mongols did eventually break in, they took their revenge, inflicting huge damage on the walls and buildings. The destruction was so severe that within a few months Julian was forced to sell Sidon 'to the Templars, because he did not have the resources to repair the walls which had been thrown down'.

Even with his exemplary track record of courage and *noblesse oblige*, Julian was still criticised for his gambling. 'This Julian was a gallant knight, hardy and vigorous,' wrote one contemporary chronicler, but he was also 'quite reckless and lacking in good judgement, with a big frame and limbs and large, well-built bones; he indulged the lusts of the flesh, and was an avid gambler, and beggared himself by playing.' People still thought the loss of his lordship was at least partly self-inflicted: no matter how well you behaved in other respects, your gambling habits would come back to haunt you.[14]

By an extraordinary chance, corroborating physical evidence of this bloodthirsty incident has recently come to light. Archaeologists working in Sidon (now in southern Lebanon) have discovered a mid-thirteenth-century grave pit, hastily dug into the ditch on the landward side of the old city walls. This pit, not far from the castle of St Louis (the 'inland' castle into which Julian had withdrawn), was presumably near the last line of retreat – the path along which the townsfolk and some remnants of the Frankish urban militia fled from the Mongol horsemen as they broke through into the city.

A total of some twenty-five bodies were found in the grave; however, the bones may also represent the remains of other bodies, too, as many of the skeletons are incomplete. The vast majority of the corpses, probably all of them, were male. This hopefully indicates that the women and children had already been evacuated into the castle precincts, leaving the men behind to conduct the defence of the city walls as best they could and buy their families time to get away.

The evidence presented by the bodies suggests strongly that they were part of the grisly massacre that Julian and his retinue had sought to prevent. The majority of the men in the pit had perhaps died *en route* from the walls, as the last defenders tried in vain to fall back on foot, pursued by the fearsome Mongol cavalry.

Their DNA, where it is possible to carry out testing, gives a good indication of the type of ethnicity one would expect in a 'crusader' garrison of this type. Some of the men were clearly of European origin. Others, perhaps local Arab Christians or Armenians, were native to the region. Still others were of mixed race, reflecting the diverse demographic make-up of the cosmopolitan 'Latin' population of the crusader states – even the royal families were mixed-race settlers (the *pulani* as the chroniclers referred to them). This ethnic melting pot was mirrored in death as much as in life, as the bodies were thrown into the makeshift pit together, their bones mingling together over time.

The manner of the men's death reveals much of the trauma they experienced in their last few minutes of life. Broadly, they can be divided into two groups: those who died quickly in the fighting, probably cut off while fleeing towards Sidon's castles; and those who died shortly afterwards in captivity. For both groups, the grim story played out as one might have anticipated.

Those who died in the retreat from the walls seem to fit the pattern of the events described by the Templar of Tyre. They were men running in panic, painfully aware that their chances of survival were slipping away with every passing second. They found themselves the prey of the tough Mongolian steppe cavalry. Inevitably under these circumstances, they suffered a disproportionate number of wounds on the back of their bodies.

As they were infantry running away from adrenaline-filled cavalrymen, they suffered all the kinds of predictable, but traumatic wounds that went with their desperate situation – glancing blows to the head, as horsemen overtook them; slashing sword wounds on the shoulders and upper arms; and stabs in the back as they tried, but failed, to evade their attackers. Tellingly – given that the mace was the preferred sidearm of many Mongol cavalrymen – some also suffered hideous concussive wounds to the head, appalling injuries which reflected the viciousness of the weapon and the transferred kinetic energy of a charging horse. The injuries were horrific.

And yet those victims were perhaps the lucky ones.

The other group of bodies seems to consist of Christian prisoners. These men suffered traumatic injuries to the back of the neck, reflecting the traditional Mongol predilection for beheading prisoners. Not all had died so quickly, however: some of the bodies had the tell-tale signs of thorough torture on the interminable path to an inevitable death. One Frankish soldier had suffered more than twelve wounds before he died. It appears that the Mongols, enraged by their inability to capture the two castles of Sidon, vented their fury by torturing and executing their prisoners – perhaps in full view of the garrison of the castle of St Louis, in an effort to antagonise those who had escaped and thwarted them.

Life in the crusader states was already tough. Working for an inveterate gambler who could not afford to maintain the city's defences was dangerous and demeaning – but, for the inhabitants of Sidon, the Mongols were there to make things even worse.[15]

A gambling problem was viewed (not entirely illogically) as a broader symptom of a flawed and weak character, as well as a cause of difficulties in its own right. Raymond of Poitiers, prince of Antioch, for instance, had a reputation not only for being a degenerate gambler, but also for having 'a habit of acting on a hasty impulse' and being prone to outbursts of anger. Gambling in his case was seen as an obvious indicator of his underlying personality defects – just one more manifestation of the rash disposition that made him a flawed leader for his people. Unhappily for his subjects, he was said to be 'seldom lucky', either in his gambling or, more importantly, in his handling of affairs of state; and it is clear how closely the two things were linked in the public mind.[16]

Like a drug, gambling caused men to be remiss about their duties. Taking the example of Raymond of Antioch once more, we find that at the siege of Shaizar in 1138 he allowed his addictive habit to overshadow his military priorities. 'While others were engaged in strenuous conflict,' wrote the Frankish chronicler William of Tyre, Raymond and Count Joscelin II of Edessa, 'let themselves be drawn away by the frivolous pursuits common to [young] men of their age. They were continually playing at games of chance to the great detriment of their own interests.' Even more dangerously, this lethargy was infectious: the torpor and lack of leadership were corrosive and 'influenced others to take a less active part in the siege'. This poor behaviour may well have been a political statement of sorts. The Frankish leaders were sulking at the prospect of having to fulfil their treaty obligations by helping the Byzantines. But petulance, a lack of self-control with gambling and other vices were natural companions to a flawed personality.[17]

This disgraceful dereliction of duty was echoed in the visual portrayals of the siege. While the Byzantine commander is shown in manuscript illustrations as leading from the front and energetically prosecuting the attacks, the crusaders' leaders are portrayed idly gambling together – although it is interesting to note that, perhaps for reasons of social status, they are shown to be gambling over a game of chess, rather than with the less intellectually demanding dice that were their real preference.[18]

In practice, seeking an outright ban on gambling or gaming was rare: stopping it altogether was usually felt to be too draconian and, more to the point, impossible to enforce. Instead, the authorities tried to compromise. There were times and places when gambling would be tolerated – in bars, for instance, and when not on campaign. But there were other times – such as in the middle of a siege – when it was considered extremely unhelpful. Weakness, a flawed character and the loss of support from an all-seeing God were a toxic combination.[19]

The other sport of kings

Even kings were not immune. On the contrary, with plentiful resources to (literally) play with, they could indulge themselves far more easily than most. If a prince or young king was lucky, it was a habit he grew out of – an edgy memory of a dissolute youth that could be quietly put behind him.

Baldwin III, for instance, became an excellent leader for his people. In the early years of his reign, however, because of his youth and the normal predisposition of men of his class and rank, he had had a couple of bad habits, too. In 'pernicious games of chance and dice,' one otherwise admiring chronicler wrote, 'he indulged more than befitted royal majesty. In pursuit of the desires of the flesh, also, he is said to have dishonoured the marriage ties of others. This was in his youth, however, for . . . after he took a wife, he is said to have been entirely faithful to her.' Gaming, whoring and drinking were all of a piece: and the sooner a man with responsibilities left them behind, the better.[20]

As they got older, some people became increasingly less tolerant of gambling and everything that went with it. When King Louis IX sailed back to the Latin Kingdom of Jerusalem in 1250, he was suffering from the post-traumatic stress of captivity and the very real threats of torture which he had experienced while held as a prisoner of war in Egypt. He was also still mourning the death of his brother, Robert of Artois. Entirely understandably, Louis was not in a good mood.

In mid-voyage, 'weak as he was through illness', Louis found his other brother, Charles of Anjou, gambling over a game of backgammon with lord Walter of Nemours. The king had a massive sense of humour failure. Louis staggered towards the players and threw their gaming board over the side. The quick-witted Walter anticipated what was about to happen and scooped all the money into his gown ('there was a lot of it', wrote John of Joinville, approvingly) before the game reached its sudden and watery conclusion.[21]

This was an experience that stayed with Louis long after he had returned to the West in 1254. Once he got back to France, he introduced a series of legal reforms which included specific anti-gaming legislation. Instructions were issued 'that all our *prévots* and baillis . . . should avoid games of dice and taverns'. Even more ambitiously (and just as forlornly), he also tried to stop gaming equipment being made, declaring that 'we desire the manufacture of dice to be banned throughout our kingdom'. Not surprisingly, there is little evidence that any of these bans were effective. But, from Louis's perspective at least, it showed that he was acting against something which he felt was an affront to honour and general perceptions of decency.[22]

Louis was generally a well-meaning king, but he was prone to being rather 'holier than thou'. He was, after all, soon to become a saint. But he and his family had not always been so sanctimonious, and stories of gambling in the royal household were rife.

Certainly his far less saintly brothers were not above such temptations – the rudely interrupted game on board the ship was no isolated incident. In 1250–1251, while the French army was still in the Latin Kingdom of Jerusalem, John of Joinville saw the royal family hard at play. As he later wrote: 'While the king was in Acre, his brothers resolved to play dice. The count of Poitiers was such a courteous player that when he won he opened up the room and had all the gentlemen and gentlewomen summoned, if there were any about, and handed over fistfuls of money, his own as well as what he had won.'[23]

The debts that gambling accumulated could be huge; but such reckless, flamboyant largesse was important – Louis's brothers believed that generosity and the visible display of wealth were central features of leadership and monarchy. If one were to look for the roots of the extravagant gaming gestures of Versailles and the court of the Sun King, the camp of Louis's army on the coast of Palestine would be a good starting point.

The predilection for gaming among the royal family was so famous that it even became known among the local Muslim states, and began, in its own small way, to have an impact on foreign policy. When envoys from the Assassins brought tribute to King Louis from their leader, the

Old Man of the Mountain, in 1250–1251, they clearly knew how much the French nobility in general, and the royal family in particular, enjoyed gambling. Louis was given 'backgammon and chess sets', each of which was 'decorated with ambergris, which was fixed to the crystal with fine gold settings'.[24]

Joinville does not mention whether the king himself enjoyed gaming at that time, just that his brothers did. Perhaps he was being discreet on behalf of his patron. But it was odd – perhaps even suspicious – that the Old Man of the Mountain, generally very informed about such things, seemed to think that he did.

Much the same was true of the Muslim world: sometimes, in that violent age, even playing a game of chess could be dangerous. One noble chess player, Count Walter IV of Brienne, had been captured by the Mamluks at the battle of La Forbie in 1244. Six years later he was still languishing in prison, but seems to have struck up a rapport with the emir, who was his captor. The two men started playing together.

Despite the absolute clarity of the rules, they began to squabble. During one game, matters deteriorated so badly that the emir punched Walter in the face. The count, who was also the brother-in-law of King Henry of Cyprus, was outraged. He grabbed the chess board, hit the emir round the head with it, and killed him. There could be no ultimate winner in this contest, however: the prison guards rushed in 'and instantly strangled the count'.[25]

Gambling was also frequently associated with defeat, disaster and lethargy – there were moral, as well as physical dangers. Just before the battle of Antioch in 1098, Kerbogha, the Turkic commander, was said to have been frittering away his time playing chess. With such dissolute activities at the forefront of his mind, it was no wonder, thought the judgemental chroniclers, that the catastrophic defeat of his armies followed soon afterwards.[26]

But sometimes the moralistic association between gambling and the punishments that might follow such dissolute behaviour could be all too literal. The sultan of Egypt in 1249, for instance, was a ruler named as-Salih Ayyub, who was in the habit of playing chess barefoot on a mat. One day, according to John of Joinville, his enemies hatched a plot to exploit this habit in order to poison him.

While the sultan was besieging the Muslim lordship of Hama, one of his servants was bribed to kill him. The servant was aware

> that the sultan would come and play chess on the mats at the end of his bed each afternoon, and so he placed poison on the mat on which he knew the sultan sat. It so happened that the sultan, who was bare legged, shifted his weight on to an open sore on his leg, and straightaway the poison entered his exposed flesh and took all power of movement from the side of his body into which it had entered. Each time the venom surged to his heart the sultan was unable to eat, drink or speak for two days.

In Joinville's account, he became severely ill, declined into semi-paralysis, and died soon afterwards.[27]

The story may well be apocryphal – Joinville confuses 'Hama' with the town of Hims, for instance; and we know that as-Salih Ayyub was already seriously ill before the alleged poisoning incident even took place. But the message Joinville was trying to convey is clear: gambling, like alcoholism or promiscuity, is dissolute behaviour. It will not end well.[28]

11

Drinking, Bars and Bar Brawls

Intoxicating recreational activities are a powerful modern link to the medieval underworld: they are an area in which we can find common experiences. They were both a focal point and a stimulus for criminality in the Middle Ages, just as much as they are now.

Pubs and bars provided opportunities for consuming alcohol and gave their customers, once disinhibited, opportunities to try a range of legally dubious activities, including robbery and paid-for sex. Fighting was also a traditional consequence of drinking too much. The correlation between alcohol and violence, particularly among males, is substantial: fights are not inevitable, but the links are easily observable. In modern crime statistics, the connection between testosterone, alcohol and aggression is clear.

Pubs and crusading sound like particularly incongruous partners. But strangely, there was a genuine and enduring connection between the two.

Pubs and taverns in the West largely grew up to cater for the pilgrim trade and for travelling merchants – they were places where strangers could stay on their travels, at a time when few ever left the village of their birth. The crusades, as grand international pilgrimages, were a major boost to the hospitality industry – and, not surprisingly, the twelfth century saw a burgeoning, symbiotic growth in the pub trade.[1]

This growth was driven by the practical needs of religious tourism; but this was not, from a moralist's perspective, without its dangers. As James of Vitry wrote in his sermons to pilgrims (c.1229–1240), 'certain pilgrims and crusaders who do not keep themselves from sins but in returning to their vomit [a charming biblical turn of phrase, redolent of the language of the counter-reformation] befoul their pilgrimage'. In this context, alcohol could quickly become an issue, even for those who were not habitually heavy drinkers.[2]

Pilgrim groups, quite sensibly, tended to put their money into a communal fund. The downside of this, however, was that if one member of the party started to drink heavily, then everyone else (since they were all part-funding their comrade's alcohol consumption) would be motivated to join in. James claimed, entirely plausibly, to have seen 'many pilgrims who, fatigued from their journey, used to drink until they were dead drunk and others who, although they were not thirsty, when they saw their companions drinking, without any need to, began to drink lest perhaps they be cheated'.[3]

The problem was not just about financial morality, however. There was a wider, and more practical, rationale underpinning the dangers of drinking. James of Vitry, sunny as ever, was continually exhorting pilgrims not to go into pubs, in order to avoid the unscrupulous innkeepers, prostitutes and petty criminals they would meet there. The problem, as he saw it, was less about the alcohol itself, and more about the consequences of a loss of control. 'In fact,' he wrote, 'a drunkard is not so much he who drinks wine as he who is drunk or absorbed by wine.' Alcohol was a disinhibitor that led to other sins, such as lust. And committing such sins, so the internal logic ran, would undermine the success of any holy enterprise, whether it was an elaborate crusade or a simple pilgrimage.[4]

A relaxing drink down the pub

There were temporal, as well as spiritual downsides, however. Staying in pubs and over-indulging in alcohol might have very practical consequences. In an age before credit was widely available, travellers needed to carry cash. Theft was accordingly widespread – and if you had your money stolen, you would be unable to proceed on crusade. James, of course, had something to say about this as well: when pilgrims or crusaders 'have become inebriated then their possessions will be stolen from them by evil tavern keepers or even by wicked companions. Certainly there is no love among hostellers. They live from theft. The guest is not safe from his host.' Indeed.[5]

Perhaps not surprisingly, given the skewed demographics of the region, there seem to have been many pubs in the major crusading cities. The thirteenth-century Uppsala map of Jerusalem, for instance, shows the location of two pubs (*taberna*): one near Mount Zion Gate and the other at the junction of the Street of Mount Zion and David Street.[6]

Wine, rather than beer, was the common drink. As in antiquity, it seems to have been watered down, according to taste or purchasing power. Joinville and his men certainly had a taste for it, and the extent to which that wine was diluted was in inverse relationship to social status. He later described being on crusade in Caesarea:

When the feast of Saint Rémy approached [i.e. in late September], I . . . [bought] wine to provide for the household all winter. I did this because supplies became more expensive in winter due to the sea, which is more treacherous in winter than in summer. I bought at least a hundred barrels of wine, and I always had the best one drunk first. I diluted the valets' wine with water and that of the squires with less water. At my own table my knights were provided with a large flask of wine and a large flask of water, and they diluted the wine as they pleased.[7]

The watering down was partly in response to the strength and body of the local wine. The wines imported from Frankish Cyprus, for instance, were said by the pilgrim William of Oldenburg in 1212 to be 'so rich and dense that sometimes they are boiled down and eaten with bread in the same way as honey'. The recuperative powers of a rich and undiluted wine were felt to be so positive that even the normally strict military orders legislated for its use in treating convalescing brothers. The practice of 'improving' the infirmary wine for sick brothers (which presumably meant not diluting it) was written into the statutes of the Hospitallers.[8]

Another characteristic drinking habit of the crusaders, and a very expensive one, was to drink chilled diluted wine in the hotter months. James of Vitry wrote that 'all through the summer . . . cold snow is brought down to Jerusalem in two or more days journey from Lebanon, which, when mixed with wine, makes it as cold as ice. This snow is preserved by being covered in straw.'[9]

The link between pubs, alcohol and other vices was not just a useful trope for moralists to play upon. In 1268, for instance, Sultan Baybars refused to put a truce in place with the lord of Jaffa. According to the chronicler Ibn al-Furat, Baybars claimed that '[the Franks] have set up a tavern in Jaffa and put a number of Muslim women into it, and they have deliberately undertaken other things that are not covered by truce terms'. Presumably, under the circumstances, the women were sex workers.[10]

The notoriety of Frankish pubs spread widely: there were even records among the Jewish community in Egypt reproving some local shellfish gatherers for drinking 'white Egyptian beer' in a Frankish tavern of 'bad repute' – and, it was implied, maybe doing more than just drinking.[11]

Violence was also very closely associated with bars, and members of the military orders were explicitly forbidden by their rules from entering them. This violence could even extend, on occasion, to murder. In 1134, Hugh, the crusader lord of Jaffa, went into revolt against King Fulk of Anjou. He was found guilty by his peers and ordered into exile for three years. Hugh enjoyed the drinking and gambling opportunities offered by the capital, however, and as he waited for his sea passage out of the country, was lingering in Jerusalem as he was wont to do. One day he happened to be playing dice on a table before the shop [presumably a pub] of a merchant named Alfanus in the street which is called the street of the Furriers. The count, intent upon the game, had no thought of danger. Suddenly, before all the bystanders, a knight of Brittany drew his sword in hostile fashion and stabbed the count again and again.[12]

Hugh survived the immediate aftermath of the attack, but died not long afterwards. His assailant, in true Frankish fashion, faced gruesome punishment. King Fulk

ordered a sentence commensurate with his guilt to be pronounced upon the man. The court accordingly convened, and the assassin was sentenced by unanimous consent to suffer the penalty of mutilation of his members. The judgment was reported to the king, who ordered the sentence to be carried out.[13]

As there was a history of bad blood between Fulk and Hugh, however, the king went to great lengths to ensure that the process was transparent. Anxious to avoid any appearance of a cover-up, he insisted 'that the tongue should not be included among the members so mutilated. This exception was made lest it be said that the tongue had been removed purposely so that the criminal would be unable to confess the truth of the matter, namely, that he had been sent by the king.'[14]

Other examples of criminality in medieval France give an indication of just how rough things could get. In the late thirteenth century, in Arras in northern France, a bar-keeper had an argument with one of his neighbours, a man named Karon de Bairy. We do not know their exact relationship. The neighbour may have been a disgruntled customer or, more likely in the light of subsequent events, an erstwhile partner in one of the pub's less wholesome side ventures.

There was nothing subtle about the affair. At the end of the argument, the publican stood in the street outside the house of his victim, and threw lighted torches through the windows. The arsonist was initially arrested, but later released after concerted lobbying from his friends and associates, among whom, appropriately enough for semi-organised crime, were the local priest and the mayor.[15]

The scale and reach of the publican's criminal activities is striking. We know – but only by coincidence – that at least one of the witnesses, a certain Peter de Savie, was a well-known murderer. And the bailli, the senior police official on the case, who was responsible for the arrest (and subsequent release) of the bar-keeper, was himself later convicted on major charges of bribery and corruption. We will never know the full story of all the criminal relationships in this case, but they were clearly pervasive.[16]

Violence in pubs was far more usual, and far more expected, than in other environments – hence all the sermons exhorting people to avoid them. Even this expectation of trouble could have unfortunate consequences, however. In Abbeville in the 1280s, for instance, a customer enjoying a refreshing drink died with his wine in front of him. This was sad, of course, and unusual, even by the poor standards of medieval restaurant hygiene. But in the event, the death was found to have been from natural causes. Tellingly, however, because everyone associated with pubs was also presumed to be connected with criminality and violence, the publican and his entire customer base were arrested, as being the obvious 'usual suspects'. The bailli and his men turned up and, lazily but not surprisingly, just assumed the worst.[17]

This level of negative expectation, and of a presumption of guilt, grew to the point where people did not even bother to question the motives or narrative behind violence in bars. It was presumed, often correctly, that alcohol was behind a lot of it, and, more generally, that it was just the kind of thing that went on in pubs.

Taking late-thirteenth-century Abbeville as a continuing example, we find that in one instance of violent fighting and murder in a local pub the police did not even try to find out what the circumstances of the fight had been. In another incident, a customer got into a fight and was eventually chased out of the pub. He was pursued, but not caught – or at least that was what everyone told the police. His body was found in mysterious and unexplained circumstances seven days later; but again, nobody bothered to resolve the matter fully. Yet another man in a separate pub murder in Abbeville was later found drowned after a bar brawl, floating in a nearby pond. Again, everyone was content just to leave the crime 'unsolved'. The concept of going down the pub for a quiet drink was still several centuries in the future.[18]

These cases all seem enigmatic and mysterious to us, but were probably viewed in a far more pragmatic light at the time. Often they were not really 'mysterious' at all: the identity of the perpetrator was well known, but for various reasons nobody wanted to pursue things too closely. Or things were left un-investigated precisely because they were the opposite of enigmatic: on the contrary, they were felt to be exactly what one would expect – the consequence of the illegal activities that arose all too frequently in pubs, and which were felt to be far too mundane to be worthy of more investigation. Then as now, violence and murder among known criminals received less police attention than crimes involving innocent bystanders.[19]

There were a lot of manslaughter cases arising from a trip to the pub. Many men carried knives. Arguments between armed men might, not coincidentally, escalate quickly and end in an accidental, or at least unintended, death. The tiny fines that were often exacted as punishment, and the quick departure of an unpursued perpetrator from a village show just how common such incidents were. Although formal cases of murder might have been relatively rare in the Middle Ages, unlawful death or manslaughter was not.[20]

Less-violent crime could also start in a bar, and then be played out elsewhere, fuelled, as ever, by alcohol and high passions. In 1341, for instance, a woman named Agnes de Payenne got into a drunken argument in a pub. Her antagonist, a certain Guerin le Pioner, had publicly insulted her, and claimed that she was talking 'through her rotten teeth, like an old whore'. Not surprisingly, Agnes was unimpressed by this vivid and enduring image. Knowing she would lose in a fist fight, Agnes took her debate elsewhere: she went off on her own and destroyed Guerin's crops by way of riposte.[21]

Sometimes men in pubs fought merely for the fun of it. One of the largest, old-style bar brawls of the age took place in Paris, at Sainte-Geneviève, in 1288. It started, predictably enough, with an argument between a pimp and a disgruntled customer. By the end of that lively discussion, however, almost the entire pub had joined in, just for the sport – a violent, uninhibited celebration of the moment. Luckily for the participants, this colossal punch-up remained just that – a series of punches. When things became more serious, as they often did, it was generally because the ubiquitous knives had been drawn.[22]

Sex and bars

Particularly in the larger towns or cities, where there was rather more anonymity, a wide range of dubious pleasures were available in taverns and bars. Access to sex, either through a chance encounter or through prostitution, was an obvious one. Where sex workers and pimps were concerned, there was always potential to argue about money, however: a bill not paid, services not adequately provided, or men failing to rise to the occasion and blaming their companion.

Pubs and sexual indiscretion went easily together: 'After all, when she's drunk,' wrote James of Vitry, hopefully on the basis of little personal experience, 'does Venus care about anything? She doesn't know the difference between the head and crotch.' It was all too easy to end up with the pox, long before you arrived in the war zone of the Holy Land. And as commanders in all major wars before the invention of antibiotics knew to their cost, Cupid's arrows could take as many men out of the front line as enemy ones.[23]

Even when you got to the crusader states, many of the local bars were operating as brothels. Usama Ibn-Munqidh, the semi-itinerant diplomatic 'fixer' and memoirist, had several entertaining tales to tell about the Frankish prostitutes he had encountered – or, more discreetly, that 'a friend' had told him about. Perhaps not surprisingly, and proving James of Vitry's point, one of these stories involved a pub.

Usama wrote of a time when he stayed with a 'friend' in Nablus, 'whose home was the lodging-house for Muslims'. This house 'had windows that opened onto the road and, across from it on the other side the road, there was a house belonging to a Frankish man who sold wine'. Usama claimed to have seen a situation unfolding whereby the landlord came back unexpectedly from delivering some wine to a customer, only to discover his 'wife' in bed with another man.

The anecdote was used as an excuse to make a snide comment about the lack of control which the crusaders exerted over their women: 'the Franks', Usama wrote piously, know 'nothing in the way of regard for honour or propriety'. But it is clear that what he really observed was the interaction between a prostitute, her client and the landlord-pimp of the establishment.[24]

The binge that saved the crusades

It was easy to talk about the evils of visiting taverns. But in practice it was far more difficult to stop them. And that was reflected in many of the more unruly incidents along the paths of crusaders on the way east. Alcohol, xenophobia and religious intolerance all encouraged extraordinarily poor behaviour. The passage of the Second Crusade was no exception, particularly when the different Catholic armies from the West converged on the Christian, but Orthodox, lands of Byzantium.

Mutual suspicion was the norm. Language problems, inflamed by drunkenness and cultural suspicion, meant that arguments were quick to boil over. And the fact that so many of the participants were heavily armed soldiers meant that the consequences were disproportionally lethal.

Constantinople itself was easy to characterise, particularly by the clerics who often wrote the chronicles, as the consummate destination for sin and temptation. 'The city itself is squalid and fetid and in many places harmed by permanent darkness,' wrote one disapproving French priest, 'for the wealthy overshadow the streets with buildings and leave these dirty, dark places to the poor and to travellers; there murders and robberies and other crimes which love this darkness are committed . . . In every respect she exceeds moderation; for, just as she surpasses other cities in wealth, so, does she surpass them in vice.'[25]

This sort of comment was deeply unfair. But the monk who wrote it was not alone – everyone was quick to blame foreigners, whoever they might be. As one French source succinctly put it, adding yet another layer of drink-fuelled xenophobia to the already heady mix of prejudice on the Second Crusade, 'the Germans were unbearable even to us'. They, according to the French at least, 'disturbed everything as they proceeded, and the Greeks therefore fled from our peaceful French king, who followed after'. The French were having a difficult journey and they were not shy of allocating blame: it was, as one of their chroniclers wrote, 'the fault of the Germans who preceded us, since they had been plundering everything'.[26]

Perhaps not surprisingly, relationships were problematic as the two main western armies of the crusade approached Constantinople. The French army attributed this to the poor behaviour of their German comrades – and doubtless the German contingent held similar views about their French allies. Alcohol and xenophobia were always close companions. And the more you drank, the wider you cast the net of prejudice.

One particularly serious incident occurred when the armies got to Philippopolis in 1147. 'We also found', wrote a disgruntled French commentator, that stragglers from the German army

> had burned certain settlements outside cities; for the following incident must unfortunately be related. Outside the walls of Philippopolis was located a fine settlement of Latins [that is, westerners] who sold a great many supplies to travellers. When the Germans had got

settled in the tavern, by ill chance a juggler came in and, although ignorant of their language, nevertheless sat down, gave his money, and got a drink. After a prolonged guzzling he took a snake, which he had charmed and kept in his inside pocket, and placed it on top of a goblet which he had put on the floor, and thus, among people whose language and customs he did not know, he indulged in other jugglers' pranks.[27]

Whatever the entertainer's act consisted of, much of the humour was lost in translation. Something he, or his snake, did was massively misinterpreted. 'As if they had seen an evil portent,' the chronicler wrote, 'the Germans immediately rose up, seized the juggler, and tore him to bits; and they attributed the crime of one man to all, saying that the Greeks wished to poison them.'[28]

It was not just Europeans who tried to drink each other under the table, often with criminal consequences. The Turkic and Mongol steppe warriors who were the crusaders' most effective opponents may not have had tables when they arrived in the region, but they certainly knew how to drink. Despite a nominal adherence to Islam, the habits of their ancestors took a long time to die out. Taking violence and insanitary alcohol consumption to a new level, the steppe tribesmen even took pride in decapitating their enemies and using the heads as celebratory drinking vessels, to be brought out at parties and family gatherings.

A Dominican brother named Julian told his fellow monks about his encounters with the Mongols in around 1235, and described them as drinking from the skulls of their victims. Shortly afterwards (in 1245–1247), a Franciscan brother named John of Plano de Carpini travelled out to the Mongol lands and also wrote of their constant and heavy drinking habits.[29]

But even against such stiff competition for crazy drinking, it was a Turkic warlord, Il-Ghazi, the lord of Mardin, who had the really standout alcohol-addiction issue. Most steppe warriors could drink; but luckily for the crusaders, his was a spectacularly serious and debilitating problem. Even one of his Muslim admirers wrote that 'when Il-Ghazi used to drink wine, he would be drunk for twenty days'.[30]

Il-Ghazi could have stopped the crusades when they had barely started. In 1119, he gathered a huge army of like-minded nomadic tribesmen and rampaged across the northern crusader states. The crusaders' territories were so overwhelmed that they found it difficult to gather information about what they were facing. They sent out scouts. The scouts never came back.

The army of Antioch, commanded by their prince, Roger of Salerno, rode out to defend their lands – but they never knew what hit them. On 28 June 1119, they were overrun on the march, surrounded and massacred in a matter of minutes. Roger and his picked men died in a last-ditch stand around their mobile chapel, guarding relics containing a fragment of the True Cross. The battlefield was afterwards called, with characteristic medieval bluntness, Ager Sanguinis – the Field of Blood.

The northern crusader states were almost bereft of troops. And with the land route to Byzantium lost, the thin strip of land in Palestine that the southern Franks held would rapidly become indefensible. Il-Ghazi was poised to change the course of history.

Instead, he had a celebratory drink. And once he had started drinking, he just could not stop. As one Muslim chronicle put it, 'he took to drink after destroying the Franks and killing them, going on a drunken spree'.[31]

Everyone knew that the northern crusader states were his for the taking; but instead of exploiting the situation, Il-Ghazi settled down to entertain himself. He sent his men out on low-level raids, opting for the easy money that could be raised by taking prisoners and selling them into slavery. His senior commanders needed little encouragement: they quickly followed his alcoholic example.[32]

The Turkic leadership spent two weeks in a stupor. The only thing which diverted them from drinking was the chance to torture and mutilate the prisoners of war. Several captives were thrown with every single limb cut off into the squares and districts [of Aleppo], as a spectacle . . . and the more the . . . drunkenness raged, the more the perversity of their tortures increased. This was made known to many as the result of drinking in the master's palace [of Il-Ghazi]; for indeed on that day when Il-Ghazi lay drunk by the madness of wine in his palace after the battle, all of the distinguished Christian prisoners, as many as were in Aleppo, were brought before him together on his own orders.[33]

At this nerve-racking meeting, random prisoners were decapitated as a way of focusing the minds of the survivors. Il-Ghazi was described as showing a ghastly 'exuberance from horrific drinking', beheading captives 'while under the influence of drunkenness'. Several days later, a mass execution of prisoners was arranged for public entertainment, during which Il-Ghazi, nothing if not consistent, 'was [still] intent upon celebratory drinking with leading members of Aleppo's entire nobility'.[34]

But even Il-Ghazi could not keep operating at this pace indefinitely. Eventually he was 'placed in his tent by gangs of his own men, overcome by wine as was his custom, and he lay as if dead in the stink of his own shit for a period of fifteen days'. He was, wrote a Frankish survivor, with some understatement, 'very often exhausted by this kind of disgraceful passion'.[35]

By the time Il-Ghazi and his commanders had come to their senses, a Christian army from the south had rushed to shore up the Franks' military positions. Civilians were escorted to safety, and the castles, previously almost emptied to fill the field army that had been lost at Ager Sanguinis, were re-garrisoned. The army of Jerusalem was more cautious now that it knew the size of the enemy forces it was facing, and, ably led by the tough soldier-king, Baldwin II, it was able to beat off the nomads at the second battle of Tell-Danith on 14 August 1119.

With the chance of easy pickings gone, Il-Ghazi's mercenary tribesmen started to return home – and the opportunity to roll up the nascent Frankish settlements was gone.

Alcohol was not always the friend of the crusaders. As their moralists never tired of preaching, pubs and drinking brought a lot of problems in their train. But ironically, there was a time, whether it was recognised or not, when it had its uses. Alcoholism was, on one occasion at least, the saviour of the Holy Land.

12

Gangsters – and Prisoners of War

The phrase 'gangsters and prisoners of war' is a discordant, almost jarring, combination. Prisoners are, by definition, helpless and trapped – people (usually men) at the mercy of the states and the communities they have offended. Gangsters, on the other hand, are presumably at the other end of the social spectrum – powerful, independent figures, throwing their weight around and deliberately showing their contempt for the society that spawned them. What could these two, wildly disparate, groups possibly have in common?

Bizarrely, the conditions in thirteenth- and early-fourteenth-century Cairo were ideal for the creation of a unique hybrid community out of that most unlikely of combinations. In this ethnic and cultural melting pot, there were prisoners of war who reached out beyond the confines of their captivity – ostensibly powerless men who, in the absence of alternatives, carved out their own unorthodox society within a society.

The most extraordinary mafia

This was a time and a place when newly arrived foreigners struggled to make their way in an often harsh and prejudiced world – a world in which the only way for their communities to survive was to control those activities that were secretly in great demand, but that were also too dangerous (and too illegal) for the locals to involve themselves in openly.

These marginalised groups eventually created their niche by exploiting an enforced ban on alcohol. They started with bootlegging, but gradually branched out into the adjacent business opportunities to be found in prostitution and drugs. But this is not the social history of Prohibition, of Al Capone or Vito Corleone: it is the extraordinary story of how Frankish prisoners of war cornered the vice market in one of the centres of the Muslim world.

To create the strange phenomenon of these 'POW gangsters', three preconditions needed to be in place.

First, there had to be plenty of prisoners of war. In the violent world of the crusader Middle East, this was the least of the problems. Secondly, there was the challenge of developing the necessary infrastructure. This was a far bigger problem. There had to be plenty of military prisons to hold these captives; and in a world with little economic surplus, jails were expensive to build and even harder to maintain. Lastly, and despite the relatively high degree of central control required to fund the costly infrastructure of captivity, there simultaneously had to be a sufficiently loose approach to prison discipline to allow the POWs the freedom to set up their own nefarious freelance activities.

This was a rare and almost mutually contradictory set of preconditions. But in medieval Cairo, strangely enough, they all came together.

The infrastructure of confinement was already in place. Ironically, however, this was largely driven by the need to imprison Muslim soldiers, rather than crusaders. The Mamluks of thirteenth-century Egypt created a unique society: it was governed, controlled and maintained by slave-soldiers imported from across the Middle East and the western stretches of the Eurasian steppes. But in a world dominated by hardened, highly trained slaves or ex-slaves, discipline had to be harsh. This harshness was reflected in the quantity and quality of the prisons and dungeons that were required. Accordingly, unlike the rudimentary jail facilities of the crusader states, there were many military prisons in Mamluk Egypt and Syria – most of them geared up to accommodate their own wayward slave-soldiers, rather than prisoners of war.[1]

The main military prison in Cairo was the prison of al-Jubb, which was part of the citadel. It was built by Sultan Qalawun towards the end of the crusader period, in 1282. The degradation of the accommodation that it offered was legendary (even by comparison with other medieval prisons) and its reputation as 'the abominable prison' was well deserved. It was famous for its filthy bat colonies and, not coincidently, for its appalling smell. Conditions were so despicable that it was entirely demolished in 1329: the lucky inmates were rehoused in other parts of the citadel.[2]

There was another well-known prison nearby called Khizanat Shama'il, which housed dangerous criminals – and disturbingly, given the rock-bottom hygiene of the accommodation, those who were either already amputees or about to become so. It was built in the period 1218–1238, and was also used to hold Mamluk military prisoners, rather than the more traditional prisoners of war. It was eventually demolished in 1415, when a previous inmate became sultan. He was finally able to express his views about the prison experience in a very practical way.

Yet another prison in the citadel of Cairo was the Khizanat al-Bunud. It had previously been an arsenal under the Fatimids; but by 1069 it had been ravaged by fire, and was converted into a jail. It was successively used as a prison for Muslim military prisoners under the Fatimids, Ayyubids and, latterly, the Mamluks. In 1309, however, it began a new life as a compound for Frankish and Armenian prisoners of war, together with their families. It remained in that use until 1392, when it was pulled down and replaced with residential buildings.[3]

The availability of prisoners was not a problem either – and that availability was driven by demand, rather than by humanitarian considerations. There was no Geneva convention in the crusades. Captives were held because they were useful, and killed if they were not. Prisoners of war would habitually be executed on the spot if they proved problematic, or if transporting and storing them was difficult. And in extreme cases, killing them might just be seen as more entertaining than dragging them around with the baggage train.

But there were often good reasons for keeping prisoners alive. Quite apart from the cash-generative possibilities of ransom, they provided slave labour for agricultural or building projects. And skilled artisans, such as masons or carpenters, had an obvious commercial value. Importantly, Cairo in the period of the crusades was one vast building site. Saladin had begun the construction of a citadel there, which was to be the largest in the Middle East. And, in an even bigger project, the adjacent town of Fustat was being incorporated within the Cairo city walls. Any labour was welcome, but the skilled labour of experienced artisans was doubly attractive.

The Mamluks were experts in institutional slavery, but the economic logic of free labour was powerful enough to transcend cultural barriers – the exploitation of prisoners was the norm across all societies. For the Franks, who were always desperately short of manpower, the economic value of prisoners of war was so great that it could even disrupt foreign policy and peace treaties.

In 1263, Baybars, the sultan of Egypt (r. 1260–1277),

> sent messengers to the Christians in Acre, saying that he wished to exchange the Christian slaves which he held for the Saracen slaves which the Christians held, at a rate of two Saracens for one Christian. The Christians held a council about this matter, and it seemed to them a good and charitable arrangement. But the Templars and the Hospitallers would not agree to it, saying that their slaves brought them great profit, since they were all craftsmen, and that it would cost too much to hire other craftsmen, and therefore they did not wish to agree to this.[4]

Baybars (himself an ex-slave) was unamused by this stance, and soon made the military orders pay for their intransigence. Even their fellow

Christians were unimpressed. As one contemporary commentator reflected, 'although what they said was true, nonetheless they ought to have made the exchange, for the sake of God and the deliverance of the poor Christian slaves'.[5]

Everyone took advantage of prisoners of war. Women were habitually used for domestic service. Male prisoners tended to be used for hard physical labour, in the fields or sugar plantations, or on building sites. Under the Mamluks, the urban poor of Cairo and foreign prisoners of war were often employed to undertake the harshest, least attractive construction projects – they were to be found working the stone quarries behind the citadel (1337) or banking up the dykes on the Nile in the hottest weather (1348). And, in the unending war (and earthquake) zone that was the medieval Middle East, there was never any shortage of castles, town walls or citadels to be built and repaired.[6]

Prisoners of war were a convenient source of hard labour. They were cheap. They were easy to control. And they could be forced to do the jobs that no one else wanted to do. As a result of this convenience, many of the Frankish prisoners of war captured during the interminable fighting of the twelfth and thirteenth centuries ended up working on the construction projects of Cairo and its suburbs. The Muslim traveller Ibn Jubayr noted that 'Rumi' (Roman) captives were being put to hard work on the construction site of the citadel of Cairo when he was there in the 1180s. Proving him correct, the poignant marks of Christian stonecutters have recently been found on a gate of the Ayyubid walls of the city.[7]

The Franks were held at first in prisons, from which they could be shepherded off to the building sites each day. Over time, however, they settled into their new lives. They came to realise that escape back to Europe or to any of the increasingly beleaguered crusader states was not really feasible. And once they had made that mental shift, their behaviour and status underwent a subtle change.

They were gradually allowed to spend increasing time out in the community. Many assumed a status more akin to that of an indentured labourer, than the inhabitant of a dungeon. These 'involuntarily indentured' Frankish prisoners became more and more assimilated into local society. They grew beards. Their complexions became more tanned in the sun – many of them were of mixed European and Arab Christian blood anyway. And they began to dress like the locals.

There were limits, however. They might look the part, but, as Franks and Christians, they were never fully assimilated. They knew how things worked and where the opportunities might be, but they were always going to be outsiders. And as most of them had been warriors, adventurers or long-term mercenaries, they had the skills, and the muscle, to move into some very interesting areas of business.

The age of the Frankish gangster-POW had arrived.

Interminable imprisonment

Surprisingly, it was indeed an age. The European prisoners of war – ordinary soldiers and knights, mercenaries and warrior monks – were a disreputable feature of the Egyptian underworld for a large part of the Middle Ages. Almost a hundred years after the fall of the crusader states, there were still references to 'Frankish captives' in Muslim hands.

But surely, you say, this chronology is mistaken? Life expectancy was far shorter than nowadays, not longer – and life expectancy in a dungeon was even more limited. How could there possibly be Frankish POWs in Cairo so long after the crusades had ended? The timescales have such obvious discrepancies that the whole narrative must be called into question.

So what exactly was going on?

The story of an English knight named Roger of Stanegrave provides part of the answer. His experience is a good example of what captivity in Egypt might mean in practice: he was only released in 1315, nearly twenty-five years after the fall of the last major crusader stronghold in the East.[8]

Roger was a Hospitaller brother, one of the order's elite military monks. He was a talented and respected knight: he had been employed as an ambassador by the Lord Edward (later King Edward I) at Acre in 1271, and was part of the Hospitaller garrison at Margat in 1280. He was captured by the Mamluks at the battle of Hims on 30 October 1281 and remained a prisoner in Egypt for thirty-four years. He eventually returned to England, where he wrote a short (and, despite his experiences, surprisingly enthusiastic) text about the need to recover the Holy Land. Roger was also resilient, resourceful and, given the hardships to which he was subjected, probably very lucky: we know that he was still alive in 1332, over fifty years after his initial capture.[9]

Ironically enough, in one of the many twists with which the crusades is strewn, he had been captured while fighting as an auxiliary for the Mongols, with whom the Hospitallers had allied themselves. We know that three hundred of these Mongol prisoners of war were working on the construction of a new religious complex in Cairo in 1284–1285. It is likely that Roger and those of his Frankish comrades who were lucky enough to survive the carnage of the battle were also set to work on the same or adjacent sites.

By a strange chance, the buildings still exist to this day, and there are indeed echoes of the European Gothic style of architecture to be found in both the windows of the tomb chamber and in the nearby madrassa-mausoleum of one of the wives of Sultan Qalawun, built in 1283–1284. At least part of Roger's involuntary foray into the Middle Eastern building trade seems to have survived.[10]

The experiences of Roger and his comrades were every bit as trau-matic as one might expect. Even high status was not enough to guar-antee respite from the hardships and sometimes shocking ordeals associated with being a prisoner in medieval Cairo.

The men were often under pressure to change their religion, to apos-tatise; and if they refused, they were frequently subjected to mock (or real) executions. They were often held in chains, at least at first, and were poorly fed. One Templar knight, Gerard of Châtillon, described his experiences after he had been ransomed. He refused to go into detail (presumably because of the emotional scarring), but he was prepared to say that

> because of the multitude of his sufferings, it would almost challenge credibility to tell how many misfortunes and hardships and how much suffering from hunger, toil and grief he had sustained, when he was incessantly carrying stones on his shoulders for building the walls of the . . . Sultan [of Egypt].[11]

By chance, we even have some of the details about where Roger and his comrades were housed. In the late thirteenth century, when the crusader states finally collapsed, most Frankish prisoners of war were kept in the citadel of Cairo, or in other parts of the city's defences. Our hero, Roger of Stanegrave, was held in five different prisons before his eventual release, several decades later. At first, he was held in the basement of a tower, which, with no light, must have been extremely unpleasant. After seven years he was given slightly better conditions and went on to spend fourteen years (higher up) in a tower. He was eventually moved out of the tower to spend three years in the citadel of Cairo. This was followed by seven years in yet another tower, this time in Alexandria. His final two years were spent in another citadel, probably back in a part of the fortress of Cairo, which Roger described as being used as a prison for foreign captives – the 'prison of Joseph'.[12]

Even the circumstances of his release were suspicious. Roger was ransomed in 1318. The sum allegedly paid was the extraordinarily (and suspiciously) large sum of 10,000 gold florins. This seems to have been a fraudulent procedure, but, given his circumstances, Roger probably had little alternative but to go along with the deception.

Ransom negotiations had proceeded in an interminable and unsatisfactory fashion for many years. Eventually, to break the logjam, Roger and an Egyptian Jew named Isaac came up with a plan. Isaac agreed to provide the initial capital, take on the risk and pay the ransom upfront. His reward for doing so was to accompany Roger back to Europe, and, when they got there, to ask for an inflated sum to be 'repaid' to him. One has to assume that Roger was entirely complicit in the process, and that there was a relationship of trust and friendship between the two men: if not, the whole deal would have unravelled very quickly, once Roger was freed and back among his own people in England.

The charismatic duo eventually made their way safely to London. Isaac came to the court of Edward II and lobbied successfully for his money. By 1322, he had converted to Christianity, perhaps out of conviction or perhaps for convenience, and presumably settled down in his new home. So, prosperous and free, there was a happy ending of sorts for all concerned.[13]

Pilgrims as POWs

There is another, remarkably similar, story about Frankish prisoners of war in Cairo and their all-too-extended adventures, but this time the central figure was an upmarket German pilgrim, rather than an English warrior-monk.

Henry I, lord of Mecklenburg (r. 1264–1302), later known as 'Henry the Pilgrim', ruled over large swathes of northern Germany, stretching up to the icy Baltic. Henry was full of military bravado and daring. Even by the high risk-taking standards of the time, he was reckless and impetuous. He had fought against a Russian army commanded by the son of the famous Alexander Nevsky in 1268, for instance, and in the aftermath had become entranced by a young pagan girl. He adopted the girl as his daughter and had her baptised – much, it seems, to the chagrin of his suspicious wife. Perhaps not surprisingly, the young woman was soon sent off to a nunnery.[14]

By 1271, Henry had decided that he should look further afield for glory. He chose to commit himself and his men to a crusade to the Holy Land. This was the supreme military expedition, and the ultimate status symbol for someone like Henry, who was both genuinely pious and seriously warlike. Having started out on the eastern frontiers of

Christendom, he wanted to try his luck on the other 'Wild East' – the Mediterranean frontiers of the Christian settlements in Palestine.[15]

This was a time when the Holy Land was in dire straits. It needed, so Henry thought, all the help it could get from the faithful of Europe. This was, from his perspective, a perfect time for an armed pilgrimage. The crusade of King Louis IX had just come to a dismal end outside Tunis in August 1270. And in Palestine, Sultan Baybars was using his huge Mamluk armies to good effect: his highly trained slave-soldiers were deployed on campaign after campaign, piling pressure upon the already sorely diminished crusader states. This was the moment for a warlike Christian such as Henry to come to the aid of the beleaguered defenders of the Latin East.[16]

Henry and his entourage (including a certain Martin Bleyer, his squire) set off in the winter of 1271–1272. The exact itinerary of their journey is unknown, but they seem to have overwintered in southern Europe and waited for the spring fleets to ship them over to the eastern Mediterranean. They arrived in Acre, the capital of what remained of the Latin Kingdom of Jerusalem, in the summer of 1272. Henry was enthusiastic and eager to offer his services.[17]

Medieval communications were frustratingly slow, however. The political situation that Henry found when he eventually arrived in Palestine was radically different from what he had expected. What Henry could not have known when he originally decided to set off was that Sultan Baybars would be prepared to sign a ten-year truce with the Christians in April 1272. There was never peace in the Holy Land – only time-limited truces. But this truce deeply inconvenienced Henry and his small force: they were looking for action, and there was none to be found.

The geographical limits of the truce showed the depths to which the Franks had been reduced: it covered just the city of Acre itself, together with the plains immediately outside, and the pilgrim roads to Nazareth. The safe area created by the agreement was tiny, but the Franks were grateful to have any respite at all. And irritatingly from Henry's perspective, it was enough to make his offers of military assistance at best entirely irrelevant, and at worst, an embarrassing nuisance.[18]

It was all a huge anti-climax, particularly for a restless, proud man such as Henry. The Mecklenburg contingent were forced to kick their heels in Acre. Henry set up his lodgings with the Teutonic Knights, the German military order with which he had close associations back home. He doubtless enjoyed training with the knights and discussing the intricacies of the military situation in this, the most dangerous outpost of Christendom.

But that was not enough. Henry was bored. He could not fight because of the truce. And ironically, because of the geographical limitations of that same truce, he could not even fulfil his religious devotions in Jerusalem, or travel beyond the Holy City to visit the other holy places, eastwards towards the River Jordan: all of these involved travelling into active war zones.[19]

But Henry was impatient by nature. He was also, even more dangerously, used to getting his own way. By January 1273, he had had enough. He and his squire Martin decided to visit Jerusalem, regardless of the dangers this entailed.

This was not a popular decision, even among his co-religionists. The Church of the Holy Sepulchre was still nominally in Christian hands, but on the sufferance of the local Muslim authorities – and even then, only because they used it as a cash cow. Any pilgrim brave enough (or foolish enough) to attempt the journey was charged the enormous sum of between 36 and 40 silver *gros tournois* for the privilege – if they made it through. Ironically, the drain on Christian resources, which were sorely needed for the war effort, was such that going on pilgrimage to Jerusalem was explicitly forbidden, on pain of excommunication by the Frankish authorities in Acre.[20]

Nothing, not even the threat of excommunication, was going to stop the headstrong Henry, however. He set off with his men on the road to Jerusalem on 25 January 1273. Predictably enough, soon after they left the area protected by the truce, Henry and the squire were both captured. Like Roger of Stanegrave, the two men were sent to the less-than-salubrious prisoner-of-war camps of Cairo. And again, like the unlucky Roger, they were probably housed in the citadel.[21]

Henry was too senior, and too valuable in terms of ransom potential, to be subjected to the dangers and rigours of life on the building sites of Cairo. Even Martin, as his companion, seems to have been spared the worst of the prison experience: he later wrote that he had worked as a silk weaver and sold the garments he produced in the markets nearby to help sustain himself and his master.[22]

Henry may have been rich, but these riches did not earn him his freedom too readily. On the contrary, his wealth and elevated social status may even have been a hindrance – they raised the expectations of his captors unduly about the size of ransom that they might expect. Not surprisingly under the circumstances, the process was slow. His Mamluk captors were in no hurry. They were prepared to hold out for the largest possible payout. Back home in Germany, the political chaos caused by his absence did not help, either – and neither did rumours that he had already died in captivity. Any desultory negotiations slowed, and then stopped altogether.[23]

It was fourteen years before any serious attempt was again made to secure his release. In 1287, a huge sum of money was raised and the process of ransoming Henry began in earnest. The Teutonic Knights agreed to handle the financial transfers, and to start discussions with his captors once more. Even this was not enough, however. For reasons that are not entirely clear, by the summer of 1289 the Teutonic Knights were forced to give up: they admitted that 'there was no hope of buying Henry's freedom from the Saracens'. They sent the ransom money that had been gathered back to Henry's family, with the rather unhelpful (but strangely prescient) comment that God would find another way to secure Henry's liberty.[24]

With only rudimentary communications at their disposal, and with biometric testing still almost a thousand years in the future, the situation became ever more complicated over time. Bizarrely, and despite the huge risks involved, pretenders began to come forward during the intervening years, each claiming to be Henry – presumably, they tried to suggest, a Henry much changed by the ordeals of his captivity. At least two conmen were tried and executed for their bold attempts to worm their way into Henry's fortune.[25]

Eventually, late in 1297, Henry and his long-suffering squire were released together. Strangely, no ransom had been paid: we know that early the following year, before news of the release had reached Germany, Henry's family still believed that he had died in captivity – a document dated 20 January 1298 refers to him in the past tense as being of 'happy memory' (*felicis memorie*).[26]

The reason behind his release probably lay in the ever-changing political situation in the Muslim Middle East. The Mongol rulers of Persia remained dangerous and implacable enemies of the Egyptian Mamluk regime – indeed, they were lobbying the European powers to launch a joint campaign against the Mamluks. Fortunately for Henry, his release seems to have been part of a diplomatic and PR counter-offensive organised by the Egyptian government to try to fend off this possibility.[27]

Henry, perhaps because everyone had given up on the idea of a ransom ever being paid for him, was chosen for the task of delivering messages from the Mamluk sultan of Egypt, Husam al-Din Lajin (r. 1296–1299), to the pope: his task was to pre-empt and discredit the Mongols' overtures. Henry was accordingly released and arrived in Rome on 25 May 1298. He received an audience with His Holiness, and probably took the opportunity to pass on whatever messages he had been sent with.[28]

By the beginning of the following year, he had taken up the rule of his lands in Mecklenburg once more, after an astounding interregnum of some twenty-eight years. His son, who had been ruling as Henry II, stood down. We do not know how popular this was with Henry Junior, but the transition seems to have been carried out entirely peacefully, so presumably he was suitably dutiful.

Perhaps the age and physical appearance of his father led him to believe that he would not have long to wait before he could again take control of the family estates. And, if this was the case, he was entirely correct: Henry was dead within three years. He passed away on 2 January 1302 and was buried near the Baltic Sea, in the German colony of Doberan, a summer residence of the rulers of Mecklenburg.[29]

His career was strangely – almost poetically – symmetrical. He had left Germany as a crusader and a pilgrim. He had spent much of his life as a prisoner of war and, bizarrely, as part of the gradually burgeoning Frankish community of Cairo, which, as we shall see, also dominated the illicit adult entertainment sector in town.

But when he returned, he was given pieces of the True Cross to bring with him. The sultan doubtless wanted him to leave on his diplomatic mission with a favourable view of the Mamluk government uppermost in his mind – and after decades of imprisonment, only a truly impressive gift would suffice. The True Cross, or even the smallest fragment of it, was just such a gift.[30]

A relic from the Cross was the ultimate prize for a devout crusading pilgrim; and, if it were possible to make up for the years of sacrifice and imprisonment, this was surely the way to do it. Bringing it back elevated Henry to the position, from a spiritual perspective, of being one of the most successful crusaders of the thirteenth century. He gave half of the relic to the Franciscan order, and the other half, perhaps sensing his imminent demise, to the Cistercian monastery at Doberan, where he would be buried. Henry was, for a time at least, peaceful, respected and back in charge of his lands. Home at last.[31]

Crusading bootleggers

Henry eventually made it back to Europe, but not all his comrades were so lucky. Many were left behind, still trying to find a way to survive in Cairo. And there was one obvious avenue open to them.

Most people like a drink.

But it is not always straightforward. Certain times, certain cultures, certain places – all can conspire to make getting that refreshing drink more than usually difficult.

Islamic Cairo in the thirteenth century was one such place, and one such time. As is often the case, a partial solution was found by outsourcing the problem – or rather the solution – to groups of outsiders who were less culturally inhibited than the locals.

Over time, as we have seen, the Frankish captives' prison conditions seem to have changed. Things remained harsh, and inevitably varied according to status or behaviour. But it also appears that they were gradually given more freedom to operate in the city, and on the different building sites on which they worked.[32]

Bureaucracies and central infrastructure in the Middle Ages were always limited, even in cash-rich Egypt. And the western prisoners of war were so far from Frankish lands that it was probably felt (entirely correctly) that they would be unlikely to try to escape. Even in 1280, while the Mamluks were still at war with the crusader states, conditions had loosened up considerably. So much so, in fact, that efforts had to be made to rein the crusader captives in a little, and it became necessary to tighten up even the most basic security provisions.

Many of the Frankish prisoners of war, and particularly the mixed-race settlers (*pulani*) were blending in far too easily with the local Mamluks and Egyptians. In order to ensure that they remained easily identifiable, Egyptian jailers were told that the 'beards of all prisoners of war must be shaved, and [they must] make sure they do so whenever their beard grows back'. It was felt necessary to ensure that they were clean-shaven, in the European fashion, as a way of making them stand out in a crowd: these were clearly not men who were expected to be in a dungeon or on a chain gang at all times.[33]

There was also an instruction that prisoners of war 'who are employed [in public building works] must not spend the night outside the jail' – implying, of course, that many of them in fact did so. Similarly, it was stipulated that 'none of them is to be allowed to go to the bath-house or to any church or any attraction' – again, indicating that many occasionally had such freedoms.[34]

Inevitably, these prisoners of war – entrepreneurial, economically productive and semi-free to roam – began to form their own communities, even in a foreign land and in time of war. Certainly, by the beginning of the fourteenth century they seem to have had their own church within the citadel of Cairo. We know of its existence, because it was destroyed in urban rioting in 1321.[35]

Prisoners of war were originally housed in a specific building, or set of buildings; but as they grew in number and in influence, this gradually became a district. And over time, they became accustomed to running enterprises of their own. Their main competitive advantage, as Christians in a Muslim urban environment, was that they were less inhibited in dealing with alcohol.[36]

Frankish prisoners in the citadel of Cairo and its environs eventually developed their own alcohol suppliers and wine production facilities. Ostensibly at least, these were for their personal consumption. Things quickly moved onto a far more commercial basis, however. There was a ready client base around the Frankish district. Whatever the theoretical strictures, Mamluk soldiers naturally liked a drink, as did the Armenian bureaucrats and the other civil servants, many of whom were, of course, still Christian at this point in Egyptian history.[37]

The prisoners also had business connections with some of the Christian villages on the outskirts of Cairo, where they developed relationships with the local wine producers. One Muslim chronicler noted that the Franks in Cairo were able to produce 32,000 jars of wine every year, but even this is probably a significant underestimate, given the extensive informal network of rural Christian wine suppliers and villages that they had access to. Half a century after the collapse of the crusader states, the flotsam of the crusading movement had become major players in the illegal wine trade of Egypt.[38]

By the mid-fourteenth century, they were definitively in control of their own district of Cairo. Sultan al-Salih Ismail (r. 1342–1345) had them under his strict and direct protection, presumably because of the taxes and other, less transparent, money that the Franks paid to him. Anyone who robbed a Frankish prisoner, the sultan proclaimed, could expect to be hanged.

The implication was not just that the Franks had protection, but that they were now also prosperous: they were the kind of people you might be jealous of, the kind of minority community which had riches to steal. The wine trade was a big and profitable business, and it explains how the Franks were able to buy official protection for their illicit trading interests and growing freedoms.[39]

Perhaps inevitably, in the fourteenth century (as much as in our own day), controlling one area of illicit activity naturally led into other illegal or borderline areas. The prisoners of war also ran what was euphemistically known as the 'entertainment trade', a polite way of describing the local brothels. The famous Egyptian historian, al-Maqrizi, (1364–1442), who was himself born in Cairo, wrote that the Franks gradually became involved in prostitution and other 'depraved' activities, such as drug dealing. Shockingly, they also dabbled with singing and dancing.[40]

But although much of the story of POW gangsterism has its own internal logic, none of this multigenerational community development makes sense without women. How could Frankish 'prisoners of war' be thriving almost a hundred years after the war had ended? The answer, of course, was that they had married local Christian (primarily Coptic) women. As the conditions of their captivity grew ever laxer, they established families and children of their own, and these 'Franco-Egyptian' children were able to carry on the family businesses.[41]

Tellingly, by the mid-fourteenth century we find the community being referred to as 'Franks', rather than as 'Frankish captives'. Clearly, there was still a memory of their ethnicity and some cultural residue; but as they had integrated so fully into the local milieu, their original status as prisoners of war had been quietly forgotten. The process of integration continued apace – in 1387, there are still references to Christian captives, but not to 'Frankish captives'. And by 1415, references to the Franks as a separate community of any kind had ceased altogether.

But these communities had not been destroyed, despite their control of what might have been described as 'antisocial' activities. Their end was far less dramatic than that. They adapted to the society in which they found themselves, prospered as best they could and were eventually completely absorbed.[42]

They just gradually blended in with the communities around them, in a vivid medieval example of the process of acculturation.

The gangs of Cairo

The Franks were not the only players in the vast and amorphous social history of the 'gangs of Cairo', however. There was plenty of local competition, too.

Medieval Cairo was famous for its organised crime. A memorandum prepared for the government of Egypt in the 1280s said that the crime hotspots were in redolently named areas that included 'the Nile bank, the cemeteries, and ponds such as the Elephant's Pool and the Abyssinian Pool . . . and certain public halls in the Husayniyya Quarter known as Qa'at al-Futuwwa, where turbulent folks hang out'.[43]

There have been suggestions that the 'turbulent folk' of the Muslim *futuwwa* gangs and the *ahdath* city militia may both be the direct heirs of the Byzantine circus factions, large groupings of the young men of the city. Both were a continual thorn in the side of the authorities, as an obvious source of criminality and violent disorder. Both were rowdy and disreputable. And interestingly enough, membership of both groups had homosexual overtones, as older members were accused of having a predilection for the younger recruits.[44]

The lineage is not as far-fetched as it may sound. The Muslim conquests in Syria and other parts of the Middle East meant that these new overlords became responsible for the same civil populations in urban areas: until their arrival, these had been Byzantine citizens, with all the associated cultural habits and behaviour. And both groups had the same name: the 'young men'.[45]

In an accurate demographic summary of gangsterism (and of those who commit most violent and disorderly crime), the word *futuwwa* may also literally be translated as 'young-manliness'. Sometimes these groups were harmless, providing occasional meeting places or social clubs for unmarried men. But, given the nature of those involved, many were not. Unsurprisingly, from the early 1260s onwards, some of these groups started to muscle in on the local criminal enterprises, and by the 1280s the term *futuwwa* had distinctly pejorative overtones.[46]

Some of what they did, and much of how they displayed themselves, was calculated to mark them out as being different – a way of setting themselves apart from mainstream society. *Futuwwa* gangsters had a reputation for being good with knives; and if one were arrested, the others in the band were expected to come and get him out of jail, by whatever means necessary. Running prostitution rackets was not unheard-of either. Gang members were even, it was said by some of their less broad-minded critics, expected to prostitute their women if necessary to help a comrade.[47]

There was also an infamous initiation ceremony that sometimes involved naked young boys and youths: as with much else about the *futuwwa*, this was viewed with suspicion by the more orthodox Muslim onlookers. Their meeting places were described as being somewhere 'in which the wicked or immoral assemble', and venues, disgracefully, 'in which are wine and instruments of music and the like'. This debauched reputation, combined with continued suggestions of homosexuality, gave the gangs a spectacularly bad name – and perhaps that suited them well enough.[48]

The coarse and almost deliberately shocking nature of the gangs was reflected in the areas in which they chose to live. The Husayniyya quarter of Cairo, where they were based, was where the more unmanageable, lower-calibre soldiers were garrisoned. And from the 1260s onwards, this cheap and turbulent neighbourhood had also seen an influx of often involuntary Mongol migrants, many of them acting as mercenaries. It was a heady mix. A rough part of town was getting rougher by the minute.[49]

Thirteenth-century Husayniyya was the most dangerous suburb in a dangerous city. It was well known for crime, and all the usual vices that went with it; but it was also famous for its toughs – young men who, when supportive of the government, were available as a hardened neighbourhood militia. It briefly became slightly gentrified (in the early fourteenth century), but quickly reverted to form – a double whammy of flooding and a strangely specific infestation of roof-eating worms pushed the district firmly back to its downmarket roots.[50]

The local *futuwwa* gangs were supplemented (or temporarily supplanted) by the occasional influx of fresh and enthusiastic new blood. The Oirats, or Kalmuks (a Mongol tribe from the western steppes), for instance, settled in Husayniyya in large numbers in 1294–1296. At this distance, it is hard to say what religion they belonged to. Perhaps it was not entirely clear even at the time. They were not always regarded as being entirely Muslim, but they may have thought of themselves as such.

Whatever their exact beliefs, however, they were certainly culturally eccentric and made a big impact. They ate horses, and they had beautiful, desirable women. And as they were, at best, on the fringes of Islam, they may well have retained their steppe predilection for alcohol. They started wearing *futuwwa* dress and carried weapons in the street. Perhaps inevitably, they too set themselves up as gangsters in the vice rackets.[51]

But however threatening the *futuwwa* might look, they also had a 'Robin Hood' or 'Artful Dodger' aspect to their reputation. They stood up for local people against government officials. If necessary, they helped defend native Egyptians against their foreign rulers and the foreign rulers' mercenaries. And they provided an alternative way of life for those with no obvious escape from their rough neighbourhood – one that at least had a semblance of its own independence and dignity.

They were occasional allies for deprived people who had few life choices – a tenuous, but welcome, protection for the *hushrat* (or 'human vermin') who constituted most of the inhabitants.

The *futuwwa* probably had far more in common with the Frankish prisoners of war than either would have cared to admit. They were all subversives in their own way, doing whatever it took to survive. They were all rebels and adventurers.[52]

And in war or in peace, they were the last defenders of people with little hope.

Part IV
MURDERERS

13

A Surfeit of Blood?

The crusades. An entire epoch riven by warfare and violence. Even the name we give to the era is an encapsulation of the violent convulsions that defined it – the wars of the renewed Muslim invasions of the Middle East in the eleventh and twelfth centuries, and the increasingly desperate attempts by the powers of western Europe and Byzantium to defend the Holy Land.

This was an age of unremitting violence.

With so much warfare around, one might have hoped that people would have had enough of violent crime in general and murder in particular; one might have hoped that, when there was so much unavoidable violence, men and women, in the occasional peaceful interludes, might have seized the opportunity to work together in harmony; one might have hoped that the civilian population would have sought to escape the unspeakable horrors of frontier warfare for a brief moment and grasped whatever chances of love and stability presented themselves.

And yet disappointingly – or perhaps predictably – this was not the case.

When the crusading armies went home (incidentally, leaving the local Christians wide open to Muslim reprisals), the violence did not stop. The clamour of war moved down in pitch, but the background noise of criminality and vice continued.

Instead of a population satiated and repelled by institutionalised murder, we find in its place a depressing moral numbness: societies that had become overly accustomed to violence and individuals who had become desensitised to brutality and slavery. In an era that aspired to spirituality, we find, ironically, communities riven by criminal blood-letting.

Murder in a time of perpetual war seems faintly ridiculous. Surrounded by unavoidable and officially sanctioned killing, why would anyone want more? Surely, whatever bloodlust people had would be more than sated by what they saw around them?

In fact, of course, the opposite was sadly true. The surfeit of rootless, armed men in the Holy Land meant that levels of violent crime were always likely to be higher than in more normal places or times.

Murder was not uncommon and had an important place in the Frankish judicial system. The nature of the crime was, somewhat strangely to our eyes, partly defined by the nature of the evidence. There were two basic kinds of murder in Frankish law. Murder, or *murtre aparant*, was an act carried out with no witnesses, and which was thus a secret killing. In such cases, the victim's body would play an important part in proceedings: the presence of the corpse was, after all, what made the murder 'apparent'. Proof of murder in these instances depended partly on the state of the body (showing that a murder had indeed taken place) and partly on the outcome of any judicial combat, which would determine guilt.[1]

Where there were witnesses to the murder, however, it was defined as homicide, and the witnesses had to come forward and lay themselves open to being challenged to trial by combat by the accused. Even being a bystander could sometimes lead to violence.[2]

A surprising degree of mutilation was anticipated on a murdered body: a shocking testimony to the prevalence of edged weapons in crusader societies. One contemporary law book suggested that 'if the body should lack its head, and it would seem that the head had been severed by a blow, the accused should answer'. It went on to suggest, with an unnecessary degree of literalness, that 'there is no worse blow than the one that cuts off the head'. Similarly, it continued, 'if there is part of the corpse, and it seems to the men of the court that this had come about by a blow or blows that the other party would have done and from which it could have received death', then the accused would also have to answer the charges brought against him. Expectations of the state of the corpse were low, and probably correctly so in many cases.[3]

Even back in the West, in places that were more peaceful than the turbulent eastern frontiers of Christendom, arguments could quickly lead to homicide. Then as now, easy access to alcohol and weapons made the escalation of a dispute far easier – and far more dramatic in terms of the outcome.

A couple of examples give a taste of what was possible and, in some instances, almost commonplace. In December 1352, seven men, Catalans and Gascons, were in the village of Mireval. The scene, as so often in these situations, was a pub. A fight broke out between them and a man was stabbed to death. The perpetrator claimed that it was a fair fight and that he had acted in self-defence. It transpired that he had previous convictions for both murder and theft, however, and so he was subjected to judicial torture; perhaps not surprisingly, he eventually confessed.[4]

Two further stories – both of which took place just a few yards from where I am writing – also serve to make the point. In 1421, a fight broke out in a London pub called 'The Moyses' (that is, 'The Moses'). A man named Arnald van Harsill pulled a knife on an armourer called John Bene, and stabbed him in the heart. As was often the case, the argument was over a woman (John's mistress); and, also in the traditional way, it was fuelled by alcohol.

Arnald argued for his innocence with a plea of self-defence. When the case came to court, the plea was accepted by the jury, because Arnald had tried to run away. Unwisely, John Bene, who was armed and doubtless disinhibited by drink, had cornered him in the back yard of the pub, leaving him with no choice but to fight. Arnald's plea was that he had had to draw his dagger to defend himself. The jury, many of whom were men who were themselves accustomed to being armed when they were at their local pub, could see his point of view.[5]

Even shopping could be dangerous. In London, on 26 August 1379, near the site of Mr Bene's murder, an intemperate reaction to a trivial jostle in the street ended up with a murder and a hanging.

This was an age when drinking urban water was a high-risk activity. Anyone with sufficient money was likely to be drinking beer for health, as well as recreation. The crowded streets of London were inevitably filled with inebriates weaving unsteadily between the horses, gutters and wet manure – in these circumstances, taking a stroll often became a contact sport. In the middle of this mundane chaos, a certain John Kirkby trod on the foot of a Genoese man with the wonderful name of 'Janus Imperial'.

Janus had been sitting outside his house at the time. He was talking to his servants when the incident occurred. Harsh words were exchanged. Words became shoves, and shoving turned to blows. Matters quickly escalated. Kirkby's companion, a certain John Algor, pulled a knife and attacked Janus's servants. Before bystanders had a chance to react, Kirkby, too, drew a dagger. When Janus tried to back off and calm matters down, Kirkby also produced a sword. By the time the argument reached its bloody conclusion, Janus had received two fatal sword cuts to the head, each wound seven inches long and penetrating his brain.[6]

Violence was always close to the surface. In London, as in the case of John Kirkby, ordinary people might be carrying weapons. But in the Latin East, the situation was even more exaggerated. The word 'civilian' could be applied in only the very loosest sense to most medieval frontiersmen. Large numbers of townsfolk, tradesmen or merchants were habitually as heavily armed as soldiers.

Even household servants might be armed, and the politics and accidents of life 'below stairs', in the servants' quarters, could be extraordinarily harsh. One of Usama Ibn-Munqidh's servants, a man named Ghunaym, almost lost his life in Mosul, where his Shaizari master was employed by the Turkic warlord, Zengi.[7]

Zengi's legendary ferocity and penchant for casual violence was seemingly contagious. It happened one day that Usama and his retainers were staying in a friend's house. 'Ghunaym,' he later wrote, 'led his mule into the stables of that friend of mine [along] with the servants of the other invited guests. Among us was a Turkish youth who got so drunk that he lost control of himself.' Ghunaym, whatever his own attitudes to alcohol, was not party to these increasingly loud revelries: he was feeling poorly, and had slipped away to bed.

The Turks at this time were newcomers to Islam, and still enthusiastically practised their ancestors' traditions of excessive drinking, alongside their famously uninhibited approach to bloodshed. The young Turkic servant managed to combine both these predilections in one frenzied evening of riotous behaviour. At one point, he

> went out to the stables, drew his knife and rushed at the [other] servants. They all fled and got out of there. But Ghunaym, because of his weakness and his illness, had thrown [his] saddle down under his head and gone to sleep, with the result that he did not even get up until everyone else had fled from the stables. So that drunkard stabbed him with his knife under his navel, slicing open his abdomen with a wound about four finger-widths wide. Ghunaym dropped on the spot.[8]

The Turk was beaten to the ground and arrested. He was taken to Usama, 'with his hands tied behind his back'. Ghunaym survived, but was close to death for some time after the attack – his wound did not heal over for two months, and meanwhile it 'continued to ooze bits of scab and yellow liquid'. Strangely, his assailant was later freed without punishment; so perhaps, by local definitions at least, this constituted a 'fair fight'. The Middle East in the twelfth century was a far cry from Downton Abbey.[9]

With warfare endemic, preparedness was of the essence. Everyone was liable for military service in the all-too-regular event of an enemy invasion. Large numbers of mercenaries, armed to the teeth, congregated in the ports of the Levant in search of regular work. Under these circumstances, even the smallest incident could quickly escalate into fighting between two armed parties; and, in extremis, might end in murder. This was a society that was disproportionately predisposed to violence as a way of resolving conflicts, no matter how trivial their nature. But even newcomers quickly joined in.[10]

For those who were travelling to the Middle East from Europe, whether as pious pilgrims or as enthusiastic crusaders, murder could be the consequence of ignorance – or at least of mistaken bigotry. New arrivals from the West were generally unaware of the rich ethnic and cultural melting pot that would await them. Most of the population of the crusader states were Christians but – bewilderingly for a religious zealot who was used to clear lines of belief and who had rarely travelled more than a few miles from home – they were culturally and ethnically far more diverse than that might suggest. Even the Frankish settlers and the old crusader ruling dynasties had all quickly intermarried. They often looked, with good reason, Arabic or Armenian. It was all very confusing.

The members of different religious groups or ethnic communities were distinguished by visual signals associated with how they dressed and how they groomed themselves. Some of these signals were more subtle than others, however, and newcomers, disoriented and bemused, did not necessarily understand what they saw around them. Local Arab Christians were bearded, for instance, much like the Muslim Arab community, and dressed in a very similar fashion.

The vast number of different languages and dialects compounded the potential for paranoia and misdirected prejudice. Newcomers often failed to interpret social nuances until they acclimatised, and this could create some very dangerous situations. In 1290, for instance, chroniclers described how visiting Italians rioted and murdered some local

Muslim peasants. They also 'killed a number of bearded Syrians who were [Orthodox Christians] (they killed them because of their beards, mistaking them for Saracens). This was ill-done indeed.'

The massacre was monumentally 'ill-done': it changed the course of history. The Muslim authorities were looking for a pretext to bring their overwhelming military might to bear. They chose to use the murder of Arab civilians as an excuse to attack the remnants of the crusader states. Within a few months, the last of the Franks had been ejected from Palestine and Syria.[11]

Once more, criminality had changed the course of crusading history.

14

Murder in the Cathedral

Murdering bishops and archbishops was unusual, even in those strangely violent times. They had entourages to protect them. And they had a moral authority which deterred many of their potential enemies.

But such attacks were not entirely unheard of. Most famously of all, the murder of Thomas Becket, archbishop of Canterbury, in 1170, caused political and religious upheaval throughout western Europe. Often these attacks had a political subtext and motivation, and were driven by local animosity – or, in the case of Becket, higher-level antagonism.

Another instance of murder among the highest echelons of the Frankish Church took place in Greece in the early thirteenth century – one of the many flashpoints of conflict in the eastern Mediterranean at this time. High-ranking religious figures were, inevitably, also involved in affairs of state, and this sometimes brought them into the heart of political conflicts.[1]

The Fourth Crusade had, in 1204, controversially ended up attacking the Christian Byzantine empire – rather than pursuing its original objective of recovering Muslim-held Jerusalem. A new 'crusader empire' had been established in its wake – the so-called Latin Empire of

Constantinople. This new political structure had several exotically named Frankish vassal states within its boundaries, including the Kingdom of Thessaloniki, the Duchy of Athens and the Principality of the Morea. To make a fragmented and fluid situation even more confusing, Byzantine political refugees also set up their own successor states, such as the grandly titled 'Empire of Nicaea', the 'Empire of Trebizond' and the 'Despotate of Epirus'. This was an over-abundance of highly competitive 'empires', and an embarrassment of different religious beliefs, cultures and local interests. As they jostled against each other, the situation was ripe for political in-fighting, and the violence that inevitably accompanied it.

This fragmented and turbulent patchwork of minor states with major family interests was Christian in belief, but nonetheless riven by religious differences. The most fundamental of these was that between the previously incumbent Orthodox clergy and the newly installed Latin (Catholic) Church. Tensions between these two hierarchies were just another unhelpful layer of conflict, adding to the more 'normal' climate of political violence and general criminality.

Opportunities for sectarian conflict abounded. A number of the Latin clergy, for instance, were murdered for political reasons by Michael I Doukas, the ruler of Epirus, in 1210; and among the Frankish religious casualties was an unnamed bishop-elect. A precedent had been set.[2]

A particularly outrageous attack took place in 1217, when William of Rouen, the Latin archbishop of Philippi, a town in the Kingdom of Thessaloniki, was murdered. The crime was infamous, even at the time, and it received widespread attention, even as far away as the papal curia in Rome; but the exact circumstances (and the name of the ultimate perpetrator) were shrouded in mystery.

A letter from Pope Honorius III in August 1217 expressed horror at Archbishop William's recent death. According to information received from many Latin clergymen in the region, including the testimony of several bishops, the murder had been carried out at the behest of the 'princeps Philippensis' – an individual tantalisingly referred to, almost as if he were a villain in a cheap Victorian novel, as 'Lord S'.

The attack was carried out in the most high-profile way, presumably to make a political point of some kind, or to reiterate the ferocity of whatever local dispute had triggered the attack in the first place. Before they killed him, the murderers were said to have captured and kidnapped William, still elaborately dressed in his episcopal robes, in full view of his congregation. The theatricality of the incident, and the implicit threat to any others who might cross the mysterious 'Lord S', was obvious. The unlucky prelate was later humiliated, tortured and killed. His body was unceremoniously dumped outside the local cemetery.

Interestingly – and however tempting it would have been to attribute the attack to different ethnicities or religious sects (notably the Greek Orthodox Church, of course) – no such accusation was made. The natural implication was that the murder was instigated by the local Frankish lord, perhaps in pursuit of a dispute whose origins were not even clear at the time.

Another papal letter, written in the spring of the following year, far from clarifying matters, just muddied the circumstances of the murder still further. Confusingly, and despite the large number of supposedly well-informed individuals who had given their testimony before the first papal letter was written, a very different version of events emerged in this second document.

The letter was dated May 1218, and related to a dispute between two different groups of clergymen, both of whom were based in Thessaloniki. In order to resolve the dispute, the priests had been instructed to travel to another location, some ten days' travel away, on the road towards Constantinople.

Regardless of how keen they might have been to end the dispute, however, both parties were agreed on one thing at least: neither was prepared to travel down that road in those dangerous times. The reason for their reluctance was made abundantly clear: they wrote that the road was extremely unsafe for travellers; as an example of the dangers in store, the monks cited the fate of the late Archbishop William. He had, they wrote, been killed on the road by Bulgarian bandits (*a Bulgaris interfectus*).

Much ink has been spilt in speculation about the details of this incident, and particularly about the identity of the mysterious 'Lord S'. Ultimately, however, we do not have a solution, either to the question of who this lord might have been or indeed, given the contradictory evidence of the second letter, whether he was in fact responsible for William's murder at all.

Perhaps in the period between the two letters (that is, from August 1217 to May 1218), 'Lord S' had successfully proved his innocence. Perhaps other culprits (such as the Bulgarian outlaws who made travel by road so dangerous) had been nominated instead. Or maybe the Bulgarians had been hired by Lord S to do his dirty work for him – though that would, of course, contradict the previous story about William's 'kidnapping' in front of his congregation.

Ultimately, no one seemed to know, even at the time; and we certainly have no definitive answer now. But it does show that being a bishop (or archbishop) in the crusader states could be dangerous.[3]

William of Rouen was not the only archbishop to be murdered in full view of his congregation. Albert, bishop of Vercelli, was appointed patriarch of Jerusalem by Pope Innocent III in 1205. Albert was an extremely capable statesman, whose carefully honed diplomatic skills were greatly needed in the fractious crusader states of the thirteenth century. He had a track record of bringing warring parties together, and had mediated in long-running disputes between the papacy and the emperor, Frederick Barbarossa.

Albert was one of the most senior clerics in Christendom and was widely respected by both the clergy and the secular authorities. Crucially, he was used by the papacy as a means of trying to resolve a debilitating civil war that was undermining the defence of Antioch. He was also galvanising support for the new king of Jerusalem, John of Brienne. In some ways, Albert had more power and authority than the king himself.

High status, widespread respect and a glittering career were not enough to save him, however. Albert was murdered in the most public way, whilst on a procession in Acre on Holy Cross Day, 1214. Ironically, the assassination was driven by a petty HR dispute, rather than any grand political or strategic agenda: the murderer was a priest who felt that he had been unfairly demoted. But in a highly armed state, riven by civil and institutional violence, even the most seemingly trivial matters could be elevated swiftly towards murder.[4]

A similarly bloody and pointless incident involving a senior member of the clergy took place in Frankish Cyprus some years later. In May 1259, Geoffrey of Sergines had been made bailli of the Kingdom of Jerusalem, based in Acre. People spoke of him glowingly as 'a very strong magistrate'. That strength was expressed most visibly in the way he cracked down hard on murderers.

In a high-profile case designed to show that no one was above the law, 'he hanged a knight called John Renier, who had killed the bishop of Famagusta' as part of a personal dispute. The murderer took refuge with his Pisan friends, and that would often have been enough to ensure his safety. But the new bailli was prepared to take the cause of justice to the limit.

Although John sought asylum in the Pisan quarter, there is no direct evidence that he was a citizen of the city state. Perhaps, like the Embriaco family, which became one of the leading noble families of the county of Tripoli, John was a Frankish knight from a family with Italian origins. Whatever his lineage, however, and despite the incessant in-fighting in the Latin East at this time, everyone seems to have been shocked by the bishop's murder. The Italian cities were notoriously strident when it came to their rights and the judicial independence of their quarters, but they made an exception in this case. The newly appointed bailli stormed in with his men-at-arms and the Pisans gave the knight up to face justice.

Geoffrey of Sergines was shown to be remorseless in pursuing a murderer, regardless of social status, from Cyprus all the way to Acre.

This commitment was reflected in the way his entire tenure in office was viewed. After his death, one chronicler, reflecting on Geoffrey's achievements, noted with quiet approval that 'he had many thieves and assassins hanged. He would never spare anyone, neither for pleas, nor presents nor friendship.'[5]

It was no wonder that murder, particularly murder involving the senior clergy, was very actively discouraged: it was socially corrosive on almost every level. The high-profile treatment of violent offenders was, as modern politicians also know, an easy route to popularity. If a lord wanted it said of him that he was effective, punishing murderers was a good move: a 'hanging judge' usually had public support to back him up.

This was tough, frontier law indeed.

'Not responsible for his wicked act'

It was early in the afternoon, but the shutters had been closed tightly to keep the harshness of the sun at bay. The murderer moved quietly across the darkened room. An older man lay stretched out on the bed in front of him, coverlet pulled back off his pale legs because of the suffocating heat. His heavy breathing indicated that he was deeply asleep, immersed in whatever images and memories possessed him that day, rehearsing, repeating and reimagining vivid highlights. His vulnerability was complete.

The heavy torpor of the room was suddenly pierced by the flash of sharpened metal, raised above the head of his assassin. The blade was brought down, its shocking parabola penetrating the quiet, the bedclothes and the helpless flesh beneath. Time in the room stood still for the briefest of moments.

Then the sword swept down for a second blow, and then a third, and the animal screams of the wounded victim broke the silence with an appalling finality. The door to the bedchamber had been locked from the inside, but retainers quickly smashed their way in. They threw themselves upon the assailant, beating his strangely passive and unresponsive body to the ground. Within a matter of seconds, the raw violence of the incident was over.

But the consequences reverberated throughout the crusader states. The murderer was no Assassin, nor even an armed robber. He was a Frankish priest. And his victim was the bishop of Acre, a diplomat and one of the senior prelates of the Latin Kingdom of Jerusalem. This was a murder that was close to home, and inexplicable in its brutality.

Murder with an obvious motive – such as theft or jealousy – was relatively commonplace. It was unpleasant, but certainly explicable. The murder of the bishop of Acre, however, which took place on 29 June 1172, was something altogether more disturbing. This was an era before psychiatry, and a society in which the will of God was the default explanation for difficult areas of judgement. A random killing, or one motivated by mental disorder, was very hard to comprehend.[6]

Not surprisingly, there are no surviving eye-witness accounts of what happened. Luckily, however, the chronicler William of Tyre, himself a local archbishop, investigated the incident and wrote a relatively detailed account of what had happened. Given the social standing of the victim, William probably knew all the parties involved. He also had an opportunity to interview the individuals who had been present at the scene of the crime.

The story William uncovered was unusual, but also strangely modern.

The early 1170s were a time of frenetic diplomatic activity in the Latin East. Saladin had taken control of the sleepy, corrupt and internally fractured Fatimid empire in Egypt. His erstwhile employer, Nur al-Din, was in command of an increasingly unified Islamic empire in Syria. The crusader states were surrounded and hugely outnumbered. King Amalric of Jerusalem was an astute and energetic leader, however, who correctly identified the last remaining strategic option for his people: they needed to recapture Egypt for Christendom, before Saladin

1. Even the supposedly incorruptible warrior monks could be guilty of the usual banal cocktail of theft, violence or 'white-cowl crime'. This satirical illumination shows Renart, the embodiment of evil trickery, trying to corrupt the whole world. The sly fox makes himself grandmaster of both the Templars and the Hospitallers after they almost come to blows over who gets to claim him as leader.

2. Chivalry, perhaps inevitably, was an aspiration rather than a guarantee. All medieval states, and particularly the crusaders and their neighbours, needed lots of armed and highly skilled fighting men. But they were also acutely aware of the dangers that these individuals posed to social order. Here, 'false' knights are seen surrendering to a rival king, leaving their true king unprotected in his pavilion.

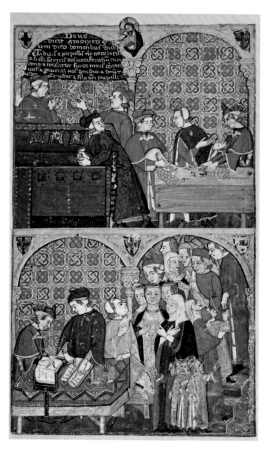

3. *(left)* This illumination, showing scenes of banking and usury, highlights the medieval ambivalence towards financial matters. This was not entirely unjustified. Bribery, tax evasion and fraud were the pervasive forms of 'white-collar crime' – they were easy to commit, hard to prevent and very profitable if you could get away with it. Relatively small-scale fraud was impossible to eradicate fully.

4. *(below)* The Inner Gate of the citadel of Aleppo. Many of Zengi's more psychopathic moments were played out behind these forbidding walls. The dungeons, too, were rightly famous for their scenes of torture and horror. Walter the Chancellor, one of the victims, chose not to revisit his personal experiences, but left a harrowing account of his comrades' extended tortures, mutilations and executions, performed for the entertainment of their Turkic jailors.

5. Mugging could quickly morph into murder. It is significant that both of these 'civilian' figures are armed – one with a knife, the other with a short sword. The crusaders and their contemporaries did not have guns but, then as now, proximity to arms and familiarity with how to use them meant that they were more likely to feature in instances of 'civilian' violence and led to more serious outcomes.

6. This gambling scene illustrates the sin of avarice – but it also shows the consequences of addiction. The man on the right holds his hands to his face as the full magnitude of what he has done sinks in. In extreme situations, crusader lords, such as the inveterate gambler Julian of Sidon, could lose so much money that they could no longer maintain their own town's fortifications.

7. *(left)* Scene in a tavern with men drinking. Below, a publican passes up more drinks as the customers, from left to right, get progressively more inebriated. Once suitably disinhibited, pubs and bars gave their customers opportunities to try a range of legally dubious activities including robbery and paid-for sex. Fighting was also a traditional consequence of drinking too much.

8. *(below)* When Louis sailed back to Acre in 1250 he was suffering from PTSD and trauma from the threats of torture which he had experienced while being held as a prisoner of war in Egypt. Louis was not in a good mood. When he found his brother gambling over a game of backgammon, Louis had a massive sense-of-humour failure and threw his gaming board over the side.

9. This beautiful but politically loaded illumination shows Raymond of Antioch playing 'chess' at the siege of Shaizar in 1138 while his Byzantine allies did the heavy lifting. It is interesting to note that, for reasons of social status, the crusader leaders are depicted playing a game of chess, rather than gambling over the far less intellectually demanding games of dice that were their real preference.

10. Northern walls, Cairo. Bizarrely, the conditions in thirteenth- and early-fourteenth-century Cairo were ideal for the creation of a unique hybrid community of captive Frankish gangsters. In this ethnic and cultural melting pot, there were prisoners of war who reached out beyond the confines of their captivity – ostensibly powerless men who, in the absence of alternatives, carved out their own unorthodox society within a society.

11. Beautiful but grim. One man is ostensibly embracing, but in reality pinning, his companion who is being attacked from behind by an assassin. It is significant that everyone in this 'civilian' scene, including the victim, is heavily armed. Murder in crusader societies, at a time of perpetual war, seems faintly ridiculous. Why would anyone want more blood? Sadly, the surfeit of rootless, armed men in the Holy Land meant that levels of violent crime were always likely to be higher than in more normal places or times.

12. Regime change in the Muslim courts of the Middle East was often accompanied by 'tragic accidents'. John of Joinville wrote a vivid first-hand account of what the transfer of power might look like in a Mamluk government. A cabal of emirs decided to kill Turanshah, the sultan of Egypt, while he was still in his low-security campaign headquarters.

13. In an illustration (c.1134) accompanying tales of the adventures of a travelling merchant named al-Harith, our hero confronts the Bedouin who has stolen his camel. What al-Harith is less willing to advertise, however, is the fact that he himself had stolen the horse he is now riding. Criminality in the Holy Land, particularly between strangers, was so predictable that it was almost to be expected.

14. This stunning illumination shows the horrors that accompanied the fall of the city of Tripoli to the Mamluks in 1289. The image is 'military' but the majority of the participants pictured are 'civilians' – always a fine distinction in the Latin East. A large number of Frankish ships are in port, in this case ferrying refugees, but normally available for piracy. Men happily butcher and behead each other, even in a church sanctuary. Everyone is desensitised to bloodshed. The crusader societies head towards an appropriately violent ending.

and his army of fierce Turkic and Kurdish horsemen had time to consolidate their hold on it.

This could only happen if the crusader states could attract military allies to help them. Such an alliance might include the Orthodox Byzantine empire of the East, the feudal Catholic powers of western Europe, or the maritime states of Italy – or preferably, all of them. A charm offensive was unleashed. It was clear that successful diplomacy was the only way to save the Holy Land.[7]

This campaign of shuttle diplomacy reached a climax at the beginning of 1171. King Amalric 'called before him all the nobles and laid before them the needs of the kingdom'. It was decided that delegations should be sent as a matter of urgency to both the East and the West. The Frankish settlers were desperate. There was no question of prioritisation. Envoys were sent to anyone who might be even remotely helpful.[8]

One mission was sent 'to explain the difficulties of the kingdom to the princes of the West and to ask for their help'. The itinerary set out for these diplomats was gruelling in the extreme. The envoys 'were instructed to visit the pope and those illustrious lords, the emperor of the Romans [Germany], the kings of France, England, Sicily, and the Spains, and also other distinguished dukes and counts'.[9]

But the most immediate source of potential help was felt to be Byzantium, 'as the emperor was much nearer to us and was besides far richer than the others, and he could more easily furnish the desired aid'. The leadership of this delegation was crucial: the fate of the entire Latin East might depend on it.

Much to the horror of the royal court, who were all too aware of the dangers involved in international travel, King Amalric declared 'that a mission of such importance could be undertaken by no one but himself and added that he was prepared to undergo all perils and hardships to relieve the desperate necessity of the kingdom. The great nobles of the realm . . . were almost overcome by this proposal and protested that the task was too arduous'. Amalric was not to be dissuaded, however.[10]

What passed for the Frankish 'diplomatic corps' (far too grand a phrase for the rudimentary bureaucracies of these fledgling states) was put into motion. But who were the diplomats? The Frankish nobility were hardened soldiers who could relate well to their peer groups in other parts of Christendom. These men were the obvious choice. But they were often barely literate; they were also on permanent military duty, thinly spread along the borders of the crusader settlements. They could not easily be taken out of the front line – or at least not in the numbers required by such an intensive diplomatic offensive.

Consequently, much of the burden of conducting King Amalric's diplomacy fell instead on the shoulders of the bishops and other clerics of the kingdom – men who were educated, articulate and trustworthy. William, bishop of Acre, was one of these honest, chosen men, and he and his retinue accompanied the king on his mission to Constantinople.

But the task was no sinecure. It was a world away from the pampered modern norms of statesmanship, with meetings and press conferences punctuated by champagne receptions in luxury hotels. This was a time when travel was slow and dangerous. Communications were cumbersome and primitive. Some men could cope with these rigours. Others could not. There were casualties, both physically and mentally.

Amalric and his delegation – clearly supplicants, but proud and eager to impress – set out for Constantinople on 10 March 1172. Following the age-old principle that banks are more likely to lend to people who do not need to borrow, they were keen to show that they had strength: they were accompanied by an armed escort of ten galleys. But even this was largely for show. As Jerusalem did not have the luxury of a standing navy, these ships were probably leased for the journey, the flotilla cobbled together as best as it could be for the occasion – an attempt to make an impoverished monarchy and a beleaguered kingdom look like an attractive going concern.

Amalric eventually arrived safely at his destination. The trip had not been easy. William of Tyre, a man who was himself no stranger to the perils of the sea, wrote that it had only been possible because 'the favour of the Lord was with him'. Somewhere on these same ships, tired, frightened and seasick, were William, bishop of Acre, and his retinue.[11]

The mission was a great success. Amalric and the Emperor Manuel hit it off. The Franks, who knew that their very survival was at stake, were prepared to offer their fealty to Manuel. The Byzantines were, for their part, gracious and supportive. They seem to have agreed to renew their joint commitment to capture Egypt, and to help the Frankish Holy Land by taking the fight to the enemy. Amalric and his delegation left Constantinople in the early summer and reached the Latin Kingdom of Jerusalem on 15 June 1171. The men got off their ships as soon as possible, disembarking at the kingdom's northern port of Sidon, rather than sailing on down to Acre. They were relieved to put their feet on firm soil once more, as grateful as only cavalrymen can be that their sea voyage was over.

But it was not over for everyone. At some point during the discussions with the Emperor Manuel, Bishop William had been sent abroad with yet another delegation, this time to Italy. His mission took many months. It was presumably partially successful, as it was arranged that instead of heading straight back to the crusader states, he would return by way of Constantinople to give the Emperor Manuel a first-hand progress report. Accordingly, he headed back to the East the following year, journeying through the 'European' lands of Byzantium. At the end of June 1172, William and his party reached the city of Adrianople, near Turkey's modern-day border with Bulgaria, and stopped for a well-earned break.

The entire group were shattered after their travels, ending an exhausting year that had been punctuated by frustration and danger. Everyone was in need of rest. But for one of the men it was already too late.

Brother Robert, one of the bishop's party, had fallen sick. He had become over-stressed during their long journeys. Although his companion was afflicted with such crippling anxiety, the bishop had been loath to leave him behind. The relationship between the two men was a close and affectionate one. We are told that Robert was a member of the bishop's staff and 'one whom he himself had raised to the priesthood and received among his personal retinue'. But Robert had not coped well with the rigours of their mission. By the time they arrived at Adrianople, 'he was recovering from a long illness during which he had suffered greatly'.[12]

The group breathed a collective sigh of relief as they settled in at their lodgings. William took the chance to relax and, 'much fatigued by his long journey, the bishop partook of food at the noon hour, and then lay down to rest his weary limbs'. With the worst of their journey over, at least in the short term, everyone must have hoped that Brother Robert would make a quick recovery.[13]

It was not to be. Robert was ostensibly unconscious in the darkened room, which he shared with the bishop that afternoon; but he seems to have been seized by what we might today call a psychotic episode. As William drifted off to sleep, Robert became deeply disturbed and 'suddenly a madness came upon him; he seized his sword and stabbed the sleeping bishop, inflicting fatal wounds'.[14]

Help was quickly at hand, but the damage had been done in seconds: 'the bishop's people outside heard his cries and recognised by his groans and outcries that their master was in the throes of death. When the door was finally broken down by force, they found their lord almost lifeless although his heart was still faintly beating.'

Bishop William was clearly dying; but, impressive to the end, he was extraordinarily charitable and measured in his response to his attacker. His retainers wanted 'to seize the murderer and deliver him over in chains to the punishment due to him according to the laws against homicide. But the bishop forbade them and most earnestly implored them that for the good of his soul full indulgence should be granted the murderer.' William died, having ensured that his deeply disturbed friend did not suffer any more torments than illness was already inflicting. As he passed away, William 'was still begging that the present deed should not be held against the young man'.

The murder was shocking and puzzling in equal measure. 'As yet we have been unable to determine the reason for this deed', wrote William of Tyre, in his rather plaintive summary of an event that clearly saddened him. 'It is said by some,' he suggested after much consideration, 'that Robert . . . had been suffering from a long illness; that, although convalescent, he was attacked by a sudden violent frenzy and therefore was not responsible for his wicked act.'[15]

Despite the vagaries of medieval justice, and the superstitions that we imagine pervaded civil life, it is interesting and heartening to see that 'diminished responsibility' was a legitimate and recognised defence, even in the twelfth century – and that even the victim of such butchery might have the good grace and nobility to forgive his attacker.

15

Murderous Monks

Headstrong and heavily armed soldiers might be hard to police, but even monks were not always easy to control. The Church was ideologically pacifistic, at least in theory. It went to great lengths to try to keep violence under control. But there were profound tensions: and nowhere was this truer than in the Latin East, where, somewhat ironically, the Church bore much of the burden of financing the defence of the frontiers.[1]

Christianity might abhor violence, but the lives of the Frankish settlers and the native Christian communities depended to a very large extent on the effectiveness of militarised monks. Three main monastic orders – the Templars, the Hospitallers and later the Teutonic Knights – had been established to help defend the Holy Land. In the absence of standing armies, they quickly took on the responsibility for looking after large stretches of vulnerable frontier lands.

For these military orders, violence was an essential and fundamental part of their very existence. Their behaviour was often inflamed by a unique and occasionally toxic combination: the testosterone of active military service, the normalising and desensitising nature of the violence which they frequently encountered, and the frustrations of celibacy.

For warriors such as the Templars, for instance, where violence was tightly directed but simultaneously glorified, the tensions this created proved particularly difficult to sustain. The possibility of murder, and perhaps even the existence of a predisposition towards it, was recognised in the ordinances of the order. 'If a brother kills a Christian man or woman,' the Rule of the Templars states at one point, 'or causes them to be killed, he will be expelled from the house.' Reference to this law was made several times – so often, in fact, that one suspects that the frequency of its appearance bore a direct relation to the frequency of offences.[2]

Case law cited in the statutes of the order gave examples of what this might mean in practice. One case recalled that 'it happened in Antioch that a brother who was named Brother Paris and two other brothers who were in his company, killed some Christian merchants'. When they were accosted about their crimes, the warrior monks had no real answer. When 'they were asked why they had done such a thing . . . they replied that sin had made them do it'. Perhaps they were drunk. Or perhaps, Templars being elite warriors, their arrogance just got the better of them.

Noble or not, the punishments were appropriately severe. The offending brothers 'were sentenced to be expelled from the house and flogged throughout Antioch, Tripoli, Tyre and Acre' – that is, they were dragged through all the main Templar regional headquarters, in order to act as a visible deterrent to anyone who might have similarly murderous impulses. 'Thus they were flogged and cried "see here the justice which the house exacts from its wicked men", and they were put in life imprisonment at Château Pèlerin and died there.' Even that was not enough to prevent a repetition, however. Soon afterwards the Templars admitted that 'in Acre a similar thing [i.e. another murder of a Christian perpetrated by a Templar] happened to another brother'. Stopping hot-headed young men from reaching for their swords was a never-ending process.[3]

But when it came to murder, even the Templars faced fierce competition from the Hospitallers, their long-standing rivals as military monks. Their professional violence was impressive and essential. There were times in the late fourteenth century when the Hospitaller garrison on Rhodes were almost single-handedly leading the defence of Christendom in the eastern Mediterranean. But the fearsome monk-knights still found time for bitter and occasionally violent fighting among themselves.[4]

By the 1370s and 1380s, the Hospitaller order on Rhodes was riven with politics, criminality and disputes. The island's effectiveness as a bulwark against further Muslim expansionism was being severely undermined by corruption and in-fighting.

Matters came to a head in 1381. Brother Bertrin of Gagnac was stationed at the Hospitaller's castle on the island. He was a rich French knight and a leading member of the order. But his reputation was highly dubious. The senior knight of the Spanish brothers at Rhodes had recently been found dead, drowned on the shore. Rumours were circulating that Brother Bertrin was implicated in the affair, and was possibly even the murderer himself. Bertrin complained about the gossip, and in April 1381, in an effort to divert attention away from his own behaviour, he tried to implicate the local master and his agents in the murder instead. Insufficient evidence could be gathered, however, and the case had to be dropped. But the affair remained ominously unresolved.[5]

As if that was not enough, the unstable and litigious Brother Bertrin went to court yet again a few weeks later, in May 1381. This time he claimed that he should be given control of the affluent Hospitaller Priory of Toulouse, with, cynics noted, all the possibilities this would open up to him for personal enrichment.[6]

But he had gone too far. In the course of the dispute, it emerged that he had already committed several other serious offences, including deserting his post in Cyprus, much to the detriment of his command. As a result of the accusations that had arisen in the process of pursuing Brother Bertrin's claims to Toulouse, an enquiry was set up to examine his conduct. Matters quickly escalated. Bertrin was suspected of having embezzled large sums of money while he was serving on Kos; and at the end of June, the accounts of Kos were audited to identify any shortfalls.[7]

More and more evidence of his criminality emerged over the coming months. On 2 November 1381, an assembly of the brothers was convened on Rhodes to try Bertrin 'for certain grave excesses and crimes he had perpetrated'. The evidence was overwhelming. He was eventually found – extremely – guilty.[8]

The brothers gathered together in the castle's main chapel, the Church of St John the Baptist at Rhodes. It was agreed that as punishment he should be expelled from the Hospitaller order and, as a symbol of this expulsion, that he should be very publicly stripped of his cloak. As the knot of the cloak's cord was being untied, however, Bertrin 'rushed at the Master with a knife, which he drew from his own sleeve, with intent to kill him. The Master, using all his strength, repulsed him with his hands to avoid being struck, but Bertrin with his knife wounded the Master in the thumb of his left hand.' Bertrin continued to try to kill the aged Master (who was about seventy years old), but several of the other brother knights 'rushed to the defence of their superior and Master, slaying the said Bertrin there within that church'.[9]

The master, Fernández of Heredia, defended himself well in the fighting. But he was certainly no saint either: apart from this episode, he was mainly famous for having enriched himself at the expense of the order, having amassed huge wealth during his career. He was also known as a ladies' man: his greed was largely driven, so it was said, by the many illegitimate children he had to support, as well as by a long line of money-hungry relatives who beat a path to his door.

Bertrin of Gagnac was even more corrupt. He seems to have been guilty of embezzlement, 'grave excesses' and, even more vaguely, 'various crimes and defects'. Far more importantly, he had been implicated in the murder of the leader of the Spanish brethren – and, given his later behaviour, his guilt seems highly likely. The fact that he had a knife hidden up his sleeve that day in court shows that he had another murder in mind as well. It was only the master's surprisingly quick reflexes that prevented a further tragedy.[10]

None of the participants came out of this incident well.

16

Murder and Power

Life below stairs could be violent, but tragic accidents at the top of society were relatively commonplace, too.

This violence could sometimes emerge as a visceral form of conflict resolution. Ironically, it was sometimes a brutal, though effective, way of changing government, whilst minimising further bloodshed. It could also be a way of attempting to gain popularity (as with the murder of Thomas Becket): killing the enemy of someone important might, in theory, be ingratiating enough to generate a reward. Or, more likely, it could just be an action taken with an eye for the main chance – regime change at its simplest.

Modern statesmen live in the expectation of a metaphorical knife in the back from their political enemies (or perhaps from their friends). The situation in the Latin Kingdom of Jerusalem was similar, but the knives were far from metaphorical.

Miles of Plancy, for instance, a rich and powerful nobleman, was not popular with his peers. He had personal qualities that many found unattractive. He could be rude. He could be arrogant. But his main failing, in the eyes of his fellow nobles at least, was that he was far too successful.

Miles was a relative newcomer in the Latin East, an unwelcome *arriviste* in the most literal sense of the word. He had left France in 1169 and quickly gained the trust of the notoriously difficult King Amalric. This in itself was enough for the old-established Frankish ruling classes to close ranks and treat him with suspicion. But worse was to come. Amalric made Miles seneschal of the entire kingdom, giving him control of much of the royal finances and many castles. Critically for the famously litigious local barons, this also made him, after the king himself, the chief judicial officer of the land.

As well as power, Miles was also given riches. Amalric allowed him to marry the daughter of the baron Philip of Nablus, and through her he became lord of the Transjordan – the all-too-proud possessor of some of the strongest castles in the Middle East, with a substantial private income derived from the tolls taken from passing caravans. Miles had quickly accumulated power, lands, castles and a rich widow – all of which, the local nobility felt, were rightfully theirs.

Miles' behaviour did not make things easier. Far from placating his rivals, he flaunted his success at their expense. According to William of Tyre, who knew him and all the main players in this story, Miles was 'far from discreet, a proud and even arrogant man, lavish of high-sounding phrases and filled with a spirit of excessive presumption'. Successful or not, being pompous and arrogant was never a popular combination.[1]

Matters came to a head in 1174. On 11 July, King Amalric, a wily operator who was still in his thirties and described even by his Muslim enemies as 'bravest of their kings, the most outstanding for policy, cunning and intrigue', died unexpectedly. The kingdom was thrown into turmoil. Amalric had only kept the faction-fighting in check by his authority – and by the force of his irritable and dour personality. On his death, things quickly began to unravel.

Miles stepped in as regent to take over the running of the country, but his appointment was unwelcome to the older families. Within weeks, opposition to Miles began to take shape. Rumours circulated that the new regent was going to be assassinated, and 'matters came to such a pass that certain men were secretly incited to plot against his life'. Perhaps gossip about the plots was deliberately leaked to intimidate Miles and persuade him to back off. If so, it did not have the desired effect.

Miles was warned that conspiracies were in train, but instead of taking a more conciliatory stance, 'he made light of it'. Events moved far more quickly than he imagined, however. One day 'while staying at the city of Acre, he was stabbed on the public street just at dusk and died after suffering ignominious and shameful treatment'.[2]

The murder was ruthlessly carried out, probably with some degree of inside knowledge – Miles seems to have been attacked when his guards and attendants were elsewhere, and the murderer was never caught. The attack was well planned and timed to take place in a port during the autumn sailing season to the West: the assassin could have been on a ship back to France or Italy within the hour.

According to William of Tyre,

> some said that he had been murdered because of the devoted loyalty which he had showed towards the king. Others, on the contrary, claimed that he was secretly taking steps to seize the royal power. It was said that he had sent messengers to his friends . . . in France . . . It is well known that Balian of Jaffa [one of his supporters] had been sent to the lands across the sea with royal dispatches and that his return was daily awaited.[3]

By the time Balian got back, the dispatches were academic – his master, a man with many enemies and a disinclination to compromise, had been disposed of. The rough political debate of the time had already moved on.

Such disputes, and their bloody forms of resolution, started early in the history of the Latin East. And given the continual jockeying for power that occurred among the highly competitive knightly classes, it is perhaps not surprising that this was so.

In the summer of 1109, the siege of Tripoli was grinding to a close. After seven long years of fighting, which had been hugely debilitating for both sides, the Muslim defences were beginning to crack. By June, the Franks were sufficiently confident of their forthcoming success to start bickering about how the spoils were to be divided.[4]

The county of Tripoli had been established by Raymond, count of Toulouse, shortly after the end of the First Crusade. Annoyingly (particularly for Raymond), he died in 1105, before the putative capital city of his new state could be captured. Two of his sons (half-brothers) argued bitterly over their inheritance. One of them, William-Jordan, count of Cerdagne, lived in the East and had been working hard to secure the new county, fighting both in the siege and on the inland frontiers. He felt that he had earned possession of the county the hard way.

His half-brother Bertrand, who had inherited Raymond's French lands, had other ideas. He raised an army of some four thousand troops, supplemented by sailors and marines, and a navy of forty galleys. He and his army sailed from the Toulousain port of Saint-Gilles, and joined up with a Genoese fleet of another eighty galleys and several thousand more troops. This was a very formidable force by the standards of the time.

In March 1109, he arrived in the crusader port of Tortosa. Bertrand's ships dominated the eastern Mediterranean, temporarily at least, and his army far outnumbered William-Jordan's exhausted feudal veterans. Backed up by this level of military muscle, Bertrand felt that he was well positioned to take over his father's lands in the East.[5]

Relations between the two brothers quickly deteriorated further. Eventually, in order to stop open fighting breaking out between the two factions, a council of the leaders of the Latin states was convened outside Tripoli in June 1109.

Practical considerations ensured that Bertrand emerged as the winner. After lengthy negotiations between all four of the crusader states, the council decided that he should be given the lion's share of the county. There was little room for sentimentality in the beleaguered Latin East – military resources for the future counted for more than hard work and heroic efforts in the past. A disgruntled William-Jordan had to be content with the two fiefdoms of Tortosa and Arqa, north of Tripoli.

The dispute was ostensibly over, but it had failed to fully satisfy anyone: resolution of the issue had merely been delayed. William-Jordan felt short-changed, as he had been given only the rump of the land, despite his tenacious military efforts. And Bertrand was clearly not happy to have a hostile half-brother occupying two of his most important ports and potentially causing trouble in the future.

In the event, it seems likely (though impossible to prove conclusively) that Bertrand took matters into his own hands. When the council was over, and once William-Jordan was away from the prying eyes of a busy siege camp, a suspiciously violent dispute arose between him and some of Bertrand's men. The details are not entirely clear, and the whole affair was, probably not coincidentally, mysterious.[6]

The Genoese had a lot at stake in the dispute, both as supporters of Bertrand and as suppliers of his naval contingent. They were eager to increase their commercial presence on the coast of Palestine and Syria. Their historian, Caffaro, whom one would expect to have been relatively well informed, later wrote that William-Jordan had been killed by Bertrand's men in a dispute that was, ostensibly at least, about forage. William-Jordan, he wrote, owned most of the agricultural land around the nearby castle of Pilgrims' Mount. 'One day,' wrote Caffaro, 'early in the morning, Bertrand's squires were in among William-Jordan's crops. William jumped straight on to his horse, and as he was charging at the squires, one of them drew an arrow and shot him through the throat; he lay dead in the cornfield. Bertrand was delighted at his death.' This looks very much like a premeditated provocation: and, if so, it was one that produced the desired results.[7]

The chronicler Albert of Aachen, reporting the views of crusaders returning to Germany, wrote that 'after a brief space of time, William of Cerdagne, on account of a vile injury and dispute which annoyed his squire, was shot through the heart by him with an arrow in a secret attack and died'. Even the contemporary Damascene historian, Ibn al-Qalanisi, was surprisingly well informed about the incident. He recorded that '[William-Jordan] de Cerdagne returned to Arqa, and finding a certain Frank in the fields there, he desired to strike him, but the Frank struck and killed him.'[8]

The contemporary Frankish historian, Fulcher of Chartres, who may well have attended the Council of Tripoli in person, was rather more coy. He wrote merely that the attack took place after dark, and that 'by some mischance which I do not understand William-Jordan was killed. He was shot from ambush by a small arrow while riding one night.' Everyone, wrote Fulcher, 'asked who had done it, but they were not able to find out'.[9]

William of Tyre, writing much later in the twelfth century, summarised the debate and added his own thoughtful and worldly slant to the affair:

A quarrel chanced to spring up from some trivial cause between the squires of the two families. William-Jordan immediately mounted his horse and rode swiftly thither in the hope of settling it but he was struck by a chance arrow, from the effects of which he died. Some claimed that Count William perished by the crafty machinations of Bertrand, but even to the present day the author of the fatal wound is not definitely known.

In a dry and possibly ironic aside, William finished his comments by noting that 'his rival and competitor for the possession of Tripoli having been removed in this way, Bertrand was left in sole command of the campaign'.

As with the murder of Miles of Plancy, the circumstances of the attack were suspiciously convenient. The incident took place out of sight of the assembled Frankish dignitaries and their armies. It was clearly started by Bertrand's men, though it was, of course, hard to prove his involvement. And, as the murder took place far away from Muslim-held lands, William-Jordan would not have been wearing any armour, hence his vulnerability to an arrow or crossbow bolt.

Whether Bertrand's squires had been instructed to provoke a fracas, and to use it as a pretext to launch a personal attack upon William-Jordan, was never discovered; but the strong suspicion, then and now, was that that had indeed been the case. This was rough justice – a bitter family dispute being resolved by violence; but once it was a fait accompli, everybody was inclined to just carry on as normal.

The occasionally murderous competition between Frankish lords continued even into the last decades of the crusader states. Although one might imagine that their terminally perilous state would encourage greater unity, the claustrophobic nature of their increasingly confined conditions meant, in fact, that they often turned in on themselves instead. In the 1270s, for instance, a mysterious legal case arose from a murder committed by the brother-in-law of King Hugh III of Cyprus and Jerusalem. Doubtless helped by his connections, he seems to have been let off lightly, or received a full pardon.[10]

The intoxicating and disinhibiting nature of power persisted to the end.

Muslim murder and political drama

The Franks had no monopoly on political violence, of course. The threat of murder was pervasive at the highest political levels of Muslim society. The usual precautions of armoured clothing, ranks of guards, body doubles and food tasters were regularly deployed. Even the animal kingdom might, on occasion, be called into service: monkeys, for instance, were used to detect poison in the food and drink of the powerful. Regardless of simian help, however, murders at the top of Muslim hierarchies were still relatively common.[11]

One such political attack took place in 1137. Shihab al-Din Mahmud, the lord of Damascus, wanted to dispose of one of his more irritating emirs. The opportunity for the hit came when Bazwaj, the unfortunate emir in question,

> visited him in the Rose Pavilion in his palace in the citadel. Now Shihab al-Din had detailed a party of the Armenian Shamsiya, who were members of his cortege, to deal with him and had given them instructions to kill him. When they were able to overpower him in the absence of his attendants, they killed him and carried him out wrapped in a cloak to the tomb built for his wife, and he was buried there.[12]

Shihab al-Din Mahmud did not have long to enjoy his success. 'On the morning of [23 June 1138]', wrote the Damascene historian Ibn al-Qalanisi,

> there was made known the plot directed against Shihab al-Din . . . and his assassination while he was asleep in his bed during the preceding night, by the hands of his accursed slaves, Albaghash the Armenian, to whom he had shown special favour and . . . the eunuch Yusuf, whom he trusted to sleep by him, and al-Kwarkawi, the groom of the bed-chamber, who used to sleep in proximity to him . . . These three accursed malefactors used to sleep around his bed.

The attack was almost too easy:

> when they were assured that he was asleep, they attacked and killed him in his bed upon his couch. Another groom who was with them called out and they killed him too. They planned out their course of action, concealed their secret, and so got out of the citadel. When the assassination became known, search was made for Albaghash, but he had fled and his house was plundered. The other two were seized and crucified on the wall over the Jabiya gate.[13]

The motivation behind the killing is not clear: other than revenge, it is difficult to see what the murderers hoped to gain. Perhaps there was a tangled backstory of jealousy or long-held grudges between the men. Or perhaps they felt Shihab was going to dispose of them as he had Bazwaj and many others, and they decided to get to him before he killed them. Either way, their strangely Shakespearian approach (which followed the plot of *Macbeth* even as far as murdering the grooms) showed how difficult it was to protect oneself from servants, guards, lovers or ostensible close friends. There was a need for security in the bedchamber, while a ruler slept: but if those men were suborned or disgruntled, the consequences could be brutal.

Though many of their predecessors had been highly enthusiastic murderers, it was the Mamluks who perfected the art of the ruthless palace coup. As slave-soldiers they were, rather like Shihab al-Din's Armenian palace guards, men cut adrift from their families and countries: these were retainers who had (initially at least) very limited distractions in terms of local relationships. In theory, this allowed them to focus on their masters' wishes; but in practice, it also meant that they had few ties of family loyalty to keep their personal ambitions in check. And once they had chosen to take a path of betrayal, they had the means, as highly trained warriors, to further their ambitions extremely forcefully.

This meant that regime change in the Muslim courts of the Middle East was often accompanied by 'tragic accidents'. A Frankish prisoner of war was a bystander at one such coup in May 1250 and survived to write a vivid first-hand account of what the transfer of power might look like in a Mamluk government.

John of Joinville had been captured whilst on crusade in Egypt with his king, Louis IX. Unluckily for both Joinville and the victorious Turanshah, sultan of Egypt, the vicious and very personal politics of the Mamluk regime erupted unexpectedly at this moment of triumph. A cabal of emirs decided to kill their leader while he was still in the relatively insecure environment of his campaign headquarters. 'So it was,' wrote Joinville, that after they had eaten and the sultan was making his way to his chamber after having taken his leave of his emirs, one of the knights of the *halqa* [men who were, disappointingly from Turanshah's perspective, his trusted bodyguard], the man who carried the sultan's sword, struck him with his own sword across the hand, between his four fingers, and split his hand open right up to his arm.[14]

Despite the agony he must have been in, the 'young and agile sultan fled . . . [and] the members of the *halqa*, who were 500 men on horseback, tore down the sultan's pavilions and laid siege to him'. The treacherous guards, sensing that they were close to receiving the kind of attractive bonus that invariably accompanied violent regime change such as this,

launched Greek fire at him, and the tower, made of fir poles and cotton cloth, was set alight quickly . . . When the sultan saw this he came down at great speed and made off in flight towards the river along the path . . . The men of the *halqa* had hacked through on to the path with their swords, and as the sultan passed on his way to the river one of them struck him a spear blow in his side. The sultan fled for the river, trailing the spear behind him. His assailants came down to the water and swam out to kill him in the river, quite close to the galley where we were. One of the knights . . . slit him open with his sword, and pulled the heart from his chest.[15]

While this unpleasantness was going on, chaos reigned in the camp. The murderers made all the Frankish prisoners of war kneel down to be beheaded. But this was either a form of intimidation, or they just changed their minds. The crusaders were eventually trussed up and thrown into the hold of one of their captors' galleys.

'We stayed there,' wrote Joinville, prosaically enough for what must have been a traumatic experience, 'in a miserable condition all that night; we were lying so close together that my feet were touching the good Count Peter of Brittany and his were right next to my face.' The smell of Count Peter's feet, bad though that might have been, was clearly more palatable to recall than the possibility (almost probability) of their imminent execution.[16]

Strangely, although disposing of a losing general (rather than a successful one) would intuitively seem to make much more sense, this same sequence of events was repeated in a similarly victorious Muslim army a few decades later. Perhaps the heady nature of victory meant that security was looser. Or maybe the smell of blood in the air just sharpened the senses to the possibilities of ambition and opportunity.

Either way, in the aftermath of the siege of Acre in 1291, the final major blood-letting of the eastern crusades, al-Ashraf Khalil, the victorious sultan who had just conquered the last major Frankish stronghold, met a similarly disappointing and anti-climactic fate: within two years of his historic victory, he was killed by his own lieutenants. One of his trusted emirs 'hacked him so that he cut him in two'. The sultan's family was evidently not a close one, as the first wound was inflicted by 'Baydara, who was his uncle'.[17]

The killing rarely stopped, even when regime change had been successfully effected, however. The business of public death continued to be a popular act of social communication, a display of power, of displeasure or caprice.

Saladin's chivalry and much-vaunted 'humanity' is an interesting case in point. He had a long and petulant history of killing prisoners of war. These were bloodthirsty times, and societies steeped in a nomadic heritage were particularly uninhibited about the shedding of blood. Saladin's propagandist, Baha al-Din, wrote that 'forty five Franks taken at Beirut were brought before Saladin'. Cheerily, he wrote, Saladin's 'young sons had asked him to allow them to kill a captive, but he refused'. His rationale for this decision was telling: 'so that they will not, as youngsters, grow accustomed to shed blood and make light of it, when they as yet do not distinguish between Muslim and infidel'. Saladin was crystal clear, then, that he was against his sons murdering prisoners of war not because it was inherently wrong for children to become murderers, or that prisoners should be protected, but because he felt it might encourage them to kill indiscriminately, rather than just focusing on killing non-Muslims.[18]

A cursory reading of a tabloid newspaper might suggest otherwise, but as a general principle, the further back in time we look, the more violence we find. The crusades were certainly no exception. On the contrary, the unremitting danger of the times was harsh – not just for soldiers, but across the entire social spectrum. Men and women, merchants and peasants, clerics and laity – all were vulnerable.

There was killing within wars. There was widespread murder of prisoners, on all sides, even after the carnage of the battlefield was over. But murder was not uncommon even in times of peace. Societies were desensitised rather than satiated by warfare: there was blood and murder even in the rare moments when the armies went home.

The past was grim – and generally far more so than we imagine.

Part V
OUTLAWS

17

Ploughshares into Swords

In 1182, a Turkic army placed the rock-cut crusader castle of the Cave de Sueth under siege. This was unhelpful, but not entirely unusual for a country at war. The castle was 'a very strongly fortified place. It was thought to be impregnable.' But it fell within five days.

Accusations were bandied around about how the disaster had happened. According to the chronicler William of Tyre, whose version of events seems plausible enough, the Muslims had 'forced an entrance into the cave from the side by mining, a feat which could easily be accomplished since the rock was of a chalky nature. They burrowed into the first storey and seized it; then after taking that, they compelled the surrender of those in the middle and top storeys.' Contemporaries were shocked. They felt the need to place the blame, very possibly unfairly, on the garrison.

For the modern reader, however, there is an altogether different and more subtle shock. As an aside which emerged from the resulting recriminations, it became clear that the men involved were not what we would expect: the entire garrison of this vital crusader castle – everyone from the commander down to the most junior squire – was Arab.

The modern trope is that crusader armies were European in appearance and religiously intolerant by nature. But William, who was born in 'Outremer', knew that the truth was different. He took it for granted that his readers, people who lived in the crusader states or who knew what the Latin East was really like, would know that, too. The garrison was a local army unit whose commands would have been given in Arabic, and it was made up of men whose equipment would probably have included many items of traditional Arab clothing and headgear. This was a normal part of the 'crusader' army which William and his readers were used to seeing every day.[1]

In the space of a few decades, a whole society had been remilitarised.

Pax Romana and the 'heretic problem'

As we have seen, the proportion of foreign, rootless armed men in the population in this unique time and place was abnormally high.

Outsiders were not the only problem, however. The impact of this influx was doubly destabilising precisely because the civil population had previously been so largely disarmed.

The Roman empire, whose eastern provinces included the Holy Land and most of the rest of the Middle East, had been a relatively stable and successful state. The Pax Romana was largely accompanied by a harshly enforced demilitarisation of the civil populations it controlled. By the time of the Turkic invasions, much of the old Christian population in the provinces of Syria, Palestine and Egypt had effectively been without their own military tradition for several hundred years.

There had, of course, been many military actions during that time. The Byzantine army was active in Syria, Cilicia and Anatolia in the tenth century, long before the Seljuks arrived. And the combination of bandits and Bedouin had always made travel in the Holy Land difficult. No one should ever pretend that Palestine was a rural idyll before the age of the crusades. But it is nonetheless true that the civilian population became increasingly militarised once the crusader states were established. This was almost entirely inevitable – the newly recovered Christian lands were hugely outnumbered and every man was needed.[2]

Potential Christian recruits were certainly present in large numbers. Burchard of Mount Sion was a Dominican friar who had spent a decade in the Middle East. In the 1280s he wrote:

> It should be noted as a matter of fact . . . that always in every place and kingdom, except for Egypt and Arabia where many Saracens and other followers of Muhammad live, for every Saracen you will find thirty or more Christians. It is true, however, that . . . although they are Christians, because they do not have much experience of arms, when they are attacked by Saracens . . . they are subjected to them and buy peace and tranquillity for tribute . . . So it comes about that that kingdom is said to belong to the Saracens, even though in reality they are all Christians except the bailiffs, tax-collectors and other members of their families.[3]

This seems strange to our eyes, as we are accustomed to a Middle East that has become very largely Muslim. And Burchard was clearly exaggerating to make a point. We now know that the process of Islamicisation undoubtedly gathered pace in the course of the twelfth and thirteenth centuries, as the crusading movement gradually lost its struggle to defend the Christian East. But the core of Burchard's argument was true. At the time he was writing there were a lot of Christians in the Middle East, and they still formed the majority of the population in the crusader states.[4]

Given the appalling military situation facing the Christian states of the East, the re-arming of these local Arab or Armenian communities was naturally a high priority for the Franks. In the more peaceful lands of western Europe, clerics might have qualms about such things. They were prone to worrying about the 'heretic problem'. In the far more pragmatic environment of the crusader states, however, the only problem was how quickly they could be trained and integrated into the army.

So, as if the waves of foreign mercenaries, volunteers and criminals were not bad enough, the number of local young men becoming acclimatised to weaponry and violence was also ratcheting up still further.

Brothers rearmed

Alongside the Catholic Franks, the main Christian groups in the crusader states were the Greek Orthodox, the Syrian Orthodox, the Armenians and the Maronites. Religious bigotry was far less prevalent than one might suppose, if only because it was a luxury that no one could afford.

The numbers of young armed men in the local communities soared. From the earliest days of the crusader states it seems that about half of the all-important cavalry arm was provided by the Arab or Armenian communities. Among the infantry, the proportion may have been even higher.

It is hard, for instance, to overestimate the Armenian military contribution. Both of the first two kings of Jerusalem had previously been counts of Edessa and, as there were relatively few Franks in the northern crusader states, intermarriage with the local Armenians was common. Most of the rulers of Jerusalem were partly of Armenian descent, and the prominence of Armenians in the crusader states was a natural recognition of their martial skills, whether as knights, mercenaries or siege specialists.[5]

Significantly, at the battle of the Field of Blood, where Il-Ghazi's vast nomadic army rolled over the northern Franks, it was an Armenian knight who led the last-ditch defence around a fragment of the True Cross, and who rallied the survivors of the Frankish army in a forlorn attempt to stave off defeat. Similarly, we also know that at this same battle, half of the ostensibly 'crusader' cavalry were in fact local Christians, as were the vast majority of the infantry.[6]

Large parts of the 'Frankish' armies that fought against Saladin in the 1180s were in reality composed of Armenian soldiers, carrying on the fight against their old enemy and his steppe-heritage cavalry armies. The chronicles are always vague, but the Armenian contribution to the war effort was immense.[7]

Like the Armenians, the Maronites were another Christian community that was generally well disposed towards the Franks. They were originally from the Antioch region, but by the early twelfth century they had taken refuge in the northern mountain ranges of what became the county of Tripoli.[8]

William of Tyre described them in glowing terms, as being 'by no means few in numbers; in fact they were generally estimated at more than 40,000 . . . They [are] a stalwart race, valiant fighters, and of great service to the Christians in the difficult engagements which they so frequently had with the enemy.' Regardless of the suspiciously round numbers involved, it is clear that there were a lot of them, and that they were eager to help in the fighting. The Franks made efforts to arm and integrate the Maronites into the Christian armies as quickly as possible.[9]

There were also significant Orthodox Christian communities in the Kingdom of Jerusalem. Their presence was taken so much for granted that they are not always singled out for special mention in the sources – but as a society at war, with chronic manpower problems, everyone was welcome. We find Arab knights in possession of several estates in the Latin Kingdom of Jerusalem in 1155 and 1158, for instance. Even the marshal of Jerusalem from 1125 to 1154, one of the most senior military positions in the country, was an Arab – he was a baron of the kingdom, in command of the Turcopole mounted archers and even, on occasion, Frankish knights.[10]

Many of the vital castle garrisons, which are traditionally assumed to have been composed of Frankish troops, were in fact manned by local Arabs. As we have seen, the 'impregnable' cave-castle which fell into Muslim hands in 1182 was manned entirely by Arab Christians. But it was not the only one. Local Christians played a much greater role in frontier defence than has generally been recognised. Most of the knights (or *milites*) of the major castle and lordship of Margat also seem to have been local Christians, rather than crusaders, as were many of their comrades.[11]

Even more importantly, large numbers of the Frankish cavalry arm – even the majority, on occasion – came from the recently remilitarised native Christian light archers who famously became known as

'Turcopoles'. Evidence regarding recruitment issues is vague in this area, largely because ethnicity was not generally seen as being particularly important or significant. But, as with the infantry, we know that local Christian cavalry were present and that they were fighting in large numbers.[12]

Although few would have been aware of it at the time, the same climatic changes that forced young armed men off the steppes and down into Syria and Palestine were also indirectly responsible for the rearming of the local populations: remilitarisation was the only way in which sedentary societies could try to stem the flow of armed migrants and defend themselves.

Win or lose, the catalysts for everyday violence were cascading down through the communities of the Holy Land.

18

Stand and Deliver: Pilgrims and Travellers

The English pilgrim Saewulf made the trip to the Holy Land in c.1101–1103, and left a very moving account of his experiences. There was only one port in crusader hands in Palestine when he arrived, and there was only one road linking it to Jerusalem: every bandit and mugger in the country knew where the easy money was to be made. The pilgrims were carrying cash for their travels; they were disorientated and often unarmed. The exhausted travellers were easy prey.

'We climbed up from Jaffa into the city of Jerusalem,' wrote Saewulf. 'The journey lasted two days and it was by a very hard mountain road. It was very dangerous too, because the Saracens, who are continually plotting an ambush against Christians, were hiding in the caves of the hills and among rocky caverns.'[1]

Danger was everywhere. The Fatimid army based in Ascalon continually attracted new men to join its ranks. The regulars in the garrison were replenished and topped up several times a year. Mercenaries from Africa and the Eurasian steppes were enticed into service. To top off the horrors awaiting pilgrims and prospective settlers from the West, there were also bandits everywhere. Some of these were doubtless supplied and encouraged by the Egyptian military; but many were freelance outlaws, looking for stragglers and parties of pilgrims that were too small or poorly armed to defend themselves.

As Saewulf later wrote, the bandits 'were awake day and night, always keeping a lookout for someone to attack, whether because he had not enough people with him, or because he was fatigued enough to leave a space between himself and his party'. The only safe way through was to move quickly and in large groups.[2]

The security problem was so intense that the road looked more like a war zone than a thoroughfare on a widely used religious route. Rotting corpses and skeletons lined the path on either side. Even Saewulf, who had experienced many hardships in getting to the Middle East, was shocked by the dystopian landscape and horrors with which he was confronted. 'Anyone who has taken that road,' he recalled, 'can see how many human bodies there are in the road and next to the road, and there are countless corpses which have been torn up by wild beasts.'[3]

It was too dangerous to stop, so the bodies were just left there to rot. Saewulf was clearly riven with guilt about leaving the dead unburied. He later felt compelled to explain that 'even if the soil were there, who would be stupid enough to leave his brethren and be alone digging a grave? Anybody who did this would dig a grave not for his fellow Christian but for himself.'[4]

In a final irony, even the lucky survivors who had run the gauntlet of muggers and scavengers still had to face the less visible dangers of dehydration and exhaustion — and those dangers affected everyone. 'In that road,' wrote Saewulf, 'not only poor and weak people have dangers to face, but also the rich and the strong. Many are killed by the Saracens and many of heat and thirst — many through lack of drink and many from drinking too much.'[5]

The hill on the approaches to Jerusalem where pilgrims could at last see the Holy City was called Mount Joy. It is generally assumed that it got its name because of the joy they felt on seeing the objective of their pilgrimage at last in sight. This is undoubtedly true, at least in part. But it was also the case, particularly in the early years when the hill acquired its name, that they had been traumatised by their journey: the emotional rush of 'joy' was perhaps as much about horrors endured, and survived, as it was about the proximity of spiritual rewards.

Saewulf faced criminality and danger from the moment he arrived in the East. This may have been a shock to him, but it would have come as no surprise to someone who knew the region.

The situation he faced did not bode well. A seemingly endless influx of foreign soldiery. Highly militarised or remilitarised societies. An involuntary mixing of cultures which often created a jarring lack of religious and social empathy. And all of this hugely exacerbated by assassinations, civil wars and, particularly, the lawlessness associated with incursions by steppe nomads and Bedouin tribesmen. Levels of violence were shocking by any standards.

The lawlessness of the Holy Land had started long before the crusades.

Even in the tenth and eleventh centuries, banditry was rife: highway robbery, particularly when aimed at disoriented pilgrims, was commonplace. Gunther, the bishop of Bamberg, led a large party on pilgrimage to the Holy Land in 1065, thirty years before the First Crusade started. By the time they had got to Latakia, on the coast of Syria, the reckless tourists were already being warned of the ever-present danger of bandits. Entirely predictably, when they moved further on down the coast of Palestine, ostensibly under Fatimid control, things deteriorated even further: their stragglers were ruthlessly picked off on the roadsides, and they were badly cut up by outlaws near the coastal city of Caesarea.

It was a relief when the survivors returned, wounded and traumatised, to Germany. Some said that only one in three of the bishop's enthusiastic pilgrim group made it back to Europe. And, just to put this into context, their trip took place in what passed for a relatively peaceful period: six years later, from 1071 onwards, law and order broke down even more definitively, as Turkic tribesmen started to pour into Asia Minor and move further south into Palestine. Similar stories, albeit on a smaller scale, were told by Muslim travellers and merchants. Lawlessness was endemic, rather than directed at specific religious groups.[6]

But it was also true that the chronic warfare and criminality of the twelfth and thirteenth centuries made an already difficult situation far worse. The journey to the Holy Land was tough; but in the early days of the crusades, it got even more dangerous when you arrived. On landing, many Europeans, raised on stories of a land of milk and honey, were shocked at the horrors they found instead: and these horrors were largely caused by the depredations of bandits.

A well-planned pilgrimage around the Holy Land in the early days of the twelfth century had, for the lucky few who could afford it, many of the characteristics of a small military expedition. Journeying from the coast to the capital, Jerusalem, was still fraught with dangers years after the foundation of the crusader states.

When the Russian pilgrim Abbot Daniel arrived in 1106, for instance, he wrote bitterly of the perils involved. On the road up to Lydda he noted that 'there are many springs here; travellers rest by the water but with great fear, for it is a deserted place and nearby is the town of Ascalon from which Saracens sally forth and kill travellers on those roads'. This was only the beginning, however. He wrote that there 'is a great fear too going up from that place into the hills and from [Lydda] to Jerusalem is . . . all in rocky hills and here the road is hard and fearsome'. Even with money and a small army to back him up, Abbot Daniel was still, very wisely, wary about how to proceed.[7]

The dangers were unremitting. Most pilgrims' accounts of their journeys were written as a form of tourist guide – a travel brochure to entice the faithful in Europe to undertake the journey. But in the early days, it was hard to avoid making the delights of the Holy Land sound more like a horror show.

Writing of the land between Hebron and Ascalon, which was relatively heavily populated by Muslims and remained a high-crime area throughout the crusader period, Abbot Daniel noted that there is a very high rocky mountain and on it a great dense forest and there is a way over that terrible mountain but it is difficult to pass along it because the Saracens have a great fortress there from which they attack. And if anyone in a small party tries to travel that road he cannot; but God granted me a good and numerous escort and thus I was able to pass that terrible place without hindrance; nearby lies the town of Ascalon from which the pagans come forth in great numbers and attack [people] on that evil road.

If you walked down the road and survived, you counted yourself lucky.[8]

Travellers often found a safe place and had to stay there until they were joined by large bodies of fellow pilgrims: they were trying to create an informal convoy system, gathering enough military power to deter potential outlaws. Abbot Daniel, despite being accompanied by armed men of his own, still felt the need to wait for reinforcements before he proceeded.[9]

As always, violence on the roads was dictated just as much by opportunity as by religion. When he was staying in a peaceful village with a mixed Muslim and Christian population – in itself, a telling example of cultural accommodation – Daniel was at pains to emphasise that it was the local Muslim authorities that helped him to avoid the all-pervasive bandits. 'We spent one night in this village,' he later wrote,

and were well received by the Christians there, and rising early on the following morning we went to Bethlehem. And the chief of the Saracens, armed, escorted us as far as Bethlehem and conducted us all round those places; otherwise we should not have reached those holy places . . . for Saracens abound and carry on brigandage in those mountains.[10]

If the south and west of the Kingdom of Jerusalem was dangerous because of the Egyptian military base at Ascalon and the Muslim coastal strongholds, travelling to Galilee in the north-east was just as fraught with danger, but this time from nomads and local bandits. Daniel felt (almost certainly correctly) that his own armed guards were insufficient for the task. He waited until he was able to accompany the entire army of the Latin Kingdom of Jerusalem on campaign before beginning his travels in the region.[11]

Daniel and his party eventually made it through to the River Jordan. As soon as the king's troops left him, however, to go raiding in the Hauran, the pilgrims were forced to hunker down: they had to wait for further military assistance before they could return to Jerusalem. Only then was it safe to return.[12]

Daniel wanted to make contact with the Maronite Christian community, Frankish allies who lived in the eastern mountain ranges of what was gradually becoming known as the county of Tripoli. A visit in person was not possible for security reasons, however, and even the local Arabs were wary of making the attempt. He wrote sadly that 'the Christians who lived there and were our guides told us of it in detail and would not let us go to the mountain because of the many pagans there'.[13]

Daniel eventually wrote about his experiences. But, far from writing a pilgrim text that would encourage other Christians to visit the area, the abbot was clearly overwhelmed by his experience – whatever his original intentions, he was not doing a great PR job.

The Holy Land was never a rural idyll, and travel of any kind was not for the faint-hearted.

Destroit Castle: a case study in outlaw control

Sometimes bandits were so numerous, and so well armed, that they posed a serious threat not only to civilians, but even to kings – in fact, they almost killed King Baldwin I and his famous horse, Gazelle.[14]

Baldwin spent much of his reign hunting down bandits; but in 1103 the quarry nearly got the upper hand. After he and his men had failed to capture the port of Acre by siege (April–May 1103) the king was profoundly depressed and needed a break. Accompanied by just ten comrades, he went hunting in the wooded valleys near Caesarea to distract himself from the horrors and failures of the recent weeks. The trip was far less relaxing than he had planned, however.

Coincidentally, at the same time 'about sixty Saracens from Ascalon and Acre descended to ambush the Christians so that they might . . . butcher them and plunder their possessions'. These bandits bumped into some Christians – perhaps pilgrims or maybe local Arab villagers. When they ran off, the bandits decided to pursue them. The king and his companions were alerted to the incursion and set off to rescue them, even though, as they were just hunting, they did not have armour, shields or lances with them.[15]

Being outnumbered was obviously a major issue. But the famous bravery, or recklessness, of the king was even more problematic. Baldwin's horse, Gazelle, was faster than the others and, eager to catch up with the bandits, the king pushed him on, ever further in front of his household knights. As a result, Baldwin 'unexpectedly found himself [on his own] next to some bushes of low woodland'. There he was ambushed, and 'pierced through thigh and kidneys', causing 'his hand to cease from fighting with his sword, until at length he fell from his horse to the ground as if dead . . . and he was believed to have expired'.[16]

The king's retainers eventually caught up and drove off the marauders. But it seemed that they had come too late. They found their king, as they thought, mortally wounded: 'streams of blood gushed ominously from this cruel wound . . . his face began to grow pale, his spirit and strength to falter'. The grieving knights placed Baldwin on a makeshift stretcher 'and took him back to Jerusalem amidst a very great weeping'.[17]

Baldwin was tough. He survived the wound, but it came hard on the heels of serious physical and mental injuries that he had received in battle the previous year. It caused him pain throughout the rest of his life. Fulcher of Chartres, a chronicler who, as his chaplain, knew the king well, believed that the wound eventually contributed to his death, some fourteen years later, in 1118.

The threat posed by bandits in the rough terrain along the well-used coastal road was so persistent that a castle called Le Destroit was later built near the site of King Baldwin's skirmish. It was only demolished in the thirteenth century, when an even more daunting castle, the massive Templar stronghold of 'Atlit, was built within sight of it, on the coast.[18]

Bandits might be beaten off for a day, but even kings knew that the danger they posed was a perennial one.

19

Brigands and Bandits

A spring evening in Syria. The Frankish and Armenian horsemen were travelling carelessly. They were familiar with the road, riding slowly through the gradually dimming light. They were relaxed because they assumed they could be – they were, after all, a large and heavily armed party, deep in Christian territory.

Their leader stopped the column and dismounted. Strangely fastidious for a military man, he moved away from his men and walked off to find some privacy in the woods. Squatting and straining, he did not want his household knights to see him.

He succeeded all too well. None of his men ever saw him again.

Bandits could change the course of history by capturing or killing people at even the highest levels of society. One such incident involved Joscelin II (the Younger), count of Edessa (r. 1131–1159). On 5 May 1150, he had made the mistake of setting out relatively late in the day for a meeting in the neighbouring crusader state of Antioch.

As dusk was falling, he 'left his escort and turned aside to relieve the needs of nature, when, unknown both to those ahead and those following, he was attacked by brigands who rushed forth from ambush'. The 'brigands' were semi-nomadic Turcoman bandits, skilled horsemen who swiftly trussed him up and sped off. They knew he was a knight of some kind, but were presumably unaware of his identity, or how valuable he might be on the ransom market. The raiders took him to Nur al-Din, lord of Mosul and Aleppo (and soon to be the ruler of Damascus). They sold their petrified prisoner for the knockdown price of 1,000 dinars and were quickly on their way.[1]

Nur al-Din was elated. Joscelin was an old enemy. Torture would provide opportunities for entertainment. When that palled, and if there was a need for cash to pay for more mercenaries, there was a massive ransom to extracted. But it did not turn out that way.

Joscelin was not a popular figure. He was contemptuously described by one Frankish chronicler as 'a lazy, idle man, given over to low and dissolute pleasures, one who spurned good ways and followed base pursuits'. A contemporary Syrian Orthodox historian was similarly underwhelmed, describing his reign as 'the tyranny of Joscelin'. In what was a remarkable achievement under the circumstances, he had succeeded in being despised by both his Frankish compatriots and the native Christians.[2]

Joscelin had presided over the loss of his entire county, and had never been forgiven. When the city of Edessa, his capital, had been besieged and captured, he was nowhere to be seen: he had chosen to set himself up in the more comfortable (and far safer) haven of Turbessel, far to the west, on the other side of the Euphrates. While his people had been enslaved and butchered, Joscelin found time 'for luxurious pleasures of every kind, and he felt no responsibility, as he should have done, for the noble city'.[3]

Being held prisoner in the medieval Middle East was a disturbingly tangible and inescapable measure of popularity. Respected leaders were ransomed as quickly as possible, even if it bankrupted their vassals. Those who were widely regarded as losers, on the other hand, were quietly forgotten about – and Joscelin fell squarely into the latter camp.

Having lost his county, Joscelin no longer had access to large amounts of money on his own account, and no one was rushing forward to make up the difference. Frustrated by the lack of ransom offers, Nur al-Din and his torturers settled in for the long haul. Joscelin was tormented for nine interminably long years in the infamous dungeons of the citadel of Aleppo. He died, missed by no one, in 1159. When his body was finally taken out of the citadel, his remains were found to be in a dreadful state. A curious crowd gathered and were said to be 'astonished at what had happened to him'. He had, wrote one uncharitable chronicler, 'reaped the result of his dissolute ways and came to a wretched end'.[4]

As Joscelin was so unpopular with the more judgemental kind of chronicler (most of them, given that the majority were priests), this was a salutary, perversely satisfying story – a suitably ignominious end for a seedy and ineffective leader.

But it also, unwittingly, tells a different story – a story of how, deep in Christian territory, even the ruler of one of the crusader states might be robbed and abducted by bandits.

Bandits as militia

Defining exactly what constituted a 'civilian' at any point in the Middle Ages is problematic; and in the violent world of the crusades, it is virtually impossible. Almost everyone would fight if they needed to, and normal citizens were, for entirely sensible reasons, often armed. In these circumstances, the line between villagers and bandits, or between civilians and militia, could be a fine one indeed.

Warfare and endemic banditry brought out the worst in people, as always – even heads of state became adept at using the criminal element to their own advantage. Using 'alliances' with bandits (in much the same way as some rulers went into business with pirates) allowed an overlord to take a personal percentage of the profits from pillaging travelling merchants – and even their own populations – without being too visibly associated with the enterprise. A disapproving obituary of Qaraja, the Muslim governor of Hims, in 1112, for instance, described him as 'an oppressive ruler, and a confederate of brigands and outlaws'.[5]

Many armies, and particularly Muslim armies operating near their major population centres, had large numbers of bandits and criminals operating alongside them on a freelance basis. These loosely affiliated groups of young men had little to lose, and were eager to scavenge. From the perspective of a Muslim general, they were of limited value on a battlefield, but they certainly had their uses: they were cheap (they fought for the opportunity of plunder, rather than a salary) and they were an easy, low-cost way of occupying the enemy's attention by sapping his strength and soaking up a lot of energy and resources. They could never stand up to a Frankish charge; but they could, as nineteenth-century strategists like Clausewitz astutely pointed out, add significantly to the 'friction' which degrades all armies on campaign.

Bandits might have an intimate relationship with governments. For states with few resources for a police force, and only limited funds for soldiers, they were a cheap form of temporary labour. They were the medieval 'expendables'.

Even enemy armies were not immune from theft: taking their supplies was yet another kind of pin-prick damage that the outlaws could inflict, primarily working on their own behalf, of course, but also acting, indirectly, in the interests of their state. Usama Ibn-Munqidh, himself often operating on the fringes of Muslim armies on campaign (albeit in a far more socially elevated capacity), had several run-ins with 'bandit-auxiliaries' skirmishing against the Franks. His anecdotes show that he was outraged and impressed by their activities in equal measure.

He wrote of one occasion in the early twelfth century in which a Frankish army from the county of Tripoli had raided into Muslim territory and 'encamped against Hama in its fields, in which there was a fat harvest of corn; they pitched their tents right in the midst of that harvest. Now, a group of robbers came out from Shaizar to reconnoitre the Frankish army and rob them, and they noticed their tents were pitched in the corn.'

The freelancers were certainly not risk averse. One of them, according to Usama, 'went before the lord of Hama and said, "tonight I will burn up the entire Frankish army" [in return for which they wanted to be given a great deal of money]. Once evening fell, the robber went out with a group of like-minded companions, and they started the fire in the corn west of the tents.' This was a spectacularly stupid plan, as they soon found out. 'Thanks to the light of the fire,' we are told, 'the night became like day, so the Franks caught sight of them, rushed towards them and killed most of them. Only those who threw themselves into the river and swam over to the other side were able to escape.'[6]

From the bandits' perspective, the raid was a dismal failure. But for the Muslim commander, it was a risk with almost no negative consequences: if the bandits had succeeded, they would have been useful; but if they all died in the attempt, it was no great loss.

On another occasion, during an invasion of Shaizar's territory by the army of the principality of Antioch, the Franks were harassed by a local bandit chief called al-Zamarrakal. This bandit had a larger-than-life reputation, and Usama heard several stories about him, gathered from multiple sources.

One evening, al-Zamarrakal, who was already an old man by this time, was found by Usama and his men dressed as a woman, together with one of his confederates, hiding on the outskirts of the Frankish camp. This naturally raised a few eyebrows. When questioned about what he was doing, the bandit replied that he was 'waiting for nightfall . . . and then I will ask God the Exalted to supply me with the horses of those infidels'.[7]

The next morning, one of Usama's household slaves 'woke early and rode out to wait for whatever the Franks were going to do, when who should [he] see but that old man sitting on a rock in [his] way, with coagulated blood all over his leg and foot'. The veteran thief said that he had taken 'a horse, a shield and a spear from [the Franks], but one of their infantrymen caught up with me while I was on my way out [of the camp], in the middle of their troops. He jabbed at me and the spear went into my thigh. But I still made off with the horse, shield and spear.' This episode was trivial on one level; but it was also the kind of bloody and debilitating encounter that characterised the everyday experience of warfare and raiding on the frontiers – too insignificant for the history books, but an important part of the texture of criminal and military life.[8]

There was another story about that same brigand, al-Zamarrakal, which showed that there was no honour, and precious little religious integrity, among thieves. In 1136–1137, the Franks were once more encamped near Shaizar. One of the Muslim soldiers was preparing to try to enter the Frankish camp and steal some horses. Just as he was about to do so, however, al-Zamarrakal warned him off, saying that he had had his eyes on these horses for some time, and did not want anyone else competing with him. When the Shaizari soldier persisted in his attempt, the brigand shouted out to alert the Frankish guards, who charged out and almost killed him.

'The Franks came out at me,' the soldier later reported, and, 'as for [the bandit], he took off. The Franks chased after me until I threw myself in the river, and I really didn't think I would escape from them.' This treachery, and the focus on plunder, rather than on defeating a common enemy, came as no surprise. There was no hint of any cultural or religious solidarity: al-Zamarrakal would rather see a fellow Muslim killed than lose the chance to steal a horse.

Usama summed up the bandit's approach to business with a nice turn of phrase which encapsulated a deeper truth about the nature of local criminals: 'people who knew that al-Zamarrakal used to say of him, "that guy would steal a loaf of bread from his own house"'.[9]

Gritty rural realism

When civil wars were raging, or when political control was looser than usual, bandits would naturally expand their activities to fill the power vacuum and exploit new opportunities. The default position on the roads and in the countryside was so dreadful, so rife with violence and crime, that chroniclers often felt compelled to comment glowingly on the occasions when travel was safe: it was so unusual that it was worthy of special mention.

In September 1204, for instance, shortly after the establishment of the Latin Empire in Greece, it was said, as an extraordinary endorsement of a rare occurrence, that 'the region from Constantinople to Salonika enjoyed such perfect peace that the roads were safe enough for all to come and go as they pleased between the cities, which was a distance of at least twelve full days' journey'. Given that the author and his potential readership were the heavily armed Frankish nobility, one may also assume, even here, that the words 'all' and 'safe' were used in the sense that armed men could travel without hindrance, rather than women and children. Standards of safety remained depressingly low.[10]

As we have seen, pilgrims, new to the Holy Land and on their way to Jerusalem, were particularly vulnerable and attractive targets. They had to carry cash with them for the expenses of their trip. Disoriented, unused to the heat and unaware of the dangers, they could be easy prey.

A scarred Arab emir once proudly told Usama how he had robbed and murdered vulnerable travellers:

We came across a group of them [that is, Frankish pilgrims]. I encountered one of them, a man carrying a spear, with his woman behind him holding a rough-ware jar with water in it. The man gave me this first spear-wound, at which point I hit him and killed him. Then his wife advanced on me and struck me with that rough-ware jar in my face and made this other scar. Both of them left their mark on my face.[11]

The mugger was based in Ascalon, and he and his men seem to have been plying their gruesome trade on foot. The mugging itself took place on the road to Jerusalem, probably in the first decades of the twelfth century. The fate of the woman is not known; but judging by other similar cases, she was probably raped and either killed or taken into slavery.

But while this was a relatively small incident in the scheme of things, it is important to remember that these attacks were not necessarily just localised instances of mugging. Banditry could also be followed by massacres on such a large scale that they were more bloodthirsty than many battles of the period.

In the late 1120s, for instance, a large group of Frankish pilgrims were travelling back from Raphaniya towards Apamea. There were, we are told, some 700–800 people in the convoy – presumably they had all gathered together for their travels, seeking greater safety. But even numbers on that scale were not enough.

The party got lost at night as it tried to move too quickly across the dangerous frontier lands and ended up in the territory of the Muslim-controlled town of Shaizar. The town's troops (its 'askar') were away at the time. But it is interesting to see how readily, and with what deadly force, the local civilians and criminal elements stepped up with equal violence, to crush the strangers.

The pilgrims were first spotted by a townsman out in the nearby fields on an errand. He presumably said a few words to a Frankish straggler that he came across; but once he realised who he was, he quickly went back into Shaizar. There he 'grabbed his sword and went out and killed him'. The alarm was raised and the 'populace rushed out and attacked the Franks, seizing what they could of their women, children, silver and beasts of burden'.

One of the women of Shaizar 'went out with the rest of the populace and took a Frank captive and brought him back to her house'. She eventually took another two prisoners, and the 'three Frankish captives were collected at her house'. Charmingly, 'after taking what suited her from their possessions, she went out and called for a group of her neighbours, who came and killed them'.[12]

Raping captives was commonplace. Slavery and a lifetime of sexual abuse was the normal fate of the more attractive female prisoners. One of the captive pilgrim women was said to have been exceptionally beautiful and was given from one Muslim leader to another, so that she could be raped at their leisure. 'My father spotted among [the prisoners] a lovely young serving-girl,' wrote Usama, 'so he said to the manager of his household, "Bring this one to the baths, repair her clothes and get her ready for a journey" . . . My father then packed her off to the emir Malik ibn Salim, the lord of Qalat Ja'bar, who was a friend of his.'

The gift was well received, and no doubt Usama's father benefited from the goodwill generated by his thoughtful present: 'Malik found the girl very agreeable, and he was pleased with her, and took her for his very own. In time she bore him a son.' Luck and beauty ensured that the Frankish slave-girl eventually assumed great power: when her 'husband' had died, her son inherited the lordship of Qalat Ja'bar and she enjoyed the many privileges of being his mother. At this point, however, extraordinarily, and for reasons that Usama could not begin to fathom, the Frankish woman managed to escape.

It emerged that she 'hatched a plot with a group of people and let herself down from the castle by a rope. The group of people took her to Saruj [a town which had been back in Christian control since 1101]. So she married a Frankish shoemaker,' wrote Usama, 'while her son was the lord of Qalat Ja'bar!' Presumably she had pretended to convert to Islam early on in this story, but had done so merely to survive and bide her time. She waited for her master to die, and her son had already come of age when she escaped. So the determined Frankish woman had clearly been playing a very long game.

These stories were always recorded by Usama to make a point. Bizarrely, the moral that he was trying to make with this uplifting anecdote was that Frankish women were foolish and racist. Usama was shocked that a woman who had been raped and held captive, who had been traded as a sex slave and seen her family butchered, did not actually engage enthusiastically with the process. Her actions in refusing to be a passive victim were even interpreted by him as 'racism'. As the bemused Usama said critically of her astonishing (to him at least) life choices, 'the Franks . . . are an accursed race that will not become accustomed to anyone not of their own race'.[13]

There was an inextricable link between theft, murder and (occasionally) targeting people from other religious groups. This led to some disinhibition, but was by no means enough to save co-religionists if the circumstances were attractive enough. Being of a different religion in this case merely helped legitimise the process of mugging, rape and murder.

Networks of religious affiliation were far more flexible, and more likely to be driven by criminal opportunity, than we might imagine. In an anecdote set at some point in the 1140s, for example, we encounter the salutary example of a Muslim man in Nablus who wanted to enter the service of Mu'in al-Din Unur, the atabeg of Damascus (r. 1140–1149) – though in practice, as we shall see, there was little real service on offer.

The backstory to this request was complex and calculated to appeal to a patriotic Damascene audience increasingly involved in jihad against the crusaders. The petitioner claimed that 'his mother had been married to a Frank, whom she had killed. Her son used to attempt various ruses on their pilgrims, and he and his mother used to work together to kill them. They [the Frankish authorities] finally [caught him and] brought charges against him.'

The Muslim bandit was captured by the Frankish authorities and subjected to trial by ordeal. He was bound and thrown into a barrel of water. If he was innocent, so the medieval logic ran, he would sink. If he was guilty, on the other hand, he would rise to the surface. Not surprisingly, the mugger tried to make himself sink – or at least to give the impression of a sinking man. But even that was, for obvious reasons, not an entirely positive alternative.

In the event he could not do so. He was found guilty of his crimes, and blinded. Under the circumstances, as he had been convicted of murder and robbing pilgrims, he seems to have got off relatively lightly. Perhaps he had been young at the time, and his mother was regarded as the main perpetrator.[14]

He eventually made his way to Damascus, where, ever the optimistic chancer, he tried to enlist in the Syrian military. This request was naturally refused (being able to see was, after all, an obvious prerequisite for becoming a mounted archer); but he was given, according to Usama, a pension anyway, perhaps for his sheer gall.

What is missing from the story, however, is much of its unspoken but obvious cultural underpinning. Presumably one of the 'ruses' that he and his mother had used in robbing and killing their victims was to pretend to be Christian and Frankish themselves, as they were both so fluent in the language and culture. The mother had almost certainly been a local Arab Christian, or had converted to Christianity when she married (that was how such things normally worked). She then appears to have converted (or reconverted) to Islam at some point. So the half-Frankish criminal – and erstwhile 'Muslim', if indeed that was the case – had presumably also been a Christian, born into a Christian family.

In fact, although he claimed to be a Muslim, there must have been a strong possibility that he was, and always had been, a Frankish outlaw. He had been hugely cheeky in approaching Mu'in for a handout. The risk was enormous – but he had little to lose at that point. Having been blinded and shunned by his own people, he had run out of options. And at least he got a pension as a reward for his audacity.[15]

Like the Franks, Muslim communities were desperate to reduce the level of crime. Lawlessness was hugely debilitating for all aspects of civic life, but particularly trade. The poor policing of the roads, the prevalence of bandits and highwaymen, and the strongarm tactics of under-employed foreign mercenaries were so commonplace that they almost became a trope. When Il-Ghazi, himself a deeply unstable and violent foreign soldier, took control of the town of Mayyafariqin, the chronicler Ibn al-Azraq gushed over his hard and effective approach to law enforcement:

He entered the city on [2 October 1118], and took possession of it . . . the people were in great distress because of the billeting [of Turkic soldiers] in their homes. Most of the city was ruined . . . The soldiers who had no homes began living in [the city] and setting up tents in the ruins of the city because most of the city was ruined and the roads were terrorised by robbers and highwaymen, to such an extent that [caravans] could only travel if escorted by an officer and cavalry . . . From the moment [Il-Ghazi] assumed power, the roads and the countryside became safe. The robbers fled and the villages flourished.[16]

This may well have been true, but it cannot be taken at face value. The prevalence of crime meant that this praise contained many stock phrases: this is what the people wanted all their leaders to be like. It was also disingenuous in the extreme, probably because Ibn al-Azraq was working for Il-Ghazi's son when he wrote his chronicle. He stepped lightly over the fact that Il-Ghazi had himself brought many of these rogue soldiers and bandits into the region. To a large extent he was just being praised for trying to keep his own men in order – but even that was better than nothing.

The little castle on the prairie?

However hard the encouraging pilgrim texts might try to promote the idea of a 'land of milk and honey', the truth was far different. Irrespective of religion or cultural background, the threat of violence and criminality was all-pervasive and debased every aspect of life.

A small selection of surviving anecdotes, this time taken from the recollections of a Muslim community which later fled to Damascus, demonstrates just how deeply fear of criminality was ingrained in the peasant experience.

The first example involves a small group of Muslim peasants and a merchant. They wanted to make the relatively short journey from their village near Nablus down to the coast, so that they could sell their goods (mainly silks and silver bowls) in the Frankish coastal town of Ascalon – a large military base that had been captured from the Egyptian government by the crusaders in 1153. The merchant had with him a servant and two beasts, both heavily loaded.[17]

Some local men had been recruited to act as guides and to provide extra security; but in a telling indicator of the lawlessness of the times, the group was intercepted by robbers before it had even set off. 'Two men, [by which] I mean Franks,' wrote one of the guides, 'came for firewood. They did not fail to notice the two men and the beasts . . . When I saw them again, they were with the Franks, tied up, and the beasts with the cargo had been taken.'

Interestingly, the Franks in question do not even seem to have been professional thieves: they were there to fetch firewood, rather than find victims for a mugging. But – and this is the important distinction – they were armed, as so many people were. And once an opportunity presented itself, they were prepared to abduct strangers and steal all their possessions without a second thought.[18]

Security was always an issue, even in peacetime and even in an overwhelmingly Muslim area, such as Nablus. The episode was noted in a matter-of-fact way, as if the reader would take it for granted that this was the way the world worked: it was obvious that a wise merchant needed guards and would only travel with great caution.

In another twelfth-century rural anecdote, we find a group of eleven Muslim peasants from the Palestinian village of Saffarin, to the north-west of Nablus, out harvesting. While they were working the fields, a group of 'infidels' (that is, Franks) came by. The peasants were petrified and feared for their lives. They later reported, however, that 'we stayed where we were, and they passed near us and did not disturb us, as if they hadn't seen us'.

Again, what is assumed and unspoken is more powerful than what is said. When strangers were around, violence and robbery were so much the norm, and so obviously to be expected, that it was worthy of comment when things went off peacefully – this was an incident to record in the village annals. There can be few more shocking indictments of the levels of fear and criminality in the countryside of the Holy Land at that time.[19]

Another story, about a similar event, was told by a Muslim headman, also in the area of Nablus. 'I went to [the small Frankish town of Magna

Mahomeria],' he wrote, 'with my son and a friend of ours. We came across a group of Franks, I mean those who had arrived from across the sea.' The mere presence of foreign pilgrims was frightening, and the Muslim group rushed to get out of their way. 'We were afraid of them and sat by the road,' said the headman, 'and they passed without addressing a word to us.' The peasant leader felt that he and his party had got off very lightly from the encounter, because he believed that 'infidels who came [from] across the sea ... whenever they meet a Muslim, they cause him harm.' Once again, the absence of casual violence and robbery was so remarkable that the anecdote found its way into the collective memory of the villagers.[20]

This was not just the Muslim experience. A pilgrim named Theoderic had an uncannily similar story to tell, but this time from a Christian perspective. While he was in the Holy Land (in the years 1169–1174), Theoderic wrote that 'when we were going along this road [ironically also near Nablus] we saw a crowd of Saracens, who were all beginning to plough with their oxen and asses a very well-kept field. And they uttered a horrid cry, which is not unusual for them when they start any work, but they filled us with great terror.' Once again, we find commentators naturally assuming that walking down a road was inevitably going to be fraught with danger, and the occasion of 'great terror'.[21]

As soon as you left your home, as soon as you were out of sight of your friends and family, the expectation was that you were in trouble. And as these examples show, this depressing view of the world in general, and of human nature in particular, was not entirely unrealistic.

Crime was everywhere. And in the absence of a police force, reliance on community and extreme caution were the only ways to protect yourself and your family. They do not often take a central role in the history books, but rural life in the Middle East was dominated by shadowy, all-pervasive figures – bandits.

20

Bedouin Bandits

Banditry was widespread in medieval Palestine. The Franks, the local settled Arabs and steppe nomads were always active players. But they were just enthusiastic amateurs compared to the Bedouin.

Long-term instability and criminality in the region pre-dated the crusades by many years. Much of this had been driven by the large-scale infiltration of restless nomadic tribesmen. From the south, these tribesmen tended to be Bedouin, coming up from the desert. And from the north they tended to be Turkic horsemen, coming down from the Eurasian steppes. These tribesmen had very little in common with each other, and in fact were often in bloody conflict.

They did have three things that they could see eye to eye on, however. First, they had their own idiosyncratic views about law and property ownership – and, perhaps not surprisingly, these rarely coincided with the ideas held by the local farmers and other sedentary communities.

Secondly, they were opportunists. If they could take something without unduly negative consequences, they probably would. And that included stealing people (as slaves), as well as cattle or other possessions. If central control was loose, as it often was in the era of the crusades, they would exploit that weakness to the full.

And finally, they were both – Bedouin just as much as Turks – tough, hardened men. Given the chance, they could strip a settlement bare in minutes, and there was very little that a small community of farmers, peasant women and children could do to stop them.[1]

The destructive and disruptive power of these nomads meant that there were, in effect, strong anthropological and cultural frontiers (as well as the more obvious religious and military borders) within the crusader states.

In areas where nomadic incursions were common, settlement was sparse and population levels were accordingly low. With sedentary societies very much on the defensive in these areas, it was understandably difficult to persuade settlers of any religion to put down roots. Land was a scarce commodity in Palestine, and people were desperate to find somewhere to live: but no matter how desperate they were, few people were prepared to live under constant fear of attack. Not surprisingly, areas that were particularly vulnerable to the nomads remained resolutely under-populated.[2]

The local Muslim sedentary population might be settled and usually accommodating, but that level of trust and cooperation was never possible with nomads. When faced with overwhelming force, nomads would normally behave. But once that force was removed, they would return to their predatory ways: all nomads, given the right conditions, were a potential danger to sedentary societies.[3]

But the most consistent, and best adapted, nomads in the region posed the most serious threat – the Bedouin.

Phrases such as 'Bedouin bandit' or 'pirate captain' were almost tautologies in the medieval Middle East.

Muslim rulers found Bedouins every bit as difficult to control as their Christian counterparts did. Saladin, for instance, who was himself of nomadic heritage, was happy to use semi-nomadic Turkic and Kurdish tribesmen in his armies; but even he deeply despised the Bedouin – and not without some cause. He devoted a lot of time and energy to weakening and controlling them wherever he could.[4]

Even western medieval observers, who were often ill-informed and ignorant in the way they viewed other cultures, were able to make clear distinctions in this regard: they knew that sedentary Arabs (regardless of religion) were a very different proposition to their nomadic counterparts. Burchard of Mount Zion, for instance, a Dominican monk writing in the thirteenth century, was clear that the local Muslim townsfolk and villagers could be polite and kind to strangers – they were people you could do business with. He described the nomads, on the other hand, as being 'exceedingly warlike' and dangerous – visitors from Europe, never famed for their cultural sensitivities, quickly found out whom to avoid.[5]

Burchard was being realistic, rather than overly cynical or prejudiced. The Bedouin (and many other nomads) lived in a different moral universe. That is not to say it was a world without morals: on the contrary, it had its own strict codes of behaviour. But they were very different.

John of Joinville similarly grew to understand the distinctions between the different enemy groups, and the impact this had on their behaviour. Once, when he and his Mamluk captors left their camp, he noted that

> the Bedouins rushed into it in great numbers. They left not one thing in that camp, carrying off everything that the Saracens had left behind. I never heard it said that the Bedouins, who were subject to the Saracens, were thought less of because they would take or steal things; taking advantage of the weak was their custom and their way of life.[6]

They were so different from the other Arab groups that John was unclear about their religious allegiances. 'The Bedouins do not believe in Muhammad,' he wrote in some confusion. 'Instead they follow the law of Ali, who was Muhammad's uncle.' In fact, most of the Bedouin were nominally Muslims, although, as they pre-dated the Islamic invasions, some were still Christians. But theology was not the key determinant of their behaviour.[7]

OUTLAWS

Usama and the Bedouin

A remarkable first-hand account has survived of what it was like to be
on the receiving end of an extended attempt at armed robbery by these
ancient Arab tribes. Usama Ibn-Munqidh, the wandering Syrian prince,
had bad luck in his dealings with the Bedouin. This was a hardship for
him, but a great bonus for us.

In many ways his bad luck was inevitable. He travelled a lot and, as
we have seen, any travel in the Holy Land was dangerous. On several
occasions he acted as an envoy operating between the governments of
Syria and Egypt. As the route along the coast and then up overland
through Palestine was blocked by the crusaders, communications
between Cairo and Damascus had to take place by a perilous overland
passage across the Sinai Desert, skirting Frankish patrols wherever
possible and moving quickly to avoid the even more dangerous attentions of the local Bedouin tribes.

No one undertook this trip lightly. Usama made the journey twice,
both times in heavily armed parties. Even so, on both occasions it
almost ended in disaster.

His first trip was a journey from Egypt to Damascus in 1150. Usama
and his companions were on a mission to lobby Nur al-Din, who
controlled most of Syria, to come to the aid of the Fatimid regime in
Cairo. Ascalon, the last remaining Egyptian military base in Palestine,
was under increasing pressure. Usama's goal was to persuade Nur al-Din
to attack the Franks, and thereby take some of the pressure off the
Egyptians. To make the task even easier, the main field army of the
Latin Kingdom was tied up elsewhere. In the event, Usama's mission
failed. Nur al-Din, shrewd and calculating as ever, saw no need to help
his Fatimid rivals. The most he felt inclined to do was to give Usama
permission to hire recruits from among the dregs of the mercenaries
that he had discarded.[8]

But successful or not, the journey itself had been extremely eventful.
There was a continual struggle to avoid local Bedouin and other bandits,

even though his was a military mission, with a large and heavily armed escort. Usama and his companions also knew that even their own people could not be trusted. They went to great lengths to ensure that their guides and guards did not know that they carried money with them for their mission.[9]

To fool their servants, Usama wrote slyly:

I put four thousand dinars in a saddle-bag on a saddle-mule being led alongside me and handed him over to an attendant. I also put two thousand dinars, along with my own petty cash, a bridle and some Maghribi dinars in another saddle-bag on a horse being led alongside me, and I handed it off to another attendant. Whenever we stopped to camp, I would put the saddle-bags in the middle of the carpet, fold up its edges on top of them, spread another carpet over it and sleep on top of the saddlebags, rising before my companions when it was time to go.[10]

Usama clearly thought he was being terribly clever and security conscious, boasting of his precautions at length. But it was all incredibly obvious. More telling was the pervasive lack of trust: the only thing you could be sure of was that you could depend on no one.

His second trip was undertaken under far more dramatic circumstances, and very nearly ended in his death. Extraordinarily, as well as having a first-hand account of the unceasing banditry that dogged the high-value caravan of Usama and his party, we also have a crusader account of what happened to the party in the latter stages of its doomed journey.

Travel between Egypt and Syria was difficult. Templar patrols in particular were always a concern. The dangers were far worse than just that, however. Setting off from Cairo on 30 May 1154 with a heavily armed group of soldiers and attendants, Usama and his party were systematically harried and attacked by Arab tribesmen along the whole route.[11]

Usama had made the mistake of backing the wrong side in the complex world of Egyptian palace politics. He had been party to (and was probably the co-instigator of) a palace coup in Cairo in 1153: once the dust had settled on the putsch, Usama's friend and employer al-Abbas was vizier of the Fatimid empire.

Things quickly unravelled, however. In the face of increasing opposition from rebel forces and dissension among his own troops, al-Abbas, his son Nasir al-Din and their confederate Usama decided to make a run for the border. Pausing only to strip the treasury of its best moveable assets, they filled their saddle bags and, with a large body of mercenaries to protect them, made a mad dash across the desert. They were desperate to get to Syria, where, they hoped, they would be able to buy their way into Nur al-Din's affections.

The Bedouin were their first concern, constantly circling, picking off stragglers and eventually closing in for the kill. Usama was himself attacked and barely escaped with his life. 'Suddenly,' he later wrote,

> the Arabs attacked me, and there I was: I couldn't find any way to repulse them, my horse couldn't help me escape, and their arrows started falling on me. I thought to myself, 'Jump off the horse, draw your sword, and have at them'. But as I gathered myself to jump, my horse stumbled and I fell onto some stones and a patch of rough ground. A piece of skin from my head was ripped off and I became so dizzy that I didn't know where I was. A group of Arabs gathered around me, while I just sat there, bare-headed, clueless, my sword lying in its scabbard.[12]

Usama was seriously concussed. 'One of [the Bedouin] struck me twice with his sword, saying "Hand over the money!" but I didn't know what he was saying. So they took my horse and my sword.' Usama was only saved when one of the Turkic bodyguards came back to get him, and the Bedouin moved off. He survived that incident, but problems with bandits continued throughout the journey.[13]

From 7 to 19 June 1154, Usama and the Fatimid group continued their march, and eventually entered crusader territory. There they were intercepted by Frankish troops, doubtless aided by the Bedouin auxiliaries with whom they had built up a good working relationship.

William of Tyre later wrote that

the Christians, apprised of [al-Abbas's] approach, had laid an ambush for him . . . and there they were stealthily lying in wait. The vizier, all unsuspecting, fell into the trap. At the first encounter he was fatally wounded by a sword thrust and at once perished . . . the immense riches which they had carried away with them out of Egypt, fell into the hands of the Christians and the booty was divided among them according to the custom. Consequently, our people returned home laden with the richest spoils, indeed fairly bending under the burden of treasures hitherto unknown to our land.[14]

Usama very wisely did not wait around to ask who they were, but we know from other sources that most of the Frankish troops he encountered were elite Templar cavalry, who operated increasingly aggressive patrols in the area from their base in Gaza.[15]

Usama's co-conspirator, the son of the vizier, was captured in the debacle. 'In the distribution of the spoils,' wrote William, 'beside other things there fell to them by a lot [Nasir al-Din], the son of Abbas.' The Templars

held this man a prisoner for a long time. He professed an ardent desire to be reborn in Christ and had already learned the Roman letters and been instructed in the rudiments of the Christian faith when he was sold by the Templars for 60,000 pieces of gold to the Egyptians, who demanded him for the death penalty. Heavily chained hand and foot, he was placed in an iron cage upon the back of a camel and carried to Egypt, where . . . the people literally tore him to pieces bit by bit with their teeth.[16]

The Templars came in for some criticism for their decision to take the ransom money, particularly given Nasir's strangely convenient conversion to Christianity. But they were undoubtedly correct in doing so. They had suffered grievous casualties in the siege of Ascalon just a few months earlier. Templar knights had made a brave but reckless assault into the centre of the town, before being cut off and wiped out: they were in no mood to be too sentimental about the fate of Fatimid commanders. More importantly, and as his own people knew, the murderous Nasir was completely untrustworthy: his conversion was far less genuine, and infinitely less tangible, than the ransom money they received.[17]

Even though Usama and some of the others managed to escape, however, Bedouin bandits proved to be every bit as dangerous and, if anything, even more tenacious than the Franks and their allies. 'We continued on through Frankish territory,' he later wrote, 'until we reached the mountains of the Banu Fuhayd (may God curse them) in Wadi Musa. We climbed through narrow and treacherous paths that led to a wide, desolate plain, full of men.' The party may have escaped from the Christians, but the Muslim 'Banu Fuhayd killed anyone who got separated from the main party straight away'.[18]

Members of yet another Arab tribe arrived and Usama was able to pay the two groups to attack each other: on receipt of one thousand dinars, the new arrivals drove off the other bandits. 'We continued on, those of us who survived the Franks and the Banu Fuhayd [and all the previous Arab tribesmen that they had encountered], reaching the city of Damascus on [19 June 1154].' The journey was a nightmare. They had been hunted down mercilessly, robbed and some killed. They even appear to have been attacked along the way by some of their own men, as the mercenaries they had employed to guard the caravan turned on them when they found out how much money was being transported.[19]

Religion was not a factor; vulnerability was everything.

Saladin and the Bedouin

Saladin also had a deeply ambivalent attitude to the Bedouin. He disliked and distrusted them, but (as mentioned above) on occasion he was also able to use them to his advantage.

In a time of perennial warfare and non-professional armies, it is perhaps not surprising to find that the boundaries between civil criminality and criminality on the battlefield were extremely permeable. Many soldiers were poorly paid. Even the upmarket knights were often forced into penury when the logistics of crusading went spectacularly wrong (as they so often did). Some men, particularly on the Muslim side, but also occasionally among the Christians, were not paid at all – they accompanied armies on the understanding that they would have access to potential booty. These were men living in poverty and trading in violence, neither of which was calculated to bring out the best in people.

At the bottom end of the spectrum were those, usually Bedouin, who specialised in the theft of children, exploiting the financial possibilities offered by the very active slave markets of the Muslim world. At the 1191 siege of Acre, for instance, with armies and their accompanying civilians in close proximity, these men came into their own. One of Saladin's biographers was present when the kidnapping of a newborn baby was brought, very forcibly, to the sultan's attention. 'One day I was on horseback in attendance on [Saladin], face-to-face with the Franks,' wrote the Ayyubid lawyer and propagandist, Baha al-Din, 'when one of the forward pickets arrived with a woman in great distress, bitterly weeping and continually beating her breast.' The biographer remembered the incident well, as it unfolded while Saladin 'was riding on Tell al-Kharruba with me and a great crowd attending upon him'.[20]

The mother, a Frankish woman, had been extraordinarily brave. It was partly her desperate dedication to her child that made the story so memorable to those who were there that day. 'When the mother missed the child,' wrote Baha al-Din, she spent the whole duration of the night pleading for help with loud lamentations. Her case came to the notice of [the crusader] princes, who said to her, '[Saladin] has a merciful heart. We give you permission to go to him' . . . So she went out to ask the Muslim advance guard for assistance, telling them of her troubles through a dragoman who translated for her.

This exceptional woman was presumably a camp follower or the wife of an ordinary soldier, as she does not appear in any of the Frankish accounts. But she made a persuasive case to both her own leaders and the Muslim pickets upon whose mercy she threw herself:

She said, 'Muslim thieves entered my tent yesterday and stole my daughter. I spent all night until this morning pleading for help. I was told, "Their prince is a merciful man. We shall send you out to him to ask him for your daughter." So they sent me to you, and only from you will I learn of my daughter.' The sultan took pity on her. His tears flowed and, prompted by his chivalry, he ordered someone to go to the army market to ask who had bought the little girl, to repay what had been given for her and bring her back.

In a display designed to showcase the sultan's power and the orderly state he presided over, Baha al-Din wrote that

hardly an hour had passed before the horseman arrived with the little girl over his shoulder. The moment the woman's eye lighted on her, she fell to the ground, besmirching her face with earth, while all around wept for what she had suffered. She was lifting her eyes to heaven, although we did not know what she was saying.[21]

The baby had already been sold into slavery: 'People went and found that it had been sold in the market.' With an eye to the theatricality of the moment, Saladin ordered the purchase price to be paid to the purchaser and the child taken from him. He himself stayed where he had halted until the infant was produced and then handed over to the woman who took it, wept mightily, and hugged it to her breast, while people watched her and wept also. I was standing there amongst the gathering [wrote Baha al-Din]. She suckled the child for a while and then, on the orders of the sultan, she was taken on horseback and restored to their camp with the infant.[22]

The incident made a powerful impact upon Baha al-Din – so much so that he told the same story twice, in two slightly different versions in different chapters of his biography of Saladin. It had everything: human interest; an excitable, desperate, foreign woman; and a wise, noble ruler to adjudicate with generosity and provide the sorry story with a happy ending.

But, as so often with cases of Saladin's carefully honed (and extremely successful) PR campaign to polish his reputation for chivalry, all was not as it seemed. Baha al-Din was so pleased with the story that he let slip certain details which show the narrative in a very different light.

Elsewhere in his biography, Baha al-Din explained that

the Muslims had thieves who would enter the enemy's tents, steal from them, even taking individuals, and then make their way back. It came about that one night they took an unweaned infant three months old. They brought it to [Saladin's] tent and offered it to him. Everything they took they used to offer to him and he would reward and recompense them.[23]

So it is clear that Saladin had explicitly organised the capture of people by thieves, and that these kidnappers were in his pay. And, by his own biographer's admission, the sultan had seen the baby earlier in the day and had personally authorised her sale in the slave markets. Having organised the kidnapping and sale of a baby into slavery, the sultan could now produce floods of tears while he 'wept mightily' and basked in a cosy (and very public) glow of magnanimity.[24]

Even veteran soldiers were vulnerable to these professional kidnappers. At the end of June 1191, as the siege of Acre ground on to its conclusion, bands of Muslim thieves launched a series of trench raids on the crusaders' lines,

> entering the camp and snatching goods and individuals. They seized men with ease by coming to them as they were sleeping, putting a knife to their throat, then waking them and saying through gestures, 'If you speak, we shall cut your throat.' Then they would carry them away to the Muslim camp. That happened many times.[25]

In the murky world of medieval soldiering, employing thieves as auxiliaries was extremely helpful. Kidnapping and the search for booty were useful for a commander with stretched resources: theft was a way of debilitating the enemy army, part of a broader war of attrition when more obvious means of attack were unavailable.

An uneasy relationship

Commercial activity in areas where Bedouin operated was extremely dangerous, and would only be attempted with numerous armed guards present – often so many that they were, in effect, small armies. There were no friends, no genuine 'co-religionists' – merely opportunities and victims. The story of a major – and heavily guarded – caravan leaving Damascus is a good example of this.

In 1112, King Baldwin I of Jerusalem was at Acre when the Bedouin came to tell him about a potential opportunity: together they could attack the Damascene caravan and steal its entire contents. The idea was compelling, as the king and his state were permanently teetering on the edge of bankruptcy.[26]

But in the relatively short space of time it took Baldwin and his Muslim helpers to get there, the convoy had already been robbed twice by other Bedouin. First, 'a part of the Banu Hawbar had seized part of the caravan'. Secondly, once that ordeal was behind them, the remainder escaped and 'reached the settlement of the Banu Rabi'a who detained them for some days but afterwards let them proceed' – presumably in exchange for a hefty ransom.[27]

This respite merely delayed the fate of the caravan, however. When it moved out along the pass of 'Azib, 'the Franks appeared above [it]. All who were with the caravan fled, and those who climbed the hill escaped with their lives, but lost their property.'[28]

This was clearly a joint effort between the Bedouin and the Franks. We are told that the Bedouin with King Baldwin 'captured most of the men, and the Franks seized all the goods and merchandise in the caravan, while the Arabs pursued those who fled and took them prisoner. Baldwin obtained more than 50,000 dinars and 300 captives from it, and returned to [Acre]'.[29]

The caravan was a massive enterprise, an encumbered army on the move, rather than a small band of vulnerable merchants. 'There was not a town [in Syria],' wrote the Damascene chronicler Qalanisi, 'but had some merchants among the victims in this caravan.' The Bedouin had wanted to enter into a partnership with the Franks precisely because the convoy was so heavily protected – they needed the muscle of heavily armoured Frankish knights to guarantee that they could overwhelm it with minimal casualties.[30]

Frankish accounts of the raid confirm the basic details and emphasise its importance to the impoverished Kingdom of Jerusalem. The main field army was very heavily engaged in the attack – in fact, it seems as though most of the kingdom's knights were involved. Albert of Aachen, presumably having been debriefed by participants, wrote that King Baldwin took 'two hundred cavalry and one hundred infantry and set out for . . . the region of the kingdom of Arabia, to seize quantities of plunder'. Given that there were only two or three hundred knights in the entire kingdom at the time, this was clearly a major commitment.[31]

The Bedouin were just as happy working for a Muslim government, of course – it all depended on the price and the circumstances. In 1249, for example, during the siege of Damietta, a letter written by King Louis's chamberlain, John Sarrasin, mentions that Bedouin bandits

> come about the army at night to steal horses, and people's heads. The sultan of [Egypt] is said to give ten besants for every head of a Christian that is brought to him, and so these Bedouin Saracens cut the heads off hanged men and dig up buried bodies to get their heads and take them to the sultan, so it is said. One Bedouin Saracen who came every night was captured, and is still being held.[32]

For large Bedouin groups, even the distinction between banditry and full-blown warfare was never clear-cut. In 1256, for instance, in the aftermath of Muslim raiding around Jaffa, the local Bedouin tried to extort plunder from the victorious Mamluk army: they presumably felt that the raiding had taken place on their territory, and that they were entitled to some of the upside.

As one Christian chronicler wrote:

> The Bedouins up in the mountains heard that the Saracens had won rich plunder from the Christians. They said they would like a share of it, and came down from the hills into the Saracen host where the plunder was kept. They told the emir whom the sultan had put in command of the army that they wanted a share of their plunder. He said that they certainly could not have any, as they had not helped to win it.[33]

This was not the answer the Bedouin were looking for. Unimpressed by the Mamluk response, fighting broke out. The Bedouin 'attacked, fought and went off with at least two parts of the livestock . . . Three thousand or more Bedouins and Saracens were killed in this conflict.' The only winners in this bloody free-for-all were the Franks.[34]

To emphasise the equal-handed nature of Bedouin banditry, it is perhaps worth mentioning another couple of anecdotes, both from the same region, and both from approximately the same period, if only to underline the depressing predictability of nomadic violence.

The Fatimid coastal fortress of Ascalon had been captured by the Franks in 1153, after a long and bloody siege. But the aftermath of the siege was ostensibly clear-cut and relatively painless. As part of the surrender negotiations, the Muslim townspeople had been guaranteed unhindered passage out of the city and an armed escort to take them back to Egyptian territory – and the Christian victors were committed to playing their part in ensuring their safety.

The Muslim troops in the town's garrison, however, included many Turkic steppe mercenaries. Inevitably, they saw Fatimid weakness as an opportunity. Once the bedraggled column had made its way over the border, they turned on their erstwhile employers and robbed them mercilessly.[35]

For the refugees from Ascalon, this was just the beginning of their troubles. The penniless survivors were left to the tender attentions of other nomadic tribesmen, this time the local Bedouin. The defenceless refugees were robbed, killed or sold into slavery – a sad ending to their long and tenacious defence against the Franks. The civilians had met such a dreadful fate that even their Christian enemies were disgusted at the way they had been treated.

Sadly, this was disappointing, rather than surprising. The ravages of the Bedouin were exactly what the refugees expected, and had been hoping to avoid by employing Turkic mercenaries. The relationship of nomads with the local sedentary communities was fundamentally an antagonistic and predatory one.

A few years earlier, even one of the senior commanders of the military base at Ascalon barely escaped with his life in an altercation with the Bedouin. The officer – a man named Ibn al-Jullanar – had ridden out with his hunting birds to look for sport. When he got to a grove of trees beyond sight of the town, he was confronted by two Bedouin who ordered him to dismount.

The Bedouin bent down to take the spurs off his feet and, as they did so, he 'grabbed one by the neck and the other by the neck, and beat their two heads together. They were locked in his grip, so he killed them. Then Ibn al-Jullanar took their horses, their weapons and his sparrow-hawk and entered the city!' The story of the failed robbery and the double killing is told as a cheery anecdote, but it conveys a deeper and far more menacing truth. Outside of town, just beyond your community, almost anything could happen, even to armed soldiers.[36]

With every stranger, every new face, you knew you were just a step away from death.

21

The Ghost-Lordships

The phrase 'crime lord' is a curious one.

It was an invention of the early-twentieth-century tabloids, designed to add some spurious kudos and interest to the actions of the leader of a criminal organisation. But the 'organisation' was usually nothing more than a loosely affiliated collection of pimps, bootleggers or drug dealers. In the period of the crusades, however, the term was strangely, and quite literally, appropriate.

The violent and shifting frontier lands of Palestine and Syria offered ample opportunities for semi-freelance activities. Outlaws and bandits were so numerous, and so well organised, that they were often more like small states or regional militia than the isolated pockets of criminality that we assume to be the norm today. Even the supposedly 'no go' areas that one occasionally hears of in large urban areas in modern times are peaceful, compared to the norm in the medieval Middle East. And with crime lords inevitably came 'crime lordships' – their own parallel, ghostly parody of feudal control which dominated large areas of (usually inaccessible) land, and operated beyond the rule of law.[1]

Bandit cave-castles

For the Franks, the scale of the problem this presented went way beyond the normal policing capacity of local viscounts and their handful of sergeants. The field army of the Latin Kingdom of Jerusalem, always stretched in terms of manpower, often had to be diverted from its usual military activities and instead deployed on major anti-bandit operations.

The mountain regions around Sidon, for instance, were famous throughout the crusader period for their lawlessness. In 1128, the royal army, commanded by Patriarch Gormond of Jerusalem, the most senior cleric in the entire Latin East, had to be sent to besiege 'a fortress in the district of Sidon called [Belhacem], which at that time was held by bandits'. The siege took its toll. Gormand 'was stricken with a serious illness' while overseeing operations in the inevitably unhygienic environment of an extended blockade, and died. His men carried on and eventually flushed out the bandits; but as was often the case, the price they paid in doing so was high.[2]

A similar situation unfolded a few years later, in dealing with another bandit-lordship, this time further south, in Palestine. The arrival of a crusading army from Europe was normally an opportunity to undertake a major military project: a chance to use the temporary additional resources to create something of lasting value for the defence of the Holy Land. In 1139, Thierry, count of Flanders, created just such an opportunity: he arrived in Palestine 'with a noble retinue' and a 'splendid force of valiant knights'. This was a chance to achieve something exceptional.

So, what was the chosen target for this force? It was the fortified base of a bandit-lordship – and the extent of the resources that needed to be thrown at the problem shows just how serious the threat was.

The centre of the brigands' power was one of the region's famous cave-castle complexes, in modern-day Jordan. It was described as a

stronghold on the other side of the Jordan, near Mount Gilead . . . This fortress was a great menace to our lands. It was a cavern, on the slope of a very high mountain, the approach to which was practically inaccessible. Above it towered a mighty precipice which reached from the top of the promontory to the depths of the adjacent valley. On one side, a narrow and dangerous path between a high projecting cliff and the precipice . . . led to the same cave.

From this impressive base the bandits had been able to dominate much of the surrounding lands and had regularly organised large-scale raids down into the Transjordan and onto the plains of Judaea beyond.[3]

Thierry and his men, along with the army of Jerusalem and the local Frankish militia, marched off to put the bandit stronghold under siege. Besieging a cave does not sound unduly difficult. But the cave-castles of the Middle East, perhaps better described as 'ledge-fortresses', were a different matter altogether. These strange but formidable structures were sited on sheer and almost vertical cliff-faces – and, because of their daunting position, they posed unique problems for besieging forces. Capturing such a 'castle' was a difficult and delicate operation, completely different from more standard sieges and requiring very specialist techniques.

The reasons why they posed such problems for conventional armed forces also made them strangely attractive for bandits. They were almost as inaccessible as it was possible to be. They were excellent lookout posts, giving criminals a spectacularly good view of any approaching pilgrims or merchants. And they were usually in the middle of fringe, lawless frontier areas where central authority was at its weakest.

The example of the Cave de Sueth (also known as Habis Jaldak), a similar cave-castle on the eastern side of the River Jordan, gives us a sense of what Thierry and the royal army saw before them, and how challenging and eye-catching these structures could be. The cave complex had been cut into a sheer rock face, and consisted of three (or possibly four) different defensive levels. These were linked by wooden steps, ladders and walkways – all of which could, of course, be removed in the event of a siege to make the attackers' task more difficult.

To make matters even worse, there were external hoardings and wooden galleries outside the most important of the cave defences, hanging precariously over the approach ledges. These allowed the defenders to throw rocks and other missiles down onto their helpless enemies below. For a potential besieger, arriving in this deserted location, far below this extraordinary fortress in the air, it is hard to imagine a more intimidating prospect.[4]

The Frankish forces eventually 'took that stronghold and returned home'. We do not know exactly how they captured it, but it was clear that bandits and raiders were so heavily armed, and so numerous, that they could tie up an entire crusader army.[5]

Even more threateningly, bandit 'ghost-lordships' sometimes controlled large territories, rather than just a single fortified base. The danger posed by large-scale confederations of outlaws was made clear when the major castle of Jacob's Ford (Chastellet) was being built on a crossing of the River Jordan in 1178. From the very outset, the historian William of Tyre stressed just how dangerous the local area was – not, as one might expect, because of the presence of the Syrian army, but rather because of the overwhelming numbers of violent bandits and lawless nomads in the region.

These bandit groups 'emerged from the land of Damascus,' wrote William,

> and so beset the highways that none could go to and from the army without peril, neither could travellers pass along any of the ways. These bandits came from a place in the mountains near Acre called . . . Bucael . . . Its inhabitants are insolent men, fierce fighters and men very proud of their great numbers, through which they have made all the surrounding fields and villages tributary to them . . . these people had become hated and abhorred by all around them, both Christians and Saracens, and frequent attempts had been made to exterminate them utterly, but without success.[6]

Intimidating bands of outlaws (*latrunculi*) on the frontiers by the River Jordan did not just raid, but even took over and operated entire localities. These 'bandit-lordships' still had their own sense of hierarchies and priorities. They functioned as a sort of informal criminal franchise operation. This even extended to offering cooperation agreements to other criminal groups: deals were made with other 'brigands and highwaymen' to provide 'a safe refuge among them, in consideration of which they receive a share of the booty and spoils taken by violence'.[7]

It was hard to stay off-grid indefinitely, however, even in the twelfth century. Eventually, the army of the Latin Kingdom of Jerusalem, despite the plethora of other things requiring its attention, had had enough. King Baldwin IV 'finally found himself unable any longer to endure their insufferable arrogance and the thefts and murders perpetrated by them. He suddenly seized the place by force of arms and put to death all whom he could apprehend.'

The main bandit stronghold, Bucael, on the site of modern-day Peqi'in, was destroyed by the royal army. But this just pushed the problem elsewhere: most of the outlaws merely escaped into Muslim territory to the east and quickly resumed their raids from new bases. From these, as William of Tyre wrote, 'they kept up their ancient habits and made frequent, though stealthy, sallies into our territory'. Within a few months they had regrouped and were making new and even more dangerous incursions. The fight against outlaws was a never-ending one.[8]

But running a bandit-lordship was a career choice not just for Muslims: the Christian communities were entirely capable of producing their own upmarket outlaws. Frankish lords, and particularly those on the frontiers, far away from central control, were quick to adapt to their local environment: they, too, could resort to banditry when the opportunity presented itself. Banyas, for example, was a dangerous frontier town on the edge of the Golan Heights which changed hands frequently – a place where the rule of law, on all sides, was regarded as something to be used for guidance, rather than as anything more definitive.

Usama, writing of a dispute in 1140 in which he had been involved, alleged that the lord of Banyas and his men had stolen several flocks of sheep from Damascene territory during a time of truce. The Muslims naturally wanted compensation for their losses. Their case was strong and the flocks were duly returned. When the sheep were counted, however, it was found that many were still missing and the issue came back to court once more to find final resolution.

Usama wanted to get compensation from King Fulk of Jerusalem for the Muslim losses, and was eventually given the sum of 400 dinars. Interestingly, King Fulk ordered six or seven of his knights to act as a jury in this case, in an effort to bring his own unruly subject back within the rule of law. Even Usama was impressed with the performance and objectivity of this jury of peers: he rarely had anything good to say about the Franks, but he forced himself in this instance to describe them as being 'the masters of legal reasoning, judgement, and sentencing'.[9]

The outlaw villages

Bandit territories, whether big or small, might occasionally be useful to the Muslim authorities: outlaws could distract the Frankish troops from more important tasks, or act as skirmishers and auxiliaries on campaign. But one should not be lulled into thinking that they were ever acting in anything other than their own interests.

The poet al-Mu'ayyad al-Baghdadi once told a salutary story, and one which he felt his listeners would be familiar with. 'The Caliph,' he said, 'had granted as a fief to my father a village which he used to frequent. A gang of young toughs lived there who engaged in highway robbery, and my father used to let them do it, and to benefit from a piece of what they took in' – i.e. what the early-twentieth-century tabloids would have called 'a piece of the action'. According to the poet's father, this gang was sixty strong, and it habitually preyed on any of the (primarily Muslim) travellers and merchants who were unlucky enough to cross its path.[10]

One day, a young Turkic servant (*ghulam*) and a serving girl encountered the poet's father. After he found out that the pair had a valuable cargo with them, the father – disappointingly but entirely predictably – 'went off to the gang to tell them about the Turk and what he was carrying with him. They then all went out to intercept him on the road.' The *ghulam* tried to put up a fight when they stopped him, but his bowstring broke and he was forced to run for his life, leaving the girl and his goods behind.[11]

The girl had to think quickly to avoid being immediately gang-raped: 'now boys, don't dishonour me', she said, all too well aware of what was about to happen. Instead, she persuaded them to let her go after the Turk – under guard of course – to tell him to part with a valuable necklace which he had hidden in his boot, as a ransom for her life. When she caught up with him, she slipped the *ghulam* a spare bowstring, and he was able to fight his way back through the bandits and recover the lost cargo.

This tale, recounted in Mosul by al-Mu'ayyad al-Baghdadi in 1169–1170, was told in a very matter-of-fact way. The substance of the tale was anything but ordinary, however – to our eyes at least. And although it is clearly a folk tale rather than a news report, it is fascinating for what it takes for granted. The poet knew that his listeners (or readers) would understand certain behaviours as 'normal'. Rape was entirely to be expected, for instance – a habitual occurrence under such violent circumstances. Similarly, the inability to trust anybody one met on the road was striking: the headman of the village was just as likely to be corrupt as anyone else, and the outlaw bands that might be encountered were so large as to be almost small armies.[12]

The lawless nature of entire villages, particularly in some of the more inaccessible rural regions is clear from many of Usama's anecdotes. At some point in the 1140s, for example, Usama was accompanying his employer, the emir Mu'in al-Din, with a large party of cavalry on the mountain paths north-west of Damascus. While they were on the road, a horseman rode up to bring news that bandits had 'captured a caravan carrying a load of raw cloth up in the pass'. The emir was keen for a bit of excitement and, accompanied by twenty of his cavalry, went after them. By mid-afternoon they were closing in on the bandits. As they approached, an attendant came riding towards them. 'There are men on foot,' the messenger said excitedly, 'bearing bolts of raw cloth on their head, down in the valley!'[13]

Usama's companions had decided not to put on their armour until they were closer to the lightly armed thieves, so that they could travel faster. When they got down into the mountain valley, however, they found that they had seriously underestimated the size of the outlaw group – to their dismay, they saw that 'the bandits were about seventy men, wielding bows and arrows'.[14]

There were men all over the mountain pass. From a distance, Usama and Mu'in had thought that many of them were local peasants chasing the bandits; but in fact they were all bandits – or were at least all co-operating together. After the event, Usama claimed (with the benefit of his habitually self-serving hindsight) that he had encouraged the emir to bring more men with him, and that they should have armed themselves properly for the fight ahead. 'Give us a second to put on our body armour,' he later claimed to have said. 'Then when we find the bandits, we can charge at them with our horses and run them through with our spears, and they won't even be able to tell whether we are many or few.' He was overruled, however, and the cavalry moved off after the bandits, down into the valley.[15]

Usama could generally construct a good tale about his own bravery; but when they caught up with the bandits, it was clear – even by his own account – that he was not much help. He later wrote that he had chased the bandits up a slope, but was then let down by his horse – he blamed the animal because it 'climbed up that rough slope but nearly breathed its last breath'. When a bandit turned and nocked an arrow on his bow, Usama fled, 'hardly believing that I had escaped from them'.[16]

Usama, irritating and duplicitous as ever, complained that the fiasco was the fault of his employer. 'If we had only had the army with us,' he later claimed to have told the emir, 'we should have struck off all the heads of those bandits and recovered everything that they had with them.' But regardless of hindsight, it remained undeniable that even the ruler of Damascus and his elite bodyguard could not bring roadside bandits to justice. Indeed, they had put themselves in great danger by trying to do so.

A very similar thing happened to Usama just a few years later (in c.1154), when he was trying to find work with Nur al-Din, the ruler of Syria – coping with the depredations of bandits was a familiar problem for anyone who needed to travel.

Usama was riding to Baalbek, where he hoped to see the famous ruins of the Hellenistic temple of Baal. When he got there, a horseman arrived from his companion, the emir Khusraw ibn Talil, with an urgent message. 'Some bandits on foot have attacked a caravan and captured it,' the emir had written hurriedly. 'Saddle up and meet me in the mountains.' The bandits, it appeared, 'had come from the territory of the Franks'.[17]

Usama quickly rode off towards the fighting, arriving just in time to see the outlaws disappearing into their mountain fastnesses. Once again, he was not keen to chase after them, and tried to persuade his companions to ride round the mountain to 'surround them' instead. He was overruled, however, and the horsemen charged down into the valley in an attempt to confront the outlaws.

The bandits climbed up the mountains, and Usama and the other horsemen tried to follow. As with the previous incident, Usama managed to avoid any fighting. He said that he could not get his horse to go up the slope ('I tried my hardest to climb up but I could not do it'). Instead, in a manner which must have provided little comfort to his brave comrades, he stood at the bottom of the valley watching the fighting.

The outlaws, he wrote, were chased by

six or seven of our horsemen on the mountain. They went on foot, leading their horses with them, towards the bandits, who formed a large group. The bandits attacked our comrades and killed two of our horsemen. They took their two horses as well as another horse, whose owner survived safely. The bandits then climbed down the opposite side of the mountain with their plunder.

The entire episode had been a fiasco. Far from seeing off the bandits, the emir's cavalry eventually 'went back, [leaving behind] two of our horsemen dead, and three horses and a caravan captured'.[18]

The outlaws in both these instances may perhaps have been Maronite tribesmen, and hence Christian: many of them were foot archers (a Maronite speciality), and the robberies took place in the mountain valleys next to 'the territory of the Franks'. But it is significant that the religion of the culprits, presumed or otherwise, is not even mentioned – the clear implication being that theology had nothing to do with their actions. Banditry and opportunity, rather than religion or community, guided their choice of victims.

It is also the case that many of these bandit attacks were clearly the consequence of 'organised' crime, with raids presumably being carried out by large numbers of people under the implicit protection of the local authorities. Criminality took place with the complicity of the villagers and their headmen – everyone was taking his cut. Banditry was a fact of life, rather than a manifestation of jihad or crusade.

Ultimately, Muslim or Frank, these bandits were not taking from the rich and giving to the poor. Neither were they 'freedom fighters', though it might occasionally have suited them to pose as such. They were just groups of predatory men, prepared to rape, enslave, extort and murder strangers of any and all religions, whenever it suited their purpose.

Part VI
PIRATES

22

Outlaws of the Sea

The fundamental demographic driver of the crusades was the need to find a seemingly limitless number of young men for the armies of each protagonist.

But it was not just for armies, of course. In addition to men-at-arms there were periodic influxes of sailors and marines (the two terms being fairly interchangeable, depending on need). By the mid-thirteenth century there were huge numbers of men manning the galleys and other ships of the Levant. But even 'peacetime' fleets could be large, and no doubt the crews had little to learn from the crusader armies in terms of poor behaviour and rowdiness. Just as the demands of war on land pulled in adventurous spirits from thousands of miles around to act as soldiers, so too did the maritime requirements of a Mediterranean war zone.

Vast numbers of ships, sailors and naval entrepreneurs were sucked into the region. Crusader pirates did not feature heavily in the chronicles of the time, but the evidence shows that they were always there in the background, often operating in large numbers.

Sometimes, as we shall see, they even changed the course of history.

Piracy and the crusades

Pirate.

It is a rich word, full of inference and meaning. For the western world, the image of piracy has been embedded in the so-called 'golden age' of piracy, the late seventeenth and early eighteenth centuries – an image focused on men who were supposedly romantic, exotic and freedom loving. These were rebels who put two fingers up to the restrictions of privilege and authority.

If pirates were the rose-tinted anti-heroes of the eighteenth century, however, their counterparts in the nineteenth century were the outlaws of the 'Wild West' of America, or any of the other European colonies – each frontier society had its own sordid, but idealised version of a Jesse James or a Ned Kelly. Both groups were romantic figures of pulp fiction, adventurous and rebellious icons for popular culture.

Strangely, the reality of their everyday existence also bore uncanny similarities – but not in a romantic way. Both groups contained large numbers of bloodthirsty men with psychopathic tendencies that quickly came to the fore. There was little romance or glamour – it was mostly just a cross between terrorism and aggravated robbery. And in both cases there were the same, depressingly predictable 'push' and 'pull' factors: the 'push' of desperation, poverty and injustice; and the 'pull' of easy money.

Even less romantically, although they live long in our imaginations, both groups were characterised by the way in which they were hunted down and hanged. Piracy might be described as a 'merry life and a short one' – but only the second half of that statement was true.[1] Most of their careers could be counted down in the alcoholic haze of a few short weeks or months. The career of a pirate or Wild West outlaw was usually sordid, reckless and brief.

Even if one is attracted by the wrong-headed romanticism of *Pirates of the Caribbean*, however, more modern definitions of piracy have misleadingly little in common with its medieval usage.

Later centuries tended to define the activity on the basis of legality. These definitions had their own problems and blurred lines, but they also had their own internal logic. If you were sailing in a government-funded vessel, for instance, operating in the interests of state policy, then you were in the navy. If you were operating a vessel that had been commandeered or hired by the state, or if you were a recognised free-lancer, preying (in theory) only on the enemies of your state, you were a privateer – you operated as an outsourced contractor, with a veneer of legality. But if you were a scavenger on the seas, just a self-employed renegade operating beyond the control of any state, you were a pirate.[2]

These distinctions existed in medieval times, too. But in practice, they were far less clear cut.

There were some places in the medieval Levant where the roles were better defined than others. Two states in the region had more rigid definitions, as they had professional, 'regular' navies (or at least what might be called 'regular' by the looser standards of the time). The Byzantine empire (Christian) had a standing fleet, whose squadrons were sometimes based in Cyprus: these ships were the ones closest to hand for day-to-day operations in the eastern Mediterranean. The Fatimid and Ayyubid empires of Egypt (Muslim) similarly had a regular fleet headquartered in Alexandria and other Egyptian ports, but with outposts and naval facilities along the coast of Palestine (until these were gradually lost to the Franks in the first half of the twelfth century).

The warships of these two imperial navies tended to be galleys. These were narrow fighting ships, with banks of oars down each side and a pointed 'beak' at the front. Contrary to our preconceptions, the 'beak' was not usually used as a ram, but rather as a raised platform from which boarding parties could jump over to an enemy ship. There are some suggestions that Egyptian galleys may have been slightly smaller and under-manned, relative to Christian-built vessels. And this may have been true, particularly at the margins. The Egyptians always found recruitment difficult, for instance, and skilled sailors were in great demand – serving in the Fatimid navy was famously unpopular. But as the evidence is unclear, in practice the differences must have been relatively slight.[3]

Beyond those formal naval powers, however, the rules of the sea were vague in the extreme. Pirates in the crusading era certainly had many things in common with the pirates of the 'Golden Age'. They were, for instance, often desperate men, involved in violent and bloody acts, and they could be a nuisance to all states, regardless of their religious leanings. But there were also major differences: the crusades were not the world of Henry Morgan or Blackbeard.

In medieval times, piracy was part of a 'portfolio lifestyle', long before anyone thought of the first-world problems of early retirement or a gig economy. The medieval word was the same (*pirati*), but the meaning was subtly different: labels were much more about what you were doing, and where you were at that particular moment in time, rather than your legal underpinning. In the world of the crusades, the role of the state was far more vague, inherently fluid and, fundamentally, far less well resourced. The scope for imaginative and entrepreneurial naval freelancing was proportionately greater.

Piracy in the Latin East was treated with a huge dose of pragmatism: largely unfettered by legal frameworks, the cynical definition of a medieval pirate was, in most instances, simply 'someone with a ship and an opportunity'.

What you did was more important than your theoretical employment status and, from the perspective of a less complex society than our own, this approach was not without its own logic. Thus, even on the same page of a particular chronicle, we find instances where Egyptian 'pirates' might be castigated for preying on Christian pilgrim vessels – and almost immediately afterwards, we read of the Fatimid navy fighting a Venetian fleet that had ventured into the eastern Mediterranean. The Egyptian ships were almost certainly the same vessels. But the difference was semantic: they were 'pirates' when attacking a stray pilgrim ship, but a 'naval squadron' when fighting a foreign fleet.

Similarly, a merchant vessel could one day be acting as a trader or a transport vessel taking pilgrims on their travels, and then the next operating as a 'pirate'. And the following week it could be commandeered by the state to operate as part of a makeshift 'navy'. It was all about what you did, rather than your (often shifting) legal position.

Although it is tempting to write of privateers in a 'crusading' or 'religious' context, it was far more complicated than such simple labels would suggest. There was a lot of raiding by Christian vessels on the ships of other Christian states, for instance, and this was a perennial problem among the Italian city states. The Fatimid government might be ostensibly Muslim, and the Byzantines were Christian, but you would often be hard pressed to guess the religious beliefs of a pirate ship from its track record, particularly once it was safely out of port and beyond the reach of the local authorities.

Above all, piracy was an equal opportunities profession – and that was a very large part of its attraction. Unusually for what could be extremely rigid and hierarchical societies, every culture and every class – from emperors and lords down to the most downmarket but entrepreneurial sailor – could play its part in piracy. And piracy offered a chance, if you were extremely lucky, to grab a life-changing opportunity.

23

The Pirate Saint

It rapidly became the stuff of legend.

Within months (which was as fast as news travelled back home from the crusader states), the manor halls of Europe were ringing with ever more elaborate versions of the tale. It was a story with three heroes, only two of whom were human. And bizarrely, the story – or at least most of it – was true.

It looked far less glamorous on the ground.

It was May 1102. The early days of the crusader states, and a time when the world was in chaos. A horse moved slowly down the road from the hills and headed towards the small crusader port of Arsuf. It was in a spectacularly distressed state, and the bedraggled knight who rode him was in little better condition. He had been wounded by arrows. He was filthy. And he had clearly been sleeping rough for several days.

His skin was blistered by the sun and, in some places, much worse than that. Livid marks on his few exposed areas of flesh seemed almost burnt. And this was literally true: the edges of his clothing were dark and scorched. As well as suffering from archery wounds, this knight, severely sunburnt and dehydrated, had also been in a fire. His mental condition was almost as distressed as his physical state. The knight was traumatised, suffering from what we would now call PTSD, and in a deep state of shock.

This was a wounded and broken man.

The unprepossessing story had an astounding and heroic ending, however. The broken man was Baldwin I, lately count of Edessa and now king of Jerusalem. He may have been bedraggled, but he was also the leader of the senior of the four crusader states that had been set up to defend the Holy Land. His horse was no ordinary beast either. He was Gazelle, Baldwin's favourite warhorse, and a minor celebrity in his own right. Both, against all the odds, would survive the story's ending.[1]

But it was the third hero of the story – a man whom Baldwin had yet to meet – who was the most striking character of all. He was an Englishman far from home, travelling around the fragile war zone that was the eastern Mediterranean of the early twelfth century. He was a ship's captain and – when he needed to be – a rough man of action. Bizarrely, adding an even more exotic job title to an already unlikely list, he was – or, rather, he was later to become – a saint.

Even more exceptionally, this man of strangely eclectic career paths and virtues was also a pirate. Extraordinarily, as well as being occasional merchants or warriors, pirates of the Middle Ages could, literally, be saints. Godric – or Saint Godric as his friends came to call him – was about to change the course of history.[2]

There was already an English heritage of pilgrimage, armed or otherwise, to the Holy Land; but the exploits of the very earliest crusaders had turbo-charged that process of militant religiosity. Stories about the larger-than-life celebrities of the First Crusade were eagerly devoured by the Anglo-Norman nobility and their knights. This quickly morphed into more active expressions of admiration – and the tradition of English crusading was born.

By July of 1102, for instance, we find a certain 'Harding of England' with a number of English ships at the crusader port of Jaffa, on the coast of Palestine. This intrepid traveller may be the same 'Harding of

Oxford' who we know travelled East to help with the crusading cause at some point before 1109. But given the popularity at that time of both crusading and the name 'Harding', it may have been a different person altogether.[3]

The pirate hero of our tale, Godric of Finchale, fits firmly into the same tradition, bringing an astonishing mixture of entrepreneurialism, piety and derring-do to an already over-rich cultural cocktail. As so often in the Middle Ages, we only know of his story by accident. By a remarkable chance, a document has survived which closely approximates to that of an autobiography of our hero – something which, for a pirate or merchant of this period, is almost unheard of.

In his later years, after he had become a hermit and gained widespread fame for his piety, Godric dictated the story of his life to the prior of Durham, Reginald of Coldingham. The finished work was thus based on Godric's own recollections, and he even seems to have had the power of final editorial veto, which he exercised from his deathbed. The 'Life of Godric', which still exists in manuscript form, is the life he was proud to have lived.

After his death he was widely recognised as an informal saint. And, as a saint, his life naturally attracted attention. The story of his later piety ironically involved recording the far more interesting (for our purposes at least) details of his all-too-active life in the secular world.

Godric had many claims to fame, and the life that emerges from this semi-autobiographical account is indeed an exceptional and profoundly over-achieving one. As a merchant and ship's captain, he made frequent trips around the British Isles, and on to Scandinavia and Rome: he was sailing from country to country at a time when most Englishmen thought walking to the neighbouring village was an exciting adventure.

As a monk, hermit and saint, he provided an example for the pious society in which he lived. He was a devoted pilgrim, but was also keen to serve the interests of his God and his fellow pilgrims in an active and, if necessary, violent capacity. He even found time to write songs, which are, bizarrely, the earliest surviving musical pieces in the English language.

To top it all, he had been a pirate. As part of his piratical role, he went on to save the life of King Baldwin of Jerusalem – and arguably, the entire crusading movement.

Godric was born around 1065–1071, into the most tumultuous period of English history – just as the old Anglo-Scandinavian culture was about to be torn apart, and England was forcibly thrust into the mainstream of European culture. This was a time of danger and change; but for those resilient enough to grasp it, this was also a time of opportunity.

He came from the bottom rungs of what might charitably be described as the lower middle classes. His forebears were firmly on the losing side, and he had an Anglo-Saxon background, rather than coming from the Norman nobility. His upbringing was a simple and conventionally pious one: he later wrote (or rather dictated) that 'his father was named Aeilward, and his mother Aedwen, both of slender rank and wealth, but abundant in righteousness and virtue'.[4]

His parents, unlike Godric, wanted a quiet life, and they particularly wanted no trouble with the authorities: unusually for Anglo-Saxons of this time, they even named their second son William, no doubt as a token of deference to the new Norman regime and to their ultimate overlord, William the Bastard.[5]

Godric was an exceptional man in many ways. Physically, he certainly looked more like a merchant-adventurer than a ploughman. He was said to be a strong and vigorous man, 'of middle stature, broad shouldered and deep-chested'. He was attractive – or at least, that is how he later described himself when he was talking, at the end of his life, to his biographer. He had 'a long face, extremely clear and piercing grey eyes, bushy eyebrows, a broad forehead . . . a nose of comely curve, and a pointed chin'. To complete the jaunty, nautical air, he also sported a beard that was 'thick, and longer than the ordinary'. Always a man of contrasts and extremes, his hair at the time of his adventures in the Holy Land was black, but in later years it became 'white as snow'.

The sea was in his blood: the family, wrote Godric's biographer, 'were born in Norfolk, and had long lived in the township [near the coast] called Walpole'. We also know that he later worked near the Wellstream estuary, which runs out to the Wash, close by the spot where King John was later said to have lost his treasure. Aeilward seems to have had a small-holding in the hamlet: the Domesday Book records that there were six 'bordars' (something approaching tenant farmers) in Walpole at this time, one of whom was almost certainly Godric's father. Aeilward was not rich, but he was a freeman, and one of the more prosperous peasants: the family probably owned a few acres and a simple cottage.[6]

As he grew up, Godric railed against this relatively safe, but predictable existence. He decided not to be a farmer, like his fathers before him. Instead, he went into riskier, and potentially more rewarding, fields of business. He chose 'to study, learn and exercise the rudiments of more subtle conceptions . . . [and] aspiring to the merchant's trade, he began to buy and sell and gain from things of greater expense'. After starting as a low-level trader and market stall holder, he gradually built up his business, travelling ever further abroad.[7]

Godric learned his core skills as a merchant-adventurer and prospective pirate on the hard waves of the North Sea. He plied his trade up the coast between East Anglia and Scotland, astutely filling his ship with profitable goods, and venturing as far north as St Andrews on occasion. And the more Godric learned about commerce, the more he realised he was good at it. He began to branch out and 'soon associated himself by agreement with city merchants'.[8]

Godric was a man of imagination. He grasped the opportunities for international trade which presented themselves. His growing business connections gradually took him further and further away from his humble origins in East Anglia. Godric became accustomed to making extraordinary journeys and he quickly expanded his nascent business empire across the North Sea: he 'laboured not only as a merchant but also as a shipman to Denmark and Flanders and Scotland'. And Godric knew what he was doing. He soon 'made great profit in all his bargains and gathered much wealth'.

His experience helped him get a grounding in the rough world of eleventh-century long-distance international trade. He travelled abroad, even as far as the Mediterranean. The turning point came when he got back from a (presumably very profitable) trip to Rome: he decided to chance his luck in the world of maritime venture capital. He set up a business partnership 'with certain other young men who were eager for commerce, [and] he began to undertake bolder enterprises, and to travel frequently by sea to the foreign lands that lay around him'.

The proceeds of his commercial activities were reinvested in shipping and what were eventually to become, as we shall see, pirate vessels. Our adventurous hero first 'purchased half of a merchant-ship with certain partners in the trade', and as business boomed, he expanded his enterprise and 'bought the fourth part of another ship'.[9]

Unlike many private-equity players, however, Godric became increasingly pious as he grew older and more successful. Although he had been intimately involved in the rough end of commerce for many years, he felt the need for repentance – to add more spiritual weight to the profit and loss ledger of his life. Pilgrimage and crusade (both terms which were largely interchangeable at this time) were the obvious way to proceed, and so Godric 'began to think of spending [his profits] on charity . . . He therefore took the cross as a pilgrimage to Jerusalem.'[10]

He visited the Latin East twice (probably once in c.1102 and again in c.1108, though the exact dates are uncertain). On both occasions, he threw himself wholeheartedly into the role of pilgrim, alongside whatever other commercial, raiding or military opportunities presented themselves. He fasted and prayed. And he visited as many of the holy places as possible, including, of course, the ancient Church of the Holy Sepulchre in Jerusalem, built on the site where Jesus was believed to have been crucified and to have risen from the dead.[11]

But he was also there as a crusader and as a man of action. He and his contemporaries saw no contradiction in this. His biographer was explicit in writing that, as a pilgrim, he bore on his shoulders 'the banner of the Lord's Cross'. And in describing the banner, he used the suitably military phrase '*vexillum crucis*'. Presumably this more active devotional role also encompassed his activities as a pirate, attacking Muslim shipping as he sailed down to the Middle East, and harassing the Egyptian naval squadrons which resupplied the Fatimid coastal cities of the Palestinian seaboard.

There was little tension in the roles: crusader-pilgrims were expected to be devout, but they were also acting as the soldiers of Christ. Godric was simultaneously a crusader, a pirate and a genuinely devout pilgrim. Each role sustained and supplemented the other. Godric and his fellow crusaders were working to recover the old Christian heartlands of the Holy Land and to defend the local Christian communities – and they knew that this was always unlikely to be achieved peacefully. Men of God also needed to be, on occasion, men of action.

Godric, as he approached saintly status later in life, described his behaviour and personality at this time as verging on the abominable: more suited (appropriately enough) to a career as a pirate or venture capitalist than to the quiet, reflective life of a hermit. He later admitted that he had lied, cheated and generally led a dissolute life.

For Godric, however, redemption was at hand – and in a very tangible way.

Disaster and deliverance

On 17 May 1102, King Baldwin I of Jerusalem set off to intercept what he believed to be a large but lightly armed Muslim raiding party. He had with him a mainly mounted force, consisting of some two hundred knights.[12]

Some claimed (after the event of course) to have counselled caution. Arpin of Bourges, who became a monk on his return to Europe, would later say that he had suggested a more measured approach. Baldwin was said to have told him, 'If you can't face a fight, go back to Bourges.' What Baldwin did not realise, however, was that this was the main Egyptian field army. His tiny cavalry force was intercepting some 15–20,000 soldiers, rather than just a few hundred bandits.[13]

When Baldwin saw them, he realised the extent of his mistake. But by then it was too late to do anything about it: Albert of Aachen, who later interviewed some of the survivors, explicitly wrote that the Fatimid forces were so close that the Franks had no opportunity to manoeuvre or to disengage.[14]

Baldwin charged, hoping to fight his way through. But his men were massively outnumbered and outflanked. Casualties among the Frankish nobility, both those who were settlers and those who were there temporarily as crusaders, were horrendous. The dead included many celebrities from the 1101 crusade, including the poignantly named 'Geoffrey who was short in stature' (or Geoffrey I Jordan of Vendome, as he probably preferred to be called).[15]

Baldwin was luckier than most. He and a group of some fifty knights punched their way through the Egyptian line. They managed to make it to the rudimentary refuge offered by a newly built tower in the nearby town of Ramla, pursued closely by Fatimid cavalry. The Egyptians quickly blockaded the tower. By dusk, the Franks realised that they were completely surrounded. During the course of the night, the enormity of the disaster gradually sank in. Half of the Kingdom of Jerusalem's nobility and government were dead. The core of the army, the heavy cavalry, had been almost wiped out. The situation was dire.

The king – brave, impetuous or reckless, depending on your point of view – decided to try to break out before the siege reached its inevitable conclusion. Mounted on his charger Gazelle, he and his squire, Hugh of Brulis, burst out through a breach in the wall of the courtyard. They were accompanied by only three knights: a tiny suicide squad to help Baldwin carve a way out through the enemy and buy enough time for him to make good his escape.[16]

For three harrowing days, Baldwin hid in the nearby foothills, evading the Egyptian cavalry who were out scouring the land for him. Exhausted and on the verge of mental and physical collapse, he eventually found a road he recognised, and stumbled down to the newly captured Frankish port of Arsuf, on the coast north of modern-day Tel Aviv.[17]

Baldwin was tough, but his ordeal during the battle and his subsequent adventures had pushed him to the limit. He seems to have suffered a temporary nervous breakdown. He did not have the luxury of being ill for too long, however – his leadership was central to the survival of the crusader states. Most of the remaining members of the Frankish government had gathered, together with their families, at the port of Jaffa. They waited to hear the latest communiqué from the front, to find out if their king was alive or dead – and if the news was as bad as many suspected, they were packed and ready to sail back to Europe. The crusades had barely started, but they were almost over.

It was essential for Baldwin to be taken back to his people, so that he could reassure those who were about to give up, and gather a new army around him. But this was enormously difficult. The Frankish garrison of Arsuf was surrounded and hugely outnumbered by the Egyptian army. The road to Jaffa was definitely blocked for the foreseeable future. The only other way out was by sea; but the port was blockaded by the Fatimid navy, with Muslim ships on continuous patrol and sailing close up to the harbour entrance. That route, too, looked impassible.

At this point our pirate hero enters history in the most spectacular fashion. King Baldwin was incapacitated and recovering himself. Despite the crisis and ensuing panic, Godric, who seems to have been trapped in the port of Arsuf when the trouble started, came up with a plan.

By 1102, he had been a merchant trader – and possibly pirate – for many years. He had seen things that few of his contemporaries had even dreamed of. And he had the experience and resourcefulness of someone you wanted by your side in a tight spot. He knew what had to be done.

While the king was recuperating, Godric studied the blockading ships and worked on an alternative exit strategy. He decided that there was a way he could get the king back to Jaffa. He prepared his ship, which was, as one might expect for a pirate coming from the North Sea, the type 'commonly called a buss'. Everything that might slow it down was stripped out. The plan was that he and his men would sail straight through the weakest point in between the blockading squadrons. But to do this, they had to set sail in broad daylight, in order to get a clear line of sight – there was no chance of surprise.

Their main advantage was the scheme's folly: it was so foolhardy, so dangerous, that the Egyptians might not immediately realise what was happening, and would react slowly as a result. It was incredibly risky, but there was no alternative – the clock was ticking. The king had taken seven days to recover. If he did not get back to Jaffa very soon, the settlers would assume the worst and return to the West. The crusading dream of recovering the Christian Middle East would be over before it had even properly begun.

Godric managed to get the king on board, together with a small bodyguard, and set sail on his unlikely mission. With only a small chance of success, Godric and the king were strangely liberated – they acted with the bravado of the desperate. Albert of Aachen wrote that the pirate ship sailed with Baldwin's 'banner fixed to a spear and raised in the air to catch the sun's rays, so that this sign of his would be recognised by the Christian citizens and they would have confidence in the king's survival' – all of which was fine in theory, but Godric still needed to fight his way through first.

Not surprisingly, the Egyptian navy 'saw and recognised his sign'. They tried, entirely correctly, to intercept the ship close in by the harbour mouth, 'at that place where the city was surrounded by sea', and where it would have a much more restricted ability to manoeuvre. The entire squadron was soon bearing down on the English pirate, and 'they met him in twenty galleys and thirteen of the ships which they commonly call *cats*, wanting to encircle the king's buss'.

The seamanship of Godric and his veteran crew was their only hope. The Fatimid ships were sluggish, turning slowly as 'the waves of the sea in front of them were swelling and resisting'. While they struggled to manoeuvre, Godric dodged through the gaps that opened up between the enemy ships and struck out for more open waters. Eventually, 'the king's buss was sliding and flying on an easy and speedy course among the stormy waters, and he suddenly arrived in the harbour of . . . Jaffa, his buss having given the enemy the slip'.

Godric, a commoner (and a pirate commoner at that), had saved the day. But the chroniclers felt the need to give Baldwin at least some of the credit. One contemporary history suggested, entirely implausibly, that the king 'shot and wounded six of the Saracens with his bow from the little vessel'.[18]

But everyone knew the truth.

It was as if Blackbeard had rescued the British Empire. An English pirate had changed the course of crusading history.

Godric made his way back to the crusader states for one last trip, possibly around 1108. This time, the visit was more visibly pious, and focused on the conventional itineraries of religious tourism and visits to the holy places. He went to the sites associated with Jesus's ministry. These doubtless included Nazareth and the Sea of Galilee, if he found it possible to do so without a large military escort – pilgrimage and crusading were acutely dangerous at this time and the eastern borders of the crusader states were still ominously fluid.

The culmination of the trip was hearing mass at the Holy Sepulchre in Jerusalem, just a couple of hundred yards from the royal palace of his friend, Baldwin I. We can only hope that Godric was not so pious by this stage that he would forgo a drink and a bout of storytelling with his old comrade.

Godric travelled with the other pilgrims along the route from Jerusalem to the River Jordan, where he underwent a second baptism. Spiritually reborn, he walked barefoot back to Jerusalem, where he worked for several months at the hospital of St John, ministering to the needs of sick pilgrims, before returning to England to pursue the next stage of his extraordinary career.

Of course, one cannot be *absolutely* certain that Godric of Finchale was the same man as 'Godric the English Pirate' who appears in Albert of Aachen's chronicle; and it is true that Godric was not an unusual name for an Englishman.[19] But there is strong circumstantial evidence to suggest that they were one and the same: we know that both were merchant-ships' captains and that they both owned a North Sea 'buss'; both were deeply engaged in the specialised and highly edgy world of medieval international commerce, which bled so seamlessly into piracy; both were men of action, well used to the need for violence when required; both were Englishmen in the eastern Mediterranean, in a period when only tiny numbers of men would venture that far from home; both were in the area in the early twelfth century, around the time of the battle of Ramla; and both were called Godric.

The case is compelling, though – like most medieval stories – certainly not definitive. But it is at least an extraordinary coincidence. And even if they were not the same person, King Baldwin – and quite possibly the entire crusading movement – was saved by the actions of Godric the English pirate.

Monks as pirates

For a pirate to have a late-life career as a hermit was, as we have seen in the case of Saint Godric, an implausible but genuine possibility. It also worked the other way, however. Astonishingly, there are numerous examples of crusader monks operating as pirates even when they were still members of a religious order.

The military orders, such as the Templars and the Hospitallers, were the elite monastic warriors of the Latin East. They always had a naval component in their arsenals. Shipping was important, even from their earliest days, if only because of the huge requirement that they had to move men and matériel from Europe out to their fortifications in the Holy Land.[20]

The Hospitallers, in particular, focused on naval warfare after Acre, the capital of the Latin Kingdom of Jerusalem, was lost in 1291 – they, like the rest of the settlers, were forced off the mainland of the Middle East. In 1344, for instance, a crusader fleet of some twenty-five ships gathered in the Aegean. No fewer than six of those vessels were contributed by the order, led by Giovanni de Biandrate, the prior of Lombardy.

Some of these ships were huge by the standards of the time. And since much naval combat in this period was conducted by hand-to-hand fighting, this made them extremely formidable. To give a sense of the scale involved, the Templar and Hospitaller ships sailing out of Marseille in 1233 and 1234 were told that in order to avoid undercutting the local shipping, they could carry a maximum of 1,500 pilgrims on each ship – and that was in addition to all the troops, merchants and cargo they also carried. There were never huge numbers of Christian ships – in 1300, the Templars, the Hospitallers and the king of Cyprus could jointly muster only thirteen galleys in the eastern Mediterranean. But they were impressive and of the highest quality.[21]

The Hospitallers had had a small regular fleet in Cyprus ever since they transferred their headquarters to that island in 1292. The grand commander defeated a Turkish fleet near Chios in 1309, for instance, when he commanded twenty-four *barques*, supported by one galley and six smaller vessels provided by the Genoese lord of Chios. When he overcame Turkish naval forces the following year, he commanded a similar fleet of four galleys and twenty-four smaller ships.

The order also had contracts to get support from Christian pirates (or privateers) when extra help might be needed. The Hospitallers thus had a very flexible relationship with piracy, if only because of the damage it did to Muslim shipping and the blocks it put on Turkish ambitions to control the eastern Mediterranean.

They used their own ships for piracy, and they encouraged freelance corsairs to do likewise. They opened their harbours up to pirates to use as bases (presumably taking a share in the profits while they did so) and they even invested in piratical expeditions on an individual basis as venture capitalists. In 1413–1416, for instance, we know that Christian pirate vessels, including ships captained on a freelance basis by Hospitaller brothers, were based in ports controlled by the order, and were allowed to attack Muslim shipping from the protection of those harbours.[22]

But piracy was not just something to be outsourced. For the disgruntled and increasingly underemployed members of the Christian military orders, this was a perfect opportunity for career diversification. Perhaps not surprisingly, some even became pirates themselves.

Roger of Flor, for instance, the famous mercenary, started his career as a Templar sergeant. He was expelled from the order because of various misdemeanours, including robbery. He quickly turned pirate. He had been a member of the Templars' navy for many years, serving on one of their galleys since the age of eight. Freed from the discipline of the order's rules, he gathered others around him and set up a thriving freelance pirate enterprise in the eastern Mediterranean.

Many of his men were unemployed Catalan knights, and so his operation was, rather pretentiously, called The Grand Catalan Company. But Roger was certainly exceptional. For a former sergeant to be commanding so many knights, and tough freelance knights at that, was extremely unusual: Roger was clearly a charismatic and forceful personality. The pirate ex-Templar died in the high-profile way that he lived: entirely fittingly, given his extravagantly implausible lifestyle, he was assassinated at Adrianople in 1305 on the orders of the Byzantine royal family.[23]

24

Crusader Pirates

We normally associate the crusaders with the vivid cliches of medieval life: armoured knights on heavy, intimidating horses, venturing out from glowering castles which dominated the stark landscape beneath them. But there is another, equally fundamental, element of life in the crusader states which is far less obvious and far easier to overlook – the sea.

The clue lies in a name.

That name is an often forgotten signpost – forgotten because it is in such plain view. We call the medieval Frankish colonies in the Holy Land 'the Latin East', or perhaps 'the crusader states'. But contemporaries had a far simpler vocabulary. In a turn of phrase that was seemingly naïve, but was in fact profound and full of meaning, Europeans at the time had a redolent way of describing them.

The colonies were simply known as the lands 'beyond the sea' – 'Outremer'.

Controlling the sea was always the prerequisite for the existence of the crusader settlement. With the sea at their backs, and a lifeline to the West in place, they still had a slim fighting chance of survival in a hostile Middle East. Without control of those shipping lanes, however, the life expectancy of the entire Frankish community of the Levant would probably be measured in months, rather than years.

A cursory glance at a map of the eastern Mediterranean confirms just how important the sea lanes were to the crusaders. Most of the major Frankish population centres had a port, with relatively secure links back to the West. This was no coincidence: the only two that did not – Jerusalem and Edessa – were plagued by military and demographic problems.

The ancient city of Edessa survived for a while, but only because of its large native Christian population of highly motivated Armenians. Even so, it was continually under pressure and was the first major crusader stronghold to fall into enemy hands. It was overrun in 1144 and never recovered.

Jerusalem, similarly, was militarily indefensible: its existence in Christian hands was only sustained by a large field army and extensive Frankish defences to its east, in the Oultrejourdain and Galilee. But with those defences gone, the city could not be held for long.

Jerusalem fell on 2 October 1187, just a couple of months after the destruction of the Frankish field army at the disastrous battle of Hattin. Even that short respite was only attributable to its inherent weakness: the Muslim commanders knew it was so easy to capture that there was no hurry – they could move on to more pressing targets.

The city was brought back into Christian hands by diplomatic means at various points in the thirteenth century. But this was only sanctioned by the Christians' enemies because they knew that the Holy City was a liability, rather than an asset: the mere act of ownership forced the Franks to devote scarce resources to its defence, even though such defences would inevitably be inadequate for the task. Militarily, the original home of the Holy Grail remained a poisoned chalice.

Under these circumstances, the Franks were understandably desperate to control the shipping lanes into Palestine and Syria. They were initially helped in this by the problems that beset their enemies in the region. The Muslim naval presence in the eastern Mediterranean was substantial at the beginning of the twelfth century, in the shape of the Fatimid Egyptian empire's large and professional navy. Luckily for the crusaders, the Egyptian fleet was better known for its incompetence, politicisation and inter-service rivalries than for its maritime skills. It had numbers on its side, and was highly dangerous when used correctly, but it never lived up to its potential.

The only other significant navy within the region was that of the Byzantine empire. This was not usually a threat. Even when relations with the Franks were poor, the Byzantines normally had far better things to worry about than harassing the crusader states: attacking fellow Christians at the very fringes of their fleet's operating range was rarely a priority.

The crusader states had problems of their own, however. They had no standing navies and, with little money and severely limited manpower, no realistic prospect of acquiring them. But if the lack of a regular navy was the problem, there was an irregular solution to hand: piracy.

The ports of the Latin East were full. They drew in many of the world's boldest sailors and their ships. The potential rewards of piracy in the waters off the crusader states were enough to attract adventurers and freebooters from all parts of Christendom.

The eastern Mediterranean was one of the major destinations at the western end of the Silk Road, the famous trade route which carried goods across the Eurasian steppes from China. As a result, there were always merchants and cargo ships in the ports of the Latin East, bringing goods to and from Europe. There were also ships carrying passengers – pilgrims, mercenaries or even contingents of knights and their men on crusade. The prospects of money and adventure – plus even occasionally religious fervour – blended together to act as a catalyst to attract skilled sailors and shipping.

It is this magnetic appeal which explains why so many groups of experienced, tough and underemployed sailors were available at short notice. These were the men who, incongruously enough, became the crusader pirates.

Pirate Franks

The bottom end of the pirate business had a relatively low cost of entry. Not surprisingly, many prospective entrepreneurs took the opportunity to pile in.

Even in the earliest days of the Latin Kingdom of Jerusalem, after the big names and their big fleets had set off home to Europe, adventurers and opportunists were to be found in the dangerous waters of the East. Having delivered their pilgrim passengers to the Holy Land, many ships' captains stayed on to see what rich prizes were still to be had. In 1110–1111, for instance, we know that 'a company of [Egyptian and Syrian] travelling merchants [were] chafing at their prolonged inaction' because of the political and military upheavals caused by the First Crusade. They decided to take matters into their own hands. The frustrated traders 'lost patience and set out from Tinnis, Damietta and Misr [that is, Fustat or 'Old Cairo'] with a great quantity of merchandise and money'.[1]

They formed a convoy and, by sheer weight of numbers, hoped to force their way through any Christian pirates that might stand in their way. The Egyptian navy, cautious and famously unhelpful, decided that it was 'unable to go to sea' to help them. But the merchants, who were rapidly running out of time and money, 'took upon themselves the risk and set sail'.[2]

This was bold. But it was also a huge mistake.

Even in a substantial convoy, accompanied by as many guards as they could muster, disaster struck. They 'fell in with some Frankish vessels and were captured, and merchandise and monies to the value of more than one hundred thousand dinars were seized by their captors, who held them as prisoners and tormented them, until they ransomed themselves by all that remained of their deposits at Damascus and elsewhere'. In the first decade after the capture of Jerusalem, skilful, ruthless Frankish pirates were already a fearsome threat.[3]

The word soon spread. Encouraged by the chance of acquiring such life-changing booty, more European ships arrived, and increasingly

proliferated in the eastern Mediterranean. These western pirates operated their own private enterprises and, particularly helpful to states
(such as the Latin Kingdom of Jerusalem) that had no standing navy of
their own, made themselves available for hire at short notice.

Many of their more enterprising 'colleagues' were already there.
Large Italian fleets had been extremely valuable in the early years of the
crusading movement, transporting armies and destroying Egyptian
squadrons when they appeared. Not coincidentally, the Italian maritime city states also acquired valuable commercial shipping and trading
rights in the East while they did so. Most of these fleets went home
once their expedition was over, but some of the more independently
inclined captains stayed on as freelancers with their ships and crews
once the main fleet had gone.

The Franks had occasional naval support from Europe to help them
with the combined land and sea sieges that were necessary to capture
the coastal cities of the Holy Land, but local pirates or privateers were
always available for hire. Their constant presence was guaranteed by the
constant opportunities. Most of them doubtless had 'day jobs' as
captains of pilgrim ships or merchantmen, but they could quickly be
encouraged to turn to warfare or state-sponsored piracy when needed.

In 1107, a few years before the destruction of the Egyptian merchant
convoy, King Baldwin of Jerusalem approached the Fatimid-held port
of Sidon and 'assembled forces from all sides, from land and sea, from
different nations of the realm of Italy . . . and all those who were accustomed to attack and despoil at sea in the manner of pirates, and besieged
the town of Sidon by sea as well as by land in the month of August'.[4]

Despite the help of these Italian and other pirates, however, the siege
eventually failed. Albert of Aachen wrote that the king's ships, presumably including the pirate vessels, had to be destroyed after the Egyptian
army and Damascene Turks came to the aid of the city, and the siege
had to be called off. King Baldwin was reluctantly forced 'to set light to
his own ships and all the siege engines and tents, until they were reduced
to ashes and embers'.[5]

Without a standing navy, the Frankish settlers in Palestine and Syria always had trouble enforcing blockades when besieging coastal towns. The impromptu flotillas they gathered for the task, largely made up of piratical freelancers, were cheap, but none too reliable. The siege and naval blockade of 1107 had failed, but the crusaders were persistent in their attempts to capture the coastal cities of the Levant – the sea lanes back to Europe were so vital that they had little choice. Sidon was eventually taken in December 1110, shortly after the capture of Tripoli and Beirut. The Christians now controlled almost all of the coast of Palestine.

Ironically, the large number of Christian pirates based in the Levant goes a long way towards explaining why the Kingdom of Jerusalem (unlike the Fatimids or Byzantines) never felt the need to invest scarce resources in a regular navy.

If the kings and princes of the crusader states required ships for a campaign, pirate ships and merchant ships (if such a distinction is possible) could be leased at short notice. And the ubiquitous nature of Frankish piracy also meant that the crucial everyday job of patrolling the coast to destroy Muslim commercial traffic could be conducted at zero cost – there was no need to pay for a hugely expensive navy, when entrepreneurs were doing the job for free. The lack of a Frankish navy was, perversely, a sign of strength, rather than weakness.

Records from this period are, as always, limited. But the sheer scale of the Christian shipping that was available at any given time is impressive. Anecdotes from the north of the Latin Kingdom of Jerusalem in the early months of 1112, for example, show that there was an abundance of vessels to be called upon.

While the main Christian forces (and most available ships) were besieging Tyre, we know that Tughtigin, the ruler of Damascus, 'set out with a detachment of his [regular cavalry] to the district of Sidon and raided its suburbs, killing a number of the seamen and burning about twenty vessels on the shore'. Even with large numbers of ships absent at the siege, it is clear that there were still plenty of other vessels in port.[6]

Just how many ships were absent at Tyre is shown by the severity of the losses the Franks sustained as the (eventually abortive) siege ground on towards its frustrating conclusion. In the course of the siege, the chronicles show that, as well as using local ships for their naval blockade, the crusading army had been cannibalising many of these vessels for their precious timber. In April 1112, as they were forced to pull out, the Franks burned 'many of the vessels belonging to them on the shore, since they had [already] removed their masts, rudders, and equipment for their [siege] towers. The number of these vessels was about two hundred, large and small, about thirty of them being war vessels, and they used some of them for the transport of their light baggage'. Hundreds of vessels had been deployed, even though, in theory at least, the kingdom had no navy of its own.[7]

Frankish pirates were so confident that they would sometimes even take on the Egyptian navy, just for the chance of booty, or to capture slaves for resale. We are lucky in having a detailed account of one such attack that took place in 1115, when a Fatimid fleet sailed up to Tyre to resupply its garrison. On its return journey, its men knew that they could expect trouble. Accordingly, when they approached the Christian port of Acre, 'they organised naval squadrons, protected with all their weaponry against the forces of the Christians'. Two large Fatimid ships, 'which were stronger and better manned acted as a rearguard, but as they were excessively laden with goods and men, they followed at a distance of more than a mile'.[8]

Frankish buccaneers, together with their friends and neighbours in the port of Acre, saw their chance – and took it. As the Egyptian navy sailed past the city, 'around 400 of [the Frankish citizens], carried in three galleys, were launched on the waves in order to try and harass and capture the trailing ships'. One of the two Muslim ships was harried and attacked until the evening, when 'it was captured and taken all the way to the port of Haifa. At Haifa . . . captured Saracens who were wounded were put under guard and left, while those who were uninjured were sent to Acre with their captured ship, along with certain wounded Christians'.[9]

But that was not the end of their bold attack. Once the wounded Franks had been landed from the three galleys, 'the rest of the Christians, who had as yet escaped unharmed, took with them other comrades in two galleys, and pursued and surrounded the [other Egyptian] ship'.[10]

There they were joined by other European adventurers, and attacked 'it vigorously now with five galleys . . . At last, after both sides had endured a great warlike struggle from dawn to midday, the gentiles' ship . . . almost repulsed them and slipped through their hands.' The Franks in Acre saw that the struggle was not going well and, keen to stop so much profit sailing away, sent yet another pair of ships out to join the attack. After much hard fighting, the Egyptian ship 'was brought into Acre by force in the evening'.

Two Egyptian ships from Tyre sailed out to try to help, but they were forced to retreat and 'made their way back home in flight'. The second of the two captured Fatimid ships had 'a thousand strong fighting men' on it, most of whom were captured. Of these, 'some of the Saracens [presumably those who were wounded, and thus of limited economic value] were beheaded, others were ransomed for a priceless sum and released'.[11]

The story itself is a fascinating glimpse into the generally unreported naval skirmishes that regularly took place along the coasts of Palestine and Syria at this time. Perhaps even more interestingly, however, it also shows the presence of large numbers of armed and aggressive Frankish ships in port, available almost literally at a moment's notice to attack Muslim shipping. This part of the eastern Mediterranean was clearly full of Christian pirates and other maritime adventurers, just looking for profitable prizes.

Pirate slave traders

Slavery was relatively little known in most of western Europe.

When they arrived in the East, the crusaders were far less accustomed to the practice than was the case in the Islamic world, or in

Africa, where it was both widespread and institutionally well established. Frankish pirates knew an opportunity when they saw one, however, and were quick learners. Slave trading was an obviously symbiotic accompaniment to a career as a pirate, if only as a profitable way to dispose of captives who might not be sufficiently valuable to command a ransom in their own right.

One such pirate-slaver was a certain 'William Jiba' – possibly a corruption of the family name of Jubail, a Frankish port where a pirate slave trader (perhaps of Italian origins) might have learnt his grim profession. 'Kilyam Jiba', as he was known to his Muslim neighbours and customers, operated out of Acre in the early 1140s, and doubtless fitted in very well with the laissez-faire commercial environment of the crusaders' biggest port. This was not a career choice calculated to improve one's popularity: even his customers called him 'a real devil of a Frank'. Not that he cared, of course.[12]

At one point, William struck it rich. He 'went out in a boat of his on a raid and he captured a ship carrying Muslim pilgrims from the Maghrib, around four hundred souls, men and women'. Usama Ibn-Munqidh was in Acre at the time, in his capacity as freelance diplomat, and started negotiations for their release. He travelled to Damascus and made the appropriate arrangements. His employer, the emir Mu'in al-Din, provided finance for Usama to pay the ransom of a few of the captives on his own account, and also pledged money on behalf of others who wanted to pay for some of the remaining prisoners.[13]

Usama then went back to Acre to complete the transaction. But there was not enough money to free all the prisoners. After the initial haggling was finished, Usama was sad to realise that there 'remained thirty eight captives still with William Jiba'. Distressingly, families had been split up in the process of negotiating for their freedom, and one of the remaining slaves was, according to Usama, 'the wife of a man that God . . . had already delivered by my hand. So I bought her [on credit] without paying her price just then. I then rode to Jiba's home . . . and asked him "will you sell me ten of them?".'[14]

Much to his chagrin, when Usama returned to William Jiba he found that all the Muslim prisoners had escaped overnight, including the one he had bought, but not yet paid for. He was suitably outraged, but a contract is a contract, even with a slaver: Usama (and, ultimately, his employer) was obliged to pay for her, even though she had run off. William Jiba, with the luck of a 'real devil', made at least some of his money back from the escaped prisoners.[15]

Some Franks clearly became accomplished slave-trading pirates; but their Christian co-religionists in the Byzantine empire could also show a suitably buccaneering spirit, if enough money was at stake.

A touching story of piracy, slave trading and a strange redemption was told to Usama while he was in Damascus in the summer of 1176. A man called Abu Bakr related to the itinerant Syrian prince how he had been taken prisoner and enslaved when his ship was captured by the Byzantines off the coast of Egypt. 'It happened,' he said, 'that I travelled from Mecca to the land of Egypt, from where I took ship on the sea heading for the Maghrib. But the Romans [that is, Byzantines] captured the ship, and I, with others, was taken captive.' The unlucky Abu Bakr was given to an Orthodox priest as his share of the plunder. The role of the priest in this story seems unusual, but perhaps he was serving onboard the ship as a chaplain; or, if the ship was a privateer, perhaps he had been one of its financiers.[16]

Thankfully, Abu Bakr had skills that placed him in a domestic and commercial role, rather than in the harsher working environments of the quarry or the building site. We know that he was literate and an accomplished bookkeeper – others later spoke of his 'fine handwriting' and mentioned that he was 'knowledgeable about accounting'.

The exact nature of the relationship between Abu Bakr and his owner is unknown, but it certainly became a very amicable one. Presumably he worked closely with his new master in managing his property and his business affairs. When the Byzantine priest became seriously ill, he changed his will and arranged for his slave, and friend, to be freed. Very considerately, he also seems to have left him a sum of money to help him to return to Muslim lands and start his new life safely.

On the death of his master, Abu Bakr, who seems to have been charming as well as skilled, made his way to the Maghreb. Once again, his talents were soon spotted, and he found employment there in managing a bakery business. He eventually became so invaluable that he was given his employer's daughter as a bride, and settled down with his own wife and family. For the lucky accountant, being taken into slavery by pirates was a career interruption rather than the unmitigated disaster that it was for most people.

As was often the case in earlier centuries, ties of affection had gradually superseded the darker bonds of obedience and servitude between master and slave. The ending of the story was a happy one, and a pleasing reminder that the gentler aspects of human nature could still find an outlet, even in a time of violence, slavery and bloodshed.[17]

25

Muslim Corsairs

Muslim corsairs have a fearsome reputation – and with good reason. The havoc they caused across the Mediterranean in the early modern period and beyond was hugely disruptive. Despite this, however, they are remarkably rare in the chronicles of the crusades. This seems surprising on one level. But control of the eastern Mediterranean seas in the twelfth century had shifted remorselessly back into the hands of the Christian powers.

This process had its own logic. The professional Byzantine fleet and marine corps patrolled the waters around their empire. The large Italian and north European fleets, when they ventured into the region on crusade, swept aside all they encountered – the Fatimid navy generally chose to stay in port, rather than confront them. And as its naval bases were captured one by one, the Egyptian fleet was effectively hounded out of the Palestinian coastal waters: it played an increasingly marginal role from 1110 onwards.[1]

Later in the century, Saladin tried to contest control of the seas once more: he knew that cutting the links of the crusader states back to Europe was vital. Once he had taken power in Egypt, he threw huge amounts of money into an attempt to revitalise its naval capabilities. But despite the massive investment he made in ships, men and port facilities, the programme was an expensive failure: the strategy was correct, but despite the extra funding, the means to implement it were still inadequate.[2]

The Christians did not have a monopoly on piracy, however – far from it. Particularly in the early years of the crusader states, the Egyptian navy fought fiercely for control of the eastern Mediterranean. The Fatimid fleet might be doomed to lose the struggle, but that final outcome was not so evident to those on the losing end of one of the many skirmishes that took place at sea every year.

On his way back from a trip to the Holy Land in 1101–1103, for instance, the English pilgrim Saewulf left a distressing account of his experiences. He had almost been killed by Muslim bandits when he arrived, but he was also lucky to survive his departure. He boarded a ship at Jaffa for the journey back to Europe, along with many other fellow pilgrims. They set off north up the coast of Palestine. Soon after they set sail, however, they were bounced by a squadron of predatory Muslim ships.

'When we were sailing between [Haifa] and Acre,' wrote Saewulf, 'there were twenty five Saracen ships to be seen, that is of the Prince of the [Muslim-held] cities of Tyre and Sidon, going to Egypt with forces to help the Egyptians fight against the King of Jerusalem.' The Christian pilgrim vessels had formed a convoy of at least six ships (probably more): wisely, they had sought safety in numbers for their journey, because of the dangers they knew they might face. Up against an entire Muslim fleet, however, their convoy was completely outclassed. It quickly became clear that their best bet lay in scattering and sailing as quickly as possible towards the nearest Frankish-held ports.[3]

This was entirely logical, but Saewulf, who was trapped on one of the larger, slower vessels, was understandably rather bitter. 'Two ships,' he wrote, 'which were coming with us and were laden with pilgrims, abandoned our ship and, since they were lighter, rowed off and escaped to Caesarea.' Left on their own, Saewulf and his companions looked like easy meat. As they desperately tried to sail away, 'all round our ship the Saracens sailed, staying about a bow-shot away, and rejoicing at such a prize'.[4]

But being on a larger vessel also had its advantages. It may have been slower, but its very size meant that it was well manned. In an age when most naval actions involved boarding the enemy, attacking a high-sided European ship full of armed men was not straightforward: they might be easy to pursue, but they were far less easy to capture. Left with little alternative, Saewulf and the others fought bravely, and the archers and armed pilgrims made a suitably intimidating show, particularly at a distance. 'Our men,' he later wrote with relief, 'were prepared to die for Christ. They took up arms, and when they were armed they defended the ship like a castle.' There were almost two hundred men defending our dromond [a large galley].'[5]

Eventually the Muslims thought better of it, and

after about an hour, when he had taken counsel, the [Muslim] prince sent one of his sailors up the mast of the ship, which was very large, to learn what he could of our action. When he learned from him of the strength of our defence, he raised his sails and went out to sea. So on that day the Lord made us escape from our enemies.[6]

Saewulf and his ship made it back into port, only to find that three other ships in the Christian convoy had not been so lucky: they had been captured by those same Muslim ships, and their passengers had been killed or sold into slavery.

Even that was not an end to their dangers, however: as they moved further up the coast, the attacks continued. Saewulf later recalled that after they had sailed north beyond Palestine, up the coast of Syria and on to Anatolia, 'we were often attacked by pirates, but the divine grace protected us, and nothing was lost to us either by enemy attacks or by storms'. He lived to tell the tale of his journeys; but he was all too conscious that many other pilgrims were far less fortunate.[7]

Like Saewulf, the Russian pilgrim Abbot Daniel, travelling just a few years later (1106–1108), encountered the dangerous pirates of Anatolia. Even though he had a well-equipped and substantial entourage with him, he was less lucky than Saewulf: his ship was boarded and robbed, but at least he escaped with his life. He wrote that near the city of Patara, also known as Arsinoe, 'pirates in four galleys met us and captured us and robbed us all. Thence we went to Constantinople which we reached in safety.' Being a pilgrim in pirate waters was a high-risk affair in the early days of the crusader states.[8]

However dangerous the pirates might have been to individual ships or travellers, however, it is interesting to see that the dynamics underpinning piracy were the same for all states, regardless of their religious persuasion. Although Muslim pirates might be useful for their rulers in terms of slowing down the influx of European settlers into the region and disrupting communications back to the West, they were also an unruly force to contend with.

The independence of spirit which piracy encouraged created an unhelpful culture of insubordination: it was easy to forget that you had an overlord, or that your interests and his might not always be completely aligned. The pirate emir Usama, for instance (not to be confused with his contemporary, the writer Usama Ibn-Munqidh) was almost as much of a liability for his ostensible friends as he was for his enemies.

Usama the pirate had established himself in Beirut in the chaotic times that followed the collapse of the Latin Kingdom of Jerusalem in the late 1180s, after the catastrophic defeat at Hattin. In true corsair style, however, Usama proved unreliable to everyone he had dealings with, Christians and Muslims alike. He managed to duck and dive, and avoided direct rule from either of the two main centres of Muslim power at the time – Damascus and Cairo. Instead, slipping in between the cracks, he set up his own pirate mini-state.[9]

He was tolerated because he had his uses – and this usefulness was just enough to maintain his position in the eyes of his masters. Helpfully, in times of war 'he used to send out galleys to interrupt Frankish shipping'. Far less helpfully, however, he continued his activities even in times of truce, much to the irritation and embarrassment of the local Muslim rulers: they were engaged in delicate diplomacy with the Franks and half a dozen other regional players at any given time. 'More than once,' wrote Ibn al-Athir, a contemporary historian from Mosul, 'the Franks complained of this to [Sultan] al-Adil at Damascus and to [Sultan] al-Aziz in Egypt, but they did not stop Usama.'[10]

The Franks eventually had enough of Usama's activities, and mustered an army to march against him. This placed the local Muslim authorities in an extremely awkward position. They had some sympathy with the Franks regarding Usama's wayward activities – after all, they had tried and failed to control him themselves. But they could not let the Christians recapture the important port of Beirut.

The sultan of Damascus tried to effect a compromise of sorts. He knew he could not trust Usama, but equally he could not let Beirut fall to the enemy. Instead he arranged a way to destroy the port: if it was going to be such a liability, they could at least deny the crusaders its facilities and fortifications. Accordingly, Damascene troops 'moved to Marj al-Ayun [near the Litani River, in early October 1197] and a detachment of the army went to Beirut with the intention of demolishing it. They [partially] razed the city wall [on 21 October] and embarked on the destruction of the houses.'[11]

With his characteristically piratical combination of charm, wheedling and (very possibly) bribery, 'Usama stopped them and undertook to hold the city [himself].' The sultan's men foolishly believed him and left Beirut. They made the gesture of having a brief skirmish with the local crusaders based in Sidon, just to show willing, and then withdrew altogether.

The Franks could not believe their luck. On 23 October they set out for Beirut. When they drew near, 'Usama and all the Muslims that were there fled, so the Franks took it with no effort and without any fighting.' This was, as Ibn al-Athir wrote bitterly, a betrayal, and with his departure Beirut was 'easy prey' for the Franks.[12]

The pirate chancer had massively over-promised.

26

❖

Vikings on Crusade

We like our history in 'boxes'.

There are labels to those 'boxes', with names like 'Romans' or 'Victorians', 'Vikings' or 'Crusaders'. It is an easy form of communication, and it resonates well with our fundamental intellectual laziness.

But these labels have more to do with structuring history courses at schools, or with firing the imagination of bored children, than they have with reality. History is never so neat on the ground. The 'boxes' bleed into each other and blur. Like Godric, the participants often fail to realise which box they belong in. For a northern world in transition, it was entirely possible for 'Vikings' to be 'Crusaders' as well. And the Norsemen, famous scourges of Christianity, could also, by the end of the eleventh century and the beginning of the twelfth, be among its most pious and fearsome supporters.

Viking twilight and crusading pirates

The crusade of King Sigurd of Norway is a good example. The story, as told by the Icelandic historian Snorri Sturluson in his famous *Heimskringla*, shows the permeable and shifting boundaries between piracy, trade and pilgrimage. As with Norse traders, the difference between a crusading expedition and a Viking pirate fleet was often slight – an almost imperceptible blend of opportunity and necessity, rather than anything more formal.[1]

In 1107, Sigurd led his people off to the Holy Land, in the same way as his not-too-distant ancestors had taken them raiding and 'aviking'. As the *Heimskringla* put it, 'so great a fleet came together for the prudent prince, picked and faithful, that sixty ships sailed, gaily planked, hence by holy heaven's decree'. They travelled down towards the southern seas, in this Nordic variant of the great crusading adventure.[2]

The trip was feasible, but not straightforward. Sigurd's fleet left Norway in the autumn of 1107, and spent the winter at the court of Henry I in England. While they were there, some pious and adventurous Englishmen like Godric may perhaps have joined the expedition. In the spring of 1108 they set sail again as the weather improved, and paused in the autumn in the north-west of Spain, on the Atlantic coastline of Galicia. This was still Christian territory, but their Viking roots remained very close to the surface: feeling that inadequate food supplies were being made available by their reluctant hosts, Sigurd and his men attacked the local castle and seized everything in it.

Their journey became ever more eventful. When they set off again, sailing down the coast of modern-day Portugal, they were at last in Muslim-occupied territory. The expedition could now take on the more legitimate appearance of a 'crusade'. They soon ran into an enemy squadron further down the coast, defeated it and captured eight ships to add to their fleet. Shortly afterwards, they arrived at Muslim-held Sintra, where they captured the castle and looted the town. From there they moved on to attack nearby Lisbon, where they similarly took huge quantities of booty.

Alcácer do Sol, further south in Portugal, was the next stop: the pilgrim-pirates attacked the town and pillaged it so thoroughly that they boasted of emptying it entirely of people and treasure. This victory was followed by a naval battle, in which they beat another Muslim fleet. That victory was quickly accompanied by a successful attack on a pirate base on one of the nearby islands.[3]

As the cold winter of 1108–1109 continued, so too did the battles and raiding. The Norwegians moved down into the Mediterranean. The formerly Christian islands of the Balearics had been lost since the Muslim invasions of the eighth century, so the Norwegians saw them as fair game for a crusading fleet. They sailed down to the islands and defeated the Muslims in further battles around Ibiza and Minorca. In the spring of 1109, the Norsemen finally arrived in Christian Sicily – a state run, appropriately enough under the circumstances, by the descendants of Viking settlers in Normandy. Friendly relations were quickly established with count (later king) Roger and his Sicilian–Norman government.[4]

The Norwegian crusading expedition finally arrived in the Holy Land in the summer of 1110. They found the naval situation in the eastern Mediterranean at tipping point. The Fatimid Egyptian regime still controlled several of the highly fortified cities of the Palestinian coast – and they did so very largely with the aid of their powerful navy. Inevitably, capturing these cities and securing supply lines back to Europe was a major strategic priority for the Frankish settlers. King Sigurd and his men could not have come at a more opportune time.[5]

As they were sailing into the Levant from the west, the Norwegians came first to the Egyptian military base at Ascalon. In the best Norse traditions, Sigurd and his army were spoiling for a fight. They had already fought at least eight battles on their way to the eastern Mediterranean and were hardened veterans. Now that they had arrived in the waters of the Latin Kingdom of Jerusalem, the Norwegians could transition seamlessly from their roles as Vikings and pirates into crusaders and *Milites Christi* – soldiers of Christ.

Most of the Egyptian fleet was in harbour further up the Palestinian coast, however, and the garrison of Ascalon was in no hurry to face off with the newcomers. The Norwegians did their best to provoke them. They were suitably intimidating, sailing close to the shore and 'with much equipment, much armour, a strong army, with sixty busses [that is, large north European ships] and ten thousand warlike men, [Sigurd] anchored in the harbour of the town of Ascalon . . . in order to see if any men from the town would meet him by land or sea'.[6]

The Fatimid troops in the town decided, very sensibly, not to give the Norwegians the fight they were so looking forward to. Instead, they 'kept quiet and did not dare to come out'. Eventually, Sigurd and his men got bored and sailed further on up the coast to crusader-held territory.[7]

The Norwegians landed at the port of Jaffa. The local Franks were delighted and suitably impressed. As one chronicler (the king's chaplain, who may have been present at their landing) later wrote, 'their leader was a very handsome youth, a kinsman of the king of that country . . . [King Baldwin I of Jerusalem] conversed with them in a friendly manner . . . begging them to remain . . . in the Holy Land for even a very little time.'[8]

But there had to be priorities. Perhaps incongruously to our eyes, these ruthless killers instantly and effortlessly morphed into pious pilgrims. Having exchanged a few pleasantries with King Baldwin, Sigurd and his warriors went to visit the holy places in Jerusalem. After fulfilling their religious devotions in the Holy Sepulchre, they then marched on to the Jordan 'where the Christian ceremony was performed in the name of Lord Jesus'.[9]

Even Muslim commentators wrote with no hint of irony of the easy way in which the Norsemen had combined the Viking pleasures of raiding with their religious duties, all conducted in the name of the ostensibly pacifistic religion of Christianity. As Ibn al-Qalanisi drily put it, they came 'for the purpose of making the pilgrimage and raiding the lands of Islam'.[10]

Once the religious fervour of the pilgrim fleet had been satisfied, discussions about military objectives could be concluded. The Christians, both Norwegians and local Franks, seem to have felt that Ascalon would be a great prize, but eventually decided against it, probably because the elaborate fortifications of the Fatimid garrison town made it too tough a nut to crack. They decided instead on a plan to attack the coastal city of Sidon. As Fulcher of Chartres wrote, the joint Christian armies 'adopted a more glorious project, to advance upon and besiege Sidon. The king moved his army from . . . Acre; the Norwegians proceeded by ship from Jaffa.'[11]

Any naval help was eagerly received in the Latin East, but the northern fleets were particularly welcome. While the Italians asked, not entirely unreasonably, for a large part of the spoils and for a permanent trading presence in the captured cities in return for their military assistance, the northerners were just religious tourists passing through. Their help came with far fewer strings attached. There was none of the hard haggling that accompanied a request for the Italians to help. The Norwegians were much more obliging: they merely said that 'wherever the king wished to go with his army, there they would gladly go by sea at the same time, provided that he would supply the necessary sustenance for them'.[12]

Disappointingly from a Muslim perspective, the reputation of the Nordic fleet preceded them, and was reflected in the passive performance of the Egyptian navy. The Fatimid

> fleet was lying hidden in the port of Tyre. From it the Saracens very often went in piratical fashion against our Christian pilgrims, and thus protected and encouraged the maritime cities . . . belonging to the [Egyptians]. But when the Saracens heard reports of the Norwegians, they dared not come forth from the port of Tyre and do battle with them.[13]

The Egyptian navy, which had been raiding along the Palestinian coast in the weeks before Sigurd's arrival, was clearly cowed by the size and ferocity of the Norwegian fleet. Even the Muslim sources were bemused at the inability or unwillingness of the Egyptian navy to intervene. As one chronicler commented laconically, 'the Egyptian fleet was then stationed at the port of Tyre but it was unable to bring support to Sidon'.[14]

With Sidon isolated, the Frankish army could begin an undisturbed and intensive siege. Large catapults were constructed and used to good effect. But the decisive weapon was a large siege tower which the Franks constructed. The city was besieged for forty-seven days and fell on 5 December 1110. The triumphant and devout King Sigurd was generous in victory: he gave his share of the spoils to the desperately poor King Baldwin to help with the defence of his young kingdom.

When he left the Holy Land, Sigurd and his men sailed first to Byzantine Cyprus, and then turned east to the imperial capital, Constantinople. There they were entertained lavishly and hospitably by Emperor Alexius Comnenus. Sigurd eventually gave all his ships to the emperor in return for horses, guides and other assistance in taking the land route back home to Scandinavia. Like the ships, many of his men also stayed behind, adding to the ranks of the famous axe-wielding Byzantine Varangian guard.

The king and his remaining followers took the roads (and, wherever possible, the rivers) back up north, travelling through Bulgaria, Hungary and Bavaria, and then further north on into Denmark. Given the length of the sea voyage to the East, the return journey went surprisingly smoothly. Sigurd and his men arrived back in Norway in 1111.[15]

This strange pilgrimage-cum-raid – a journey by Vikings who effort-lessly combined ferocious warrior skills with genuine devotion to a reli-gion of peace and love – had come to an end. The Nordic church-militant was home at last.

Northmen and their ships

So, what does this extended and supremely violent pilgrimage tell us about medieval piracy, Vikings and crusading?

Mostly, it tells us that the definitions and labels were so blurred that they were on occasion almost interchangeable. It is also clear that diver-sions were sometimes unavoidable and occasionally welcomed. Provisioning and paying for an expedition of this size was difficult. Any opportunity to underwrite the costs and replenish supplies was extremely welcome – hence the frequent and bloodthirsty pauses for raiding. It took Sigurd three years to get down to the crusader states, and that slow pace was at least partly explained by the logistical nightmare of long-distance travel by large groups of people in medieval times. Ironically, the overland trip back to Norway was far quicker, taking only a few months.

But the Norwegians were not the only northern sailors to make the long, dangerous journey down into the eastern Mediterranean.

In March 1098, for instance, an English squadron arrived in the East, carrying Italian pilgrims and equipment which they had picked up from the Byzantine military. They were probably part of the Christian fleet that occupied Jaffa in June 1099, as the Fatimid army retreated in the face of the First Crusade. Similarly, another English fleet arrived in Jaffa in May 1102, full of soldiers and pilgrims from England, Germany and France. And we know that in 1107 more ships arrived on the coast of the crusader states from Flanders and Brabant, all with large numbers of men on board.[16]

The main problem for these northern fleets was that the prevailing winds made it far easier to enter the Mediterranean than to leave it. The Straits of Gibraltar were always particularly difficult to negotiate from east to west – hence Sigurd's decision to leave his ships in Byzantium, and travel home by the overland route. But on the plus side, at least from the point of view of the Franks, it also meant that northern squadrons, once they had arrived in the eastern Mediterranean, were motivated to stay there for longer periods of time.[17]

A trip to the Holy Land was difficult, expensive and slow. But it was not impossible: with sufficient determination, it could be done. The northerners were helped in this by the robust ships they had developed. The Atlantic and the North Sea were tough places to do business, and that was reflected in the resilience of the shipping that evolved to survive in that environment.

There were two main types of northern ship. The basic distinction was between 'warships' and 'cargo ships', though of course, in practice, both types could be used in a fight. Warships tended to be long, and low in the water. They had a single, large square sail, but also a number of oars on either side. These were slender ships, designed to carry men and weapons rather than anything more substantial.

Northern cargo ships, on the other hand, were large sailing vessels often called '*keels*' at first, though by the twelfth century they were known as '*byrthings*' or, in Latin, '*bucius*'. As we have seen with Saint Godric, these ships gradually became known as '*busses*'. They had positions for a few oars, which were mainly there for emergencies or docking. The busses carried between sixty and eighty men, and had room, obviously, for cargo goods. As with King Sigurd and his Norwegian pilgrims, it is noticeable that shipping from the north of Europe tended to come down into the Mediterranean in large convoys: numbers were important, both for their own protection and to allow them to attack others they might meet along their route more easily.[18]

The north European trading vessel was useful to have in the eastern Mediterranean. It would carry more cargo (or people) than a slim, light galley, and needed a smaller crew, as it was powered by the wind and sails. This gave it significant advantages, such as a longer range, because it did not need to carry as much water for rowers as galleys did. The high sides associated with this type of ship also made it more difficult to board – particularly vital in an age before gunpowder and cannons.[19]

Northern sailors, whether pirates or not, were always welcome in the Latin East.

The northern pirate king

One sailor who realised early on that there could be an attractive interplay between commerce, crusading and piracy was Winemar, the so-called 'pirate king'. In another example of the multi-faceted, easily blended seafaring activity of the time, he and his men played a mysterious but important role in the foundation of the crusader states.

As always, the seemingly incongruous mixture of roles was rarely so contradictory in practice. It is certainly possible to describe Winemar as a 'professional pirate', for instance, operating in the region with a large number of men and ships – though it is hard to know how to define that term fully under the chaotic circumstances of the time. He operated a substantial private naval squadron in the eastern Mediterranean, and his band of followers included men from Frisia, Denmark and Flanders.

Winemar's piratical expedition came in time to help the armies of the First Crusade. Or, if one were being more cynical, to exploit the opportunities for plunder which the expedition was throwing up in its wake – like voracious seagulls following a fishing fleet. This was a co-operative but loose affiliation, born of mutual self-interest. The northern pirate fleet might be helpful on occasion, but the seamen could hardly be called 'crusaders' in the strictest sense of the word.

Winemar and his men were necessarily a fairly motley crew. But they were so numerous – and presumably so experienced by this point – that they were a very welcome addition to the exhausted crusaders.

They had arrived in the East in 1097, and docked in the mouth of the River Cydnus, just downstream from Tarsus, in modern-day Turkey. Probably not coincidently, this was soon after his compatriot Baldwin of Boulogne had captured the town. Far more coincidentally, however, this was the same Baldwin who was later to become king of Jerusalem and require rescue by yet another northern (putative) pirate – Godric of Finchale.[20]

Baldwin's men were standing guard on the walls of Tarsus. From this vantage point they

> observed from afar in the middle of the sea, three miles from the city, a great number of ships of different kinds and workmanship . . . And they saw men disembarking from these same ships onto the seashore and dividing among themselves a great deal of booty, which they had brought together over a long period of time, nearly eight years.

When they reached Tarsus, the men explained 'that they had been pirates for eight years until this day'. If true, an eight-year voyage meant, of course, that their activities pre-dated the First Crusade, making them freelance pirates who morphed into crusaders, rather than crusaders who discovered a predilection for piracy.

Such distinctions were fine indeed, however. As well as being pirates, they also said that 'they had come for the sake of pilgrimage and to worship in Jerusalem'. And, strange as it may seem to us, they may well have been speaking truthfully about their pious intent: time after time in the crusades we find the attractions of loot or conquest sitting very comfortably, with no obvious sense of hypocrisy or tension, alongside the genuine motivations of religious fervour.[21]

The bravado of these pirates even extended to claims of association with the nobility. Winemar was described, in suitably vague terms, as the leader of a 'naval association', and as 'the chief and master of all the sworn brothers [of the pirate group], from the land of Boulogne'. Rather less convincingly, he also let it be known that he was 'a member of the household of Count Eustace [of Boulogne]'.

Helpfully for Baldwin of Boulogne, who, as we have seen, seems to have had extraordinary luck where pirates were concerned, they also constituted a small, but much-needed army in their own right. These pirate-marines were willing to bolster the garrison of Tarsus, perhaps because they welcomed the opportunity to rest on dry land, having been at sea for so many years. This freed up Baldwin and his tiny band of soldiers to pursue their own interests more vigorously elsewhere.

Winemar and his pirates

> left their ships and entered the city of Tarsus with Baldwin, taking the booty and all their baggage, and they rejoiced and feasted for some days on all the good things of the land there. Then . . . three hundred were chosen from the naval force to guard and defend the city. Two hundred more were appointed from Baldwin's troops. Having arranged and organised this, they set out with their combined weapons and forces, and they marched up the royal road to the sound of trumpets and horns in a great display of power.[22]

Less helpfully, however, they soon reverted to type – for such men the lure of plunder easily trumped other, less lucrative, military priorities. During the siege of Antioch, when the success of the entire crusade was in the balance and when their assistance was most sorely needed, Winemar took the opportunity to go back to the coast in search of easier pickings.

He and his men 'sailed again for Latakia', which, incidentally, was already held by their fellow Christians of the Byzantine empire, rather than by the Muslim enemy. The pirate fleet 'laid siege to the walled town by sea and overcame it by his forces and captured it, not offering or granting any help or consideration to his Christian brothers who were besieging Antioch'. Instead, they overcame the garrison of Latakia by a naval siege and a fierce attack by land. Winemar of Boulogne, master of pirates (*piratarum magistri*), and his men were not making themselves popular with the crusaders' Byzantine allies.[23]

Having taken possession of the town, the pirates settled down for an extended bout of relaxation. The chronicler Albert of Aachen made it sound, in his understated way, like a romantic long weekend city-break: they enjoyed, he wrote, 'some leisure, and they delighted in the benefits of the territory and town'. The reality was inevitably far more rowdy.[24]

While they were busy drinking themselves senseless (as befitted pirates resting between forays), the empire struck back. The Byzantine army wanted to recover its old base and went on the offensive. When the imperial forces arrived, the drunk or severely hungover pirates were 'struck down and overwhelmed by the Turcopoles [light horse archers] and soldiers of the [Byzantines]; the town's citadel was recaptured, [and] Winemar himself was taken and put under guard in prison'.[25]

Winemar's activities seem to have caused an embarrassing diplomatic incident between the crusaders and their (entirely understandably) suspicious Byzantine hosts. Getting them out of jail required sensitive negotiations and intervention at the highest level. Winemar was 'sent to prison, but by Duke Godfrey [of Bouillon]'s intervention he was brought out of prison and from fetters after some considerable time'.[26]

Winemar's stay in the dungeons of Latakia had been a long and unpleasant one. Given that he had killed many of the garrison during his attacks, it is unlikely that anyone in the port was going out of their way to make his stay a comfortable one. Some torture was probably involved. Either way, his confinement was not congenial, and we are told that even after he was released, he still 'suffered from severe pain when he was brought back to Antioch'.[27]

And so, on that appropriately gruesome note, he disappears from history. We do not know the fate of Winemar of Boulogne. But, as was the case with most pirates, it was unlikely to have involved a long and peaceful retirement.

Viking knights

Even though Winemar was a far from universally popular man, naval assistance from the northern Christian lands was particularly important in the first decades of the crusader states, when capturing the Muslim coastal cities was a major priority. Over time, that need diminished, but the 'northern crusading-pirate' tradition continued.

Around 1150, for instance, we find Viking pirates on crusade once more. An incident is recorded in which a northern fleet on an extended pilgrimage to Rome and the Holy Land, attacked and captured a Muslim dromond – descriptions of the crew suggest that it was probably a Fatimid Egyptian vessel, largely manned by African sailors and marines. Northern sailors continued to find time to mix business with pleasure.[28]

Even a century later, in the last decades of the crusader states, the strangely linked traditions of Viking piracy and piety continued. In 1251–1252, mercenary pirates were on crusade with the French army at Caesarea. According to John of Joinville, Elinart, lord of Seninghem, arrived at Caesarea and recounted a voyage not too dissimilar to that of King Sigurd. He 'told us that he had hired his ship in the kingdom of Norway' and 'in coming to the king he skirted all of Spain and had to pass through the Straits of [Gibraltar] . . . The king retained him in his service along with his nine other knights.' Along the way, Elinart boasted that 'he and his men took up hunting lions and caught a number of them at great risk to themselves. They would shoot at the lions as they were spurring their horses on as hard as they could.' It was a story so bizarre that it was probably true.[29]

And so these Frankish and late-Viking pirates, with their lion-hunting, arrow-firing crusader knights, carried on about their eccentric business – as strange and enduring an image as one is likely to find in the crusades. They were the heirs to the traditions of restless and bloody Viking entrepreneurialism, and their eccentric activities seem endearingly appropriate. And their refusal to be put into the rigid 'boxes' we have constructed for our history remains resolutely impressive.

27

The Pirate Prince and the First Sea Lords

We tend to view piracy as a downmarket career – an option taken by desperate men on the fringes of society, pushed into desperate acts. Or perhaps as a violent gesture by defiant renegades, bitter proto-anarchists fighting back against the demeaning roles that society had forced onto them.

But that was not necessarily true in the Middle Ages. Even the most upmarket crusaders could be attracted to piracy if the conditions were right. And, once they had had a taste of the rewards that went with success, it was a habit that was hard to shake off.

Reynald the pirate prince

Reynald of Châtillon, the famous Frankish commander, was a case in point. Some men took to piracy as a last resort, but for Reynald it was often his first choice.

Reynald had many of the natural talents of a pirate. Volatile, aggressive and bold, he was, according to one contemporary chronicler who knew and despised him, 'a man of violent impulses, both in sinning and in repenting'.[1]

Born a younger son without money or lands, Reynald had clawed his way to the top with a thick skin and an over-abundance of self-belief. He was charismatic and robustly confident – many would say arrogant. Reynald had left France as a young man and had come to the Frankish colonies in the East to seek his fortune and make a name for himself. He served as a mercenary knight in the Latin Kingdom of Jerusalem, and in 1153 he was employed as part of the royal army that captured the heavily fortified Egyptian military base at Ascalon. His big break came soon afterwards.

The principality of Antioch, the northernmost surviving crusader state, was in need of a male ruler. The previous prince, Raymond of Poitiers, had died along with most of his shattered army, on the blood-soaked battlefield of Inab on 29 June 1149. His widow, Princess Constance, needed a husband to command the defences of her vulnerable principality.

Or that was what everyone said. She, however, did not see it that way.

Constance enjoyed her independence and her power too much. Although a range of rich and powerful candidates were found for her (including a member of the Byzantine ruling family), all were found wanting. And despite being penniless and without obvious prospects, she chose Reynald: his charismatic energy and raw, animal sex appeal trumped the logic of power and wealth. Constance fell in love with him, perhaps on one of the frequent trips during which the royal army of Jerusalem came to rescue her beleaguered state. Despite huge misgivings among her advisers and most other contemporary observers, she and Reynald were married in the spring of 1153.

Ironically, and despite the widespread disapproval, Constance was not entirely wrong in her choice of spouse. In many ways, Reynald was exactly the sort of man needed to rule a war-torn, medieval frontier state. He was personally strong, tirelessly brave, aggressive and restless – he was an energetic and ferocious wartime leader. Unfortunately, however useful these characteristics might be, they were also accompanied by a sense of brutality which easily tipped over beyond the normal actions of a calm and moderate ruler: when Reynald lost his temper, almost anything could happen.

The people of Christian Cyprus found out all too soon what consequences that temper might have for them.

In 1155, Reynald was offered money by the Byzantine authorities if he would intervene with his troops to stop the Armenian ruler, Thoros II, from raiding imperial territory. Eager to prove his effectiveness as a ruler and, more importantly, keen to raise ready cash to rebuild the defences of his new principality, Reynald and his small army did just that – the Armenians were put back in their box. The prince sat back and waited for his cash.

It did not come. Perhaps through incompetence or treachery, or maybe because of a misunderstanding, the Byzantines seem to have been unwilling to pay what Reynald thought he had been promised. He went ballistic.

Reynald's response was interesting – and a demonstration of just how tempting was the instant gratification offered by a pirate raid. Rather than starting the expensive and risky business of gathering an army and setting off north to besiege Byzantine castles or skirmish with Byzantine cavalry, he wanted somewhere easier to pillage – somewhere with lots of villages and poorly defended small towns with opportunities for looting. He set about creating a pirate fleet with which to wreak his revenge.

One of the easy attractions of state-sponsored piracy was the cost. Most of the expense – at least for someone like Reynald, who had control of several ports – could either be deferred or offset altogether by outsourcing. There were many freelance pirates of all religions and nationalities operating in the eastern Mediterranean at this time. There were also hundreds of merchant vessels plying the same waters.

These ships were often confined to port (or forced to restrict themselves to short journeys) for much of the year. The main crossings to Europe only took place during two relatively brief periods – one in the spring and the other in the late summer. With these unemployed or underemployed resources to hand, a naval raiding force could be gathered relatively quickly and cheaply. And in true piratical fashion, much of the cost could be defrayed by offering participants a share of the plunder.

Reynald's small pirate fleet set off for the vulnerable island of Cyprus, despite the fact that, as one Frankish historian noted, it 'had always been useful and friendly to our realm and . . . had a large population of Christians'. This was the start of Reynald's long track record as someone who put his own personal interests above those of the broader community.[2]

The Byzantine authorities were not taken completely unawares. Their spies in Antioch and the port of Saint Simeon had sent advance warnings, and there are indications that even some of the citizens of Antioch, shocked that Reynald might attack his fellow Christians, tried to warn the Cypriots of his plans.

The Cypriots mobilised their local defence forces to meet the pirates in battle. But the ferocity of the attack was too much for them: 'Prince Reynald, marching upon them, at once defeated their army and shattered their forces completely so that thereafter no one might dare to raise a hand against him. He then completely overran the island without meeting any opposition, destroyed cities, and wrecked fortresses.' With the Byzantine militia routed, most of the island was at Reynald's mercy.[3]

The punishment he inflicted on the innocent Cypriots was not merely about the money: Reynald wanted to embarrass the Byzantine government by showing just how little protection it could offer the people. His way of doing this was to allow his men to go wild – to burn, to pillage and to kill. Very visibly, and to make a point, he also encouraged his men to rape:

he broke into monasteries of men and women alike and shamefully abused nuns and tender maidens. Although the precious vestments and the amount of gold and silver which he carried off were great, yet the loss of these was regarded as nothing in comparison with the violence done to chastity.

By the time he and his men left the island, 'he had wreaked his fury upon the innocent Cypriots and had perpetrated upon them and upon their wives and children outrages abominable in the sight of both God and men'.[4]

The cash was useful too, of course. Nothing of value was left behind. 'For several days,' wrote William of Tyre (admittedly no fan of Reynald), his

> forces continued to ravage the whole country; and since there was none to offer resistance, they showed no mercy to age or sex, neither did they recognize difference of condition. Finally, laden with a vast amount of riches and spoils of every kind, they returned to the seashore. When the ships were ready, they embarked and set sail for Antioch. There, within a short time all the wealth which had been so wickedly acquired was dissipated.[5]

Even by the low standards of the time, the behaviour of Reynald and his raiders stood out as being particularly abominable. Gregory the Priest, a twelfth-century Armenian historian, wrote bitterly that

> finding the inhabitants nonchalant and unprepared [for defence], they treated them as the infidels would, devastating their towns and villages, depriving them of their homes and possessions, and maltreating many of the Greek clergymen, whose noses and ears they cut off. When the emperor and his high officials learned of this, they were deeply chagrined by what was done, but for the time being were unable to do anything.[6]

Thankfully for the Cypriots, who must have feared a repeat performance of this outrage, Reynald's inchoate career as a 'pirate prince' came to a temporary end shortly afterwards. In November 1160, he was captured by Muslim cavalry while on a typically bold long-range raid around Marash.[7]

He was taken back to Aleppo in chains, and publicly humiliated at some length (in unspecified, but doubtless imaginative ways) in front of the town's entire population. Then, when the entertainment value was exhausted, he was thrown into a hole in the citadel's dungeons. There he stayed for sixteen long years. Eventually, in 1176, after privations and tortures that he chose never to talk about, he was released.

But he was not broken. If anything, he came out of captivity even more aggressive, even more enraged than when he went in. Perhaps channelling his anger had been his way of staying sane during a captivity that would have driven less arrogant men into madness. What was indisputable, however, was that Reynald, who had never been a fan of Islam even when in a good mood, now held even firmer views about the religion and its adherents. He devoted the rest of his life to avenging himself as actively as possible on those who had tormented him for all those years in prison.[8]

His wife, Princess Constance of Antioch had died in 1163, over a decade before his release. This was far more than just an emotional jolt for Reynald. He only held his position as prince of Antioch through her, and with Constance gone, he needed to move on. Undeterred, the indefatigable and strangely attractive Reynald married Stephanie of Milly, a highly sought-after widow and heiress to the fief of the Transjordan – the frontier state within a state which the Franks called the lordship of Oultrejourdain. King Baldwin IV also gave him the town of Nablus to add to his already substantial and strategically vital lands.

By 1175, Reynald had extensive property and his own private army once again. He was back in business, and able to express in style his inner feelings about his erstwhile captors.

With characteristic, almost sociopathic boldness, and completely undeterred by the landlocked nature of his new domains, Reynald decided to revive his long-interrupted career as a buccaneer and raider. He already had some experience of long-distance raiding on land, and particularly raids designed to embarrass Saladin and disrupt his plans. In 1181 he had launched an attack on the town of Tayma, a Muslim target over two hundred kilometres from the borders of his lordship. His troops did not manage to get there, as they were intercepted by the Damascene army; but it shows the direction that Reynald was taking in his military planning – and just how audacious he could be.[9]

His next step was spectacular. Anyone unlucky enough to be standing in the Negev Desert in January 1183 would have witnessed a strange sight. Five small, prefabricated warships were being dragged and carried across the desert from Reynald's strongholds in the lordship of the Transjordan. Entirely implausibly, they were inching their way down to the Red Sea. This was not a spontaneous or impetuous act. Lack of suitable timber in the Transjordan meant that the wood for these ships had to be brought across from the coastal cities of Palestine. And the whole process of creating these 'boat-kits' involved some two years of secret preparations.

They were transported down to the Red Sea by Reynald and his men in the winter of 1182–1183, helped by the local Bedouin – men who were always for hire, and who had no love for Saladin or his new, annoyingly successful, overly centralised and irritatingly intrusive regime. There the ships were quickly assembled and launched into the water.[10]

Two of the ships, under the personal command of Reynald, began with a successful attack on the castle of Ayla (now known as Eilat), which had been lost to Saladin in 1171. Reynald seems to have stayed behind at Ayla to enjoy his new fortress and to oversee repairs and reprovisioning. This was a strategically important point on the Red Sea from which to disrupt Muslim communications between the two main parts of Saladin's empire – the cash cow of Egypt and the military powerhouse of Syria.[11]

The other ships sailed on down the Red Sea, raiding as they went. This extended seaborne raid, a kind of maritime *chevauchée*, continued for six or seven weeks, during which they attacked Muslim shipping and several coastal towns, including Aydhab.[12]

The Frankish ships on the Red Sea were eventually defeated by Saladin's admiral, Husam al-Din Lu'lu, but not before they had launched a small raiding force inland. These troops were tracked down by Muslim soldiers at some point between late January and April 1183. The cornered Franks, some 170 men in total, were offered quarter and surrendered on those terms. Saladin, whose elaborate PR programme had been severely embarrassed by the whole incident, reneged on the deal, despite the qualms of some of his advisers: he had all the prisoners ritually killed.

The raid caused problems for Saladin. There was some loss of pride, which was reflected in the somewhat hysterical nature of the executions – and, as a usurper, Saladin was always overly conscious about anything that chipped away at his legitimacy. There was also some disruption in terms of communications and trade. But these were all very short-term problems. The Ayyubid navy seems to have dealt with the small Frankish craft relatively easily. Reynald would have needed a much larger fleet to create a long-standing presence, and hence a long-standing problem. Although the Frankish force was big enough to surprise and shock, it was far too small and too far from any substantial Christian base to be anything more than a temporary nuisance.[13]

Reynald's objectives in launching the raid are still the subject of debate. It may have been designed to gather booty and cause destruction; or perhaps to cause economic disruption in the Red Sea. Both of these outcomes would have been positive from Reynald's perspective: in this they would have been similar to the objectives of his attack on Tayma, just two years earlier. He also had a long track record of attacking Muslim caravans, with, again, similar aims. Slightly more subtly, it may also have been launched to embarrass and humiliate Saladin, to show his inability to defend the *Mare Nostrum* of the Islamic world. These objectives are, of course, not mutually contradictory. On the contrary, they were, to a large extent, mutually supportive.

Some contemporary Muslim historians (though not necessarily those who were best informed) believed that the holy cities of Medina and Mecca, and the body of the prophet Muhammad, were the real targets of the attack. This does not seem very likely. Although some of the Frankish raiders were captured near Medina, they had spent the previous forty-five days sailing up and down the Red Sea – hardly the actions of men looking to launch a surprise attack on the most sensitive site in the Muslim world. They may have come to see Medina as a possible target for their attention, and identified it as an opportunity; but it does not seem to have been the strategic goal for the expedition.[14]

The raid itself was probably designed by Reynald to be a provocative (and hopefully lucrative) hit-and-run raid. It was also part of a bigger scheme, taking a broader but similarly aggressive military perspective. Reynald was an opportunistic pirate and raider, but there was always far more to him than that. His actions in attacking the towns of Tayma and Ayla, intercepting a succession of Muslim caravans, and launching raids further down the Red Sea were all consistent with a long-term strategy – that of disrupting Saladin's plans to consolidate the Muslim Middle East and of wreaking as much economic devastation as possible, in order to deflect him from his task of destroying the crusader states.

Reynald would, of course, always enjoy the short-term rewards of the booty that he could reap by such raiding. But his buccaneering career was never just about tactics. Saladin executed him with his own hands just a few years later, in 1187, after his capture at the battle of Hattin. The very personal nature of his death is, in a way, a back-handed validation that his strategy had worked.[15]

Reynald had succeeded in getting under Saladin's skin. For the first time, after five centuries of Muslim invasions into the heartlands of Christianity, a rogue pirate and ageing Frankish lord had found a way to strike back – and Saladin could not tolerate this outrage. The high-profile executions of Reynald's men in different cities around Saladin's new Ayyubid empire were deliberate: Saladin was determined to show the consequences of having embarrassed him.[16]

For Reynald, piracy was a flexible way of projecting power, even in a situation where he and his men were vastly outnumbered. It was a perfect conduit for asymmetrical warfare. For a relatively small outlay, it meant that even a minor regional power (such as the lordship of an elderly Frankish frontiersman) could at least make its presence – and its pique – felt at the highest level.

Reynald could never hope to meet and overcome Saladin's vast armies in the field. But he could take the fight to the enemy on his own terms through the bloody medium of piracy.

The first sea lords

Sadly, the cheap but effective tactic that Reynald had employed in his attack on Christian Cyprus in 1155 was soon copied.

In 1161, advanced plans were in place for the Byzantine emperor to marry Melisende, the sister of Raymond III, the proud count of Tripoli, ruler of the crusader state which occupied much of modern Lebanon. When Raymond found that the emperor's agents were secretly looking to make other arrangements, he was uncontrollably enraged.

Distraught at the public humiliation of having the Byzantine emperor renege on what he thought had been a cast-iron agreement, Raymond thrashed out in anger. In the final stages of the betrothal process he had incurred massive expenses. These included the costly commissioning of 'twelve galleys to be built and completely equipped, for he had intended to accompany his sister to her husband'. Raymond quickly found a more violent use for the wedding fleet.[17]

Piracy, as always, had attractions – when used as a form of terrorism, it was difficult to stop and allowed a much smaller state to project power in a relatively low-risk way. Although Raymond 'realized that the emperor was the most powerful monarch on earth and that his own strength was entirely inadequate to do him any injury, yet resentment drove him to action'. Piracy was the perfect way of expressing his hurt and anger.[18]

With deadly irony, he 'ordered the galleys which he had prepared [for the wedding celebrations] to be armed. Then he summoned pirates and desperados, men who had committed the most shocking crimes, and delivered the ships into their charge with orders to devastate the lands of the emperor without mercy.' The raid was to be thorough in its ghastly, remorseless retribution. As William of Tyre wrote, 'neither age, sex, nor condition was to be spared; everything was to be given to the flames without distinction, including churches and monasteries, and the work of pillage and rape carried on far and wide'.[19]

The pirate contractors were brutally effective in their task: 'both in the islands and on the lands bordering on the sea, they interpreted the count's orders in the widest sense. On all sides they plundered, burned, and massacred.' Echoing Reynald's harrying of Cyprus just a few years earlier, they deliberately sought to outrage and humiliate the Byzantine authorities and the communities that they were so visibly failing to protect. It is not clear precisely which Byzantine lands were ravaged; and ultimately, perhaps, that did not really matter. What was really important was to recoup the costs of the betrothal and provide a convenient vent for Raymond's anger.[20]

The appalling behaviour of Reynald of Châtillon and Raymond III of Tripoli in launching piratical raids, including attacks on fellow Christians, was exceptional, but not unique. Piracy was an option that clearly had attractions for a certain kind of nobleman. Other Frankish lords – and particularly, of course, those with ports in their lands – were also capable of turning to piracy when they were presented with the opportunity, or when they felt they had run out of other options.

Gerard, lord of Sidon and ancestor of Julian Grenier, the inveterate gambler, was one such renegade. As we have seen, the Latin Kingdom of Jerusalem never had a standing navy, but pirates, freebooters and mercenaries were occasionally called upon to fill the same role, at least temporarily. In the 1150s, the 'admiral' of this pop-up, rag-tag fleet was a certain Gerard, lord of Sidon. Gerard, as a member of the small group of noble warrior-leaders of the Latin East, doubtless knew Reynald of

Châtillon well. He followed his career with interest. And like Reynald, Gerard was an arrogant, intemperate and aggressive man.

During the Frankish siege of the Egyptian base at Ascalon in 1152–1153, a flotilla of rented merchant ships and self-motivated pirates was brought together in an attempt to blockade the town. This freelance squadron 'of fifteen ships, beaked [galleys] and equipped to sail, was placed in the command of Gerard of Sidon, one of the great barons of the realm. He was to prevent any approach from the sea and likewise to frustrate all attempts at escape from the city.'[21]

These ships were supplemented by new arrivals from Europe as, at 'about Easter time, the customary crossing took place which brought great numbers of pilgrims thither'. The king took steps to conscript the newcomers – always a hugely unpopular move, and only feasible in times of absolute desperation. He 'dispatched messengers from the army forbidding all sailors and pilgrims . . . to return home. All, under promise of pay, were invited to take part in the siege, a labour so acceptable to God.'[22]

This freed up a large number of Christian ships which could be used in the siege as 'all vessels also, whether great or small, were ordered to sail to Ascalon. Within a very few days, therefore, all the ships that had come in that [spring crossing from Europe] arrived before the city.' The crusaders did not have the luxury of creating a viable fleet, however. These newly arrived ships were not for use at sea. They were mostly bought by the king and stripped down for the precious wood of which they were made: timber (particularly for thick, long beams) was essential for constructing siege equipment, but – then, as now – was in very short supply in the Middle East.[23]

Having made cash payments to the hugely disgruntled shipowners, the Franks

removed the masts. Workmen were then called in and ordered to build a very high tower of the wood . . . The material which was left [over] from the wooden ships was used to construct hurling engines, which were then placed in strategic positions for battering down the walls. Covered sheds were also made from the same material under protection of which the embankments might be approached and levelled in safety.[24]

The few remaining ships of the Frankish 'navy' soon found themselves hard at work. The Egyptian fleet had been mobilised, and had set sail to relieve the city. This naval force was a substantial one, and probably contained almost all the serviceable warships in Egypt. It consisted, according to William of Tyre, 'of seventy galleys and some other ships laden to the limit with men, arms, and food. The vessels were,' he wrote, almost admiringly, 'of immense size.'[25]

The Franks did not seem to have scouting vessels posted to give advance warning of approach from the west; or if they did, they were overrun by the enemy before they could get word back to Ascalon. Surprise was total. Before the crusaders knew what was happening, 'the Egyptian fleet, borne by favouring breezes, appeared before the city'.[26]

Gerard did his best. When he saw 'that the ships were nearing the city, he tried to hinder their progress by attacking them with his small number of galleys'. The outcome was inevitable, however. Gerard and his men soon found themselves under unsustainable pressure. And as the full size of the Egyptian fleet became apparent, 'he turned back again and took measures for life and safety by flight'.[27]

The siege of Ascalon was eventually successful, but it was no thanks to what passed for the Frankish navy. Gerard's performance was unimpressive; but given the material he was working with, that was perhaps inevitable. Certainly his choice for the job of 'admiral' implies that he had some experience of organising shipping and fighting at sea. As lord of Sidon, he certainly had a significant port at his disposal; and no doubt, like Reynald and Raymond III, his position as owner of the port meant that he had working relationships with the local merchants and pirates (who were, of course, often one and the same).[28]

At some point in the 1150s Gerard seems to have grasped the potential offered by piracy. He scaled up his freelance naval activities, and turned his talents towards developing an entire pirate fleet. He equipped several ships for raids against Muslim vessels and ports, and sent them out on buccaneering expeditions. This was fine as far as it went – indeed, for a kingdom with no regular navy and in a permanent state of war, such activities could be very useful.

But Gerard, reckless like many of his class, overplayed his hand. He was a volatile man with an unfailing capacity for falling out with his overlords. Gerard's ships were supposed to focus on the enemy, but in practice they were just as likely to attack Christian vessels as Muslim ones. Complaints were made and, in colonies dependent on traffic with the West, such complaints could not be ignored.

The king tried to intervene. Rather than back down, the petulant Gerard went into open revolt. When the uprising was finally suppressed, the lord of Sidon was forced into exile. Gerard fled to Baghras, a town in the principality of Antioch. This choice of destination was no coincidence: Reynald of Châtillon, his new overlord, was, as we have seen, fairly broad-minded in his approach to piratical activities. Gerard was sympathetically received.

But even now, Gerard could not restrain himself. He soon managed to annoy his new hosts by continuing his depredations, both at sea and on land, in Antiochene territory. His behaviour was intolerable, even by the swashbuckling standards of Reynald of Châtillon: by late 1159, the goodwill in Antioch had run out, and Gerard was forced to flee once again.

The only people left for him to find refuge with were the crusaders' Turkic arch-enemies and their leader, Nur al-Din. The 'Frankish ruler of Sidon,' wrote the Muslim chronicler Ibn al-Athir, 'sought out Nur al-Din . . . ruler of Syria, to seek his protection'.[29]

Nur al-Din realised that Gerard could be used to harm their mutual Frankish enemies. He and the irrepressible Gerard set up a joint venture to launch raids into the principality of Antioch. The Muslims gave him 'guarantees [of safety] and also sent a force with him to protect him'. Frankish troops quickly put a stop to this strange alliance, however, and launched an ambush which 'overwhelmed [Gerard and his Turkic troops] on their way and killed a number of the Muslims'.[30]

These events sound extraordinary, almost implausible, but they are largely corroborated by the testimony of Michael the Syrian, a contemporary Christian chronicler of the Syriac Orthodox Church. Michael wrote of 'a Frankish brigand' at this time, based in Baghras, who 'went to Nur ad-Din, who was delighted, since [Gerard] had promised that he would make the entire coast his. [Nur al-Din] gave him troops and [he] went and entered the Franks' territory where he began to loot and destroy the Christians.' Like Ibn al-Athir, Michael suggested that Gerard and his Muslim allies had been ambushed by the king and his men on their return to his old lordship in the territory of the Latin Kingdom of Jerusalem.[31]

Gerard seems to have escaped the immediate aftermath of the ambush and to have fled to the nearby castle of Belhacem (which he knew well, as it was one of the inland castles of his old lordship of Sidon). Escape was not so easy, however. Baldwin III, the king of Jerusalem, and the royal army were in close pursuit – and we know by the accident of a surviving legal document, signed and witnessed while on campaign, that Baldwin and his leading barons (doubtless all keen to show their very visible loyalty to an understandably suspicious monarch) were still besieging the castle on 16 March 1160.[32]

Despite the enormity of his offences – including, above all else, the treacherous collusion with the kingdom's Muslim enemies – Gerard was eventually allowed to re-enter Frankish society, perhaps after yet another short period of exile. He had a final chance for redemption. There was a new king on the throne: Baldwin had died in 1163, and his successor, King Amalric, was desperate to get every able-bodied man to help him in his quest to conquer Egypt. But even now the incorrigible Gerard had not learnt his lesson.

His proud and piratical tendencies led him inexorably into more trouble. He seems to have argued violently with his new king – so violently, in fact, that people talked of the conflict for decades afterwards. Gerard's falling out with King Amalric became a *cause célèbre*. It was still being used in the thirteenth-century legal textbooks of the Latin Kingdom of Jerusalem as a definitive piece of case law. The chronicles are vague about the exact cause of the dispute, but the jurist John of Ibelin wrote that it arose because Gerard, true to form, had illegally taken lands from one of his vassals. When the king intervened on behalf of the wronged knight, civil war broke out again between Gerard and his monarch.[33]

We do not know exactly how the consequences of the conflict played out, but we do know that Gerard was once again the loser. The fighting – and the retribution that followed – was bloody. One local Christian chronicler wrote that: 'The Franks massed troops and, invoking the name of Christ, went against [Gerard], arresting this source of evil and also killing [his allied] Turkish troops. [Gerard], that vessel of Satan, was taken to Jerusalem and burned in the fire and thus his evil ended.'[34]

A troublemaker to the very end, the pirate lord was mourned, one suspects, by very few. Piracy was an option that might be taken – but rarely by the more stable members of the aristocracy.[35]

And so we come full circle.

Piracy was driven as much by greed and opportunity as it was by career path or ideology. Pirates might be traders – or saints. Vikings could be crusaders, and Viking crusaders could be pirates. Even great lords of the Holy Land became sordid criminals when it suited their interests. Almost everything refuses to fall neatly into the boxes we have made for them.

◈

Endpiece

Much of modern historical research, inevitably and correctly, focuses on the powerful celebrity figures and the grand activities they played a part in. This book, however, has tried to look both above and below that event-driven surface.

It has been the story of how climate change and migration – forces so vast as to be almost invisible to the actors on the ground – can have a profoundly scarring effect on civil society; and of how a monumental gathering of 'the usual suspects', irrespective of religion or ethnicity, creates a maelstrom of criminality and pushes local communities to the brink of collapse.

These men were not just vastly overrepresented in the population: they also had a negative halo effect on the rest of society. They made poor behaviour the norm, and other social groups inevitably felt empowered to join in. That criminality extended to all layers of crusader society and to the crusaders' neighbours. The demographic crucible of the medieval Middle East burnt fiercely across two exceptionally violent centuries.

Religion was an enabler and a focus for the wars of the crusades; but it was rarely the ultimate cause. And the same was true of criminality: people might feel more disinhibited in committing crimes against adherents of other religions or members of other communities, but ultimately most criminals were equal-opportunity miscreants who would take whatever chances presented themselves.

Palestine and Syria were dangerous places in the Middle Ages. Mugging and murder, banditry and highway robbery were endemic – almost an art form. But it was the kind of art that could destroy a society.

Modern societies face some disturbingly parallel issues of climate change and its knock-on effects. Importantly, we now have the technology and resources to understand these macro drivers with far greater clarity: unlike the crusaders, we have the luxury of knowledge and economic surplus. But that knowledge is rarely translated into strategy or action. We would do well to reflect on the profoundly negative consequences of failing to address these issues with sufficient foresight or sensitivity.

Notes

Abbreviations used in the notes

AA   Albert of Aachen, *Historia Ierosolimitana*, ed. and tr. S.B. Edgington, Oxford, 2007

BD   Baha al-Din Ibn Shaddad, *The Rare and Excellent History of Saladin*, tr. D.S. Richards, Crusade Texts in Translation 7, Aldershot, 2001

C&C   J. Bird, E. Peters and J.M. Powell (ed. and tr.), *Crusade and Christendom: Annotated documents in translation from Innocent III to the fall of Acre, 1187–1291*, Philadelphia, PA, 2013

CS   *Crusader Syria in the Thirteenth Century: The Rothelin Continuation of the history of William of Tyre with part of the Eracles or Acre text*, tr. J. Shirley, Aldershot, 1999

FC   H. Fink (ed.), *Fulcher of Chartres, A History of the Expedition to Jerusalem, 1095–1127*, tr. F. Ryan, Knoxville, TN, 1969

IA   Ibn al-Athir, *The Chronicle of Ibn al-Athīr for the Crusading Period from al-Kāmil fi'l- ta'rikh*, parts 1, 2 and 3, tr. D.S. Richards, Crusade Texts in Translation 13, 15 and 17, Aldershot, 2006, 2007, 2008

IJ   *The Travels of Ibn Jubayr*, tr. R.J.C. Broadhurst, London, 1952

Joinville *Joinville and Villehardouin: Chronicles of the crusades*, tr. C. Smith, London, 2008

JP   *Jerusalem Pilgrimage, 1099–1185*, ed. and tr. J. Wilkinson, Hakluyt Society, series II, 167, London, 1988

OD   Odo of Deuil, *De profectione Ludovici VII in Orientem*, ed. and tr. V.G. Berry, New York, 1948

Qal   Ibn al-Qalanisi, *The Damascus Chronicle of the Crusades*, tr. H.A.R. Gibb, London, 1932

Rule   *The Rule of the Templars: The French text of the rule of the Order of the Knights Templar*, tr. J.M. Upton-Ward, Woodbridge, 1992

TTT	P. Crawford (ed.), *The 'Templar of Tyre': Part III of the 'Deeds of the Cypriots'*, Crusade Texts in Translation 6, Aldershot, 2016
Usama	Usama Ibn-Munqidh, *The Book of Contemplation*, tr. P.M. Cobb, London, 2008
WC	*Walter the Chancellor's the Antiochene Wars*, tr. T.S. Asbridge and S.B. Edgington, Crusade Texts in Translation 4, Aldershot, 1999
WT	William of Tyre, *A History of Deeds Done beyond the Sea*, tr. E.A. Babcock and A.C. Krey, 2 vols, Records of Civilization, Sources and Studies 35, New York, 1943

1. The Anthropology of Crusader Criminality

1. See Chapter 7 'Women and Justice'.
2. Ibn Abi Tayyi' in C. Hillenbrand, ' "Abominable acts": The career of Zengi', in J. Phillips and M. Hoch (eds), *The Second Crusade: Scope and consequences*, Manchester, 2001, p. 121.
3. Imad ad-Din al-Isfahani in Hillenbrand (2001), p. 121.
4. Imad ad-Din al-Isfahani in T. El-Azhari, *Zengi and the Muslim Response to the Crusades: The politics of jihad*, Abingdon, 2016, p. 129.
5. Hillenbrand (2001), p. 120; El-Azhari (2016), pp. 105–06; P.M. Cobb, *The Race for Paradise: An Islamic history of the crusades*, Oxford, 2014, pp. 135–36; 'The First and Second Crusades from an anonymous Syriac chronicle', tr. A.S. Tritton and H.A.R. Gibb, *Journal of the Royal Asiatic Society of Great Britain and Ireland*, 1 (1933), p. 291; Matthew of Edessa, *Armenia and the Crusades, Tenth to the Twelfth Centuries: The Chronicle of Matthew of Edessa*, tr. A. Dostourian, Lanham, MD, 1993, p. 244; C. Hillenbrand (ed. and tr.), *A Muslim Principality in Crusader Times: The early Artuqid state*, Leiden, 1990, pp. 115–18.
6. R. Ellenblum, *The Collapse of the Eastern Mediterranean: Climate change and the decline of the east 950–1072*, Cambridge, 2012, pp. 34–35; Matthew of Edessa (1993), p. 19.
7. Ellenblum (2012), p. 24.
8. J. Phillips, *The Life and Legend of the Sultan Saladin*, London, 2019, pp. 136–40. The Nile allowed Egypt to become famous as the breadbasket of the ancient world. Weather patterns in the eastern Mediterranean might fluctuate, but Egypt could almost always be relied upon to step in to take up the slack. Importantly for the maintenance of stable sedentary societies, this meant that large and potentially volatile urban populations, such as those of Rome, Constantinople or Alexandria, could be fed.
9. Ellenblum (2012), pp. 33–40; Ibn Fadlan, *Ibn Fadlan's Journey to Russia: A tenth-century traveler from Baghdad to the Volga River*, tr. R.N. Frye, Princeton, NJ, 2005, pp. 30–31; Matthew of Edessa (1993), p. 19.
10. Ellenblum (2012), pp. 49–50.
11. See M. Widell, 'Historical evidence for climate instability and environmental catastrophes in northern Syria and the Jazira: The chronicle of Michael the Syrian', *Environment and History*, 13 (2007), pp. 47–70, for a fascinating case study of evidence for destabilising climate events in Syria in this period; Ellenblum (2012), pp. 61–122.
12. S. Tibble, *The Crusader Armies*, London, 2018, pp. 14–16.

13. R. Ellenblum, 'Demography, geography and the accelerated Islamisation of the eastern Mediterranean', in I. Katznelson and M. Rubin (eds), *Religious Conversion: History, Experience and Meaning*, Farnham, 2014, p. 66.

14. There is a considerable (and still largely unresolved) academic debate about climate change on the steppes in this period. As with all major historical events, the reasons behind the movement of the Turkic peoples of the western steppes into the Middle East are complex, and it is not always possible to be definitive from this distance in time. The Seljuk Turkic migration, for instance, was certainly also affected by political factors, such as their break with the Khazars. Similarly, climate change, given the vast areas encompassed by the term 'steppes' could be relatively localised – not all Turkic tribes left the steppes at the same time, and not all moved in the same direction. But the impact of climatic change as an underlying driver was profound, nonetheless. For the debate, see, for instance, A.C.S. Peacock, *The Great Seljuk Empire*, Edinburgh, 2015, pp. 24–25 and 286–314; and A.D. Beihammer, *Byzantium and the Emergence of Muslim-Turkish Anatolia, ca. 1040–1130*, Abingdon, 2017.

15. Matthew of Edessa (1993), pp. 143–44.

16. Ellenblum (2012), pp. 61–64.

17. ibid., pp. 23–40; P. Heather, *The Fall of the Roman Empire*, London, 2005; P. Heather, *Empires and Barbarians*, London, 2009, pp. 207–27; Tibble (2018), pp. 14–16.

18. M. Brett, 'The Near East on the eve of the crusades', in J. Stuckey (ed.), *The Eastern Mediterranean Frontier of Latin Christendom*, Farnham, 2014, pp. 285–302; C.J. Tyerman, *God's War: A new history of the crusades*, London, 2006, pp. 11–12 and 126–29.

19. The causes of the First Crusade are a mini academic industry in their own right. There are, of course, a plethora of contributory and proximate causes.

20. This overview is, of course, not meant to imply that the many different Eastern Christian communities and Frankish settler communities always shared an identical set of goals: clearly, that was not the case. Similarly, the broader Muslim community was riven with divisions: there were many occasions when Muslims and Christians even fought on the same side.

21. Not everyone was on the front line the whole time. There was enough commonality of interest, for instance, for trade to continue. Nonetheless, for ideological reasons, most of the protagonists were motivated to sustain interminable fighting, rather than a short, sharp campaign.

22. J. Riley-Smith, 'Peace never established: The case of the Kingdom of Jerusalem', *Transactions of the Royal Historical Society*, 1978, p. 89.

23. ibid., pp. 87–102.

24. ibid., pp. 100–02; C. Hillenbrand, *The Crusades: Islamic perspectives*, Edinburgh, 1999, pp. 89–255. See M. Kohler, *Alliances and Treaties between Frankish and Muslim rulers in the Middle East: Cross-cultural diplomacy in the period of the crusades*, tr. P.M. Holt, revised by K. Hirschler, Leiden, 2013, for the alliances and treaties between the Franks and their neighbours. See B. Binysh, 'Give me three good reasons for a Muslim to end a crusade: Saladin and the Third Crusade', in T.K. Nielsen and K.V. Jensen (eds), *Legacies of the Crusades, Proceedings of the Ninth Conference of the Society for the Study of the Crusades and the Latin East, Odense, 27 June – 1 July 2016*, Turnhout, 2021, for a case study of the different

factors involved, from a Muslim perspective, in bringing the Third Crusade to an end. It should also be noted that there were more substantial periods of truce (though not peace), between the Christian and Muslim states in the thirteenth century.

25. Riley-Smith (1978), pp. 87–102; Y. Friedman, 'Peacemaking: perceptions and practices in the medieval Latin east', in C. Kostick (ed.), *The Crusades and the Near East: Cultural histories*, Abingdon, 2011; J. France, 'Surrender and capitulation in the Middle East in the age of the crusades', in J. France (ed.), *Warfare, Crusade and Conquest in the Middle Ages*, Farnham, 2014; Tibble (2018), pp. 4–5.

2. Crime and Crusading

1. OD, pp. 20–21.
2. OD, pp. 42–43.
3. OD, pp. 42–45.
4. OD, pp. 44–45.
5. OD, pp. 66–67.
6. OD, pp. 72–75.
7. OD, pp. 74–75.
8. Roger of Howden, *The Annals of Roger de Hoveden*, vol. II, tr. H. Riley, 1853, pp. 140–41; Roger of Howden, *Chronica*, vol. III, ed. W. Stubbs, RS 51, London, 1870, p. 36; P.D. Mitchell, *Medicine in the Crusades: Warfare, wounds and the medieval surgeon*, Cambridge, 2004, p. 134.
9. Joinville, p. 271.
10. S. Tibble, *Monarchy and Lordships in the Latin Kingdom of Jerusalem, 1099–1291*, Oxford, 1989, pp. 99–152.
11. Joinville, p. 271. Compare this with the ritualised humiliation in the statutes of the Neapolitan 'Company of the Knot', where the 'knight was to dine alone in the middle of the hall at a special table of disgrace'. See D'A.J.D. Boulton, *The Knights of the Crown: The monarchical orders of knighthood in later medieval Europe, 1325–1520*, New York, 1987, p. 235.
12. Joinville, pp. 271–72.
13. Ambroise, *The History of the Holy War*, ed. and tr. M. Ailes and M. Barber, Woodbridge, 2003, p. 38.
14. Ambroise (2003), p. 39. 'Longebards', 'Longobards' or 'Longobardi' were the Sicilian Latins, as distinct from the Greeks (Grifons). They were not Lombards. Conversation with Peter Edbury.
15. Ambroise (2003), pp. 39–40.
16. Ambroise (2003), p. 42.
17. Ambroise (2003), p. 91.
18. Ambroise (2003), p. 91.
19. Rule p. 113; J.M. Upton-Ward (ed. and tr.), *The Catalan Rule of the Templars: A critical edition and English translation from Barcelona, Archivo De La Corona De Aragón, Cartes Reales, MS. 3344*, Woodbridge, 2003, pp. 45 and 55.
20. Rule, p. 147.
21. Rule, pp. 144–45; Upton-Ward (2003), p. 55.
22. Rule, p. 159.
23. Rule, p. 146; Upton-Ward (2003), p. 67.

24. Rule, p. 120; Upton-Ward (2003), p. 41.
25. Rule, pp. 153–54; Upton-Ward (2003), p. 75.
26. Rule, pp. 153–54; Upton-Ward (2003), p. 75.
27. Rule, pp. 153–54.
28. Rule, pp. 153–54.
29. Rule, pp. 153–54.
30. D. Jacoby, 'Aspects of everyday life in Frankish Acre', in *Crusades*, 4 (2005), p. 90.
31. A.J. Forey, 'Desertions and transfers from military orders (twelfth to early fourteenth centuries)', *Traditio*, 60 (2005), p. 165.
32. S. Tibble, *Templars: The knights who made Britain*, London, 2023, p. 91.
33. Tibble (2023), p. 112.
34. Joinville, p. 246.
35. Joinville, p. 247.
36. Joinville, p. 248.
37. Joinville, p. 248.
38. Joinville, p. 248.
39. C.J. Tyerman, *England and the Crusades*, Chicago, IL, 1988, p. 246.
40. IJ, pp. 316–18.

3. The Demographic Crime Wave

1. J. Riley-Smith, 'An army on pilgrimage', in S.B. Edgington and L. Garcia-Guijarro (eds), *Jerusalem the Golden: The origins and impact of the First Crusade*, Turnhout, 2014, pp. 23 and 58; Tyerman (2006), pp. 77 and 124. Similarly, the Christian army which besieged Nicaea in 1097 was perhaps some 60,000 strong, while the army of the First Crusade at Antioch contained around 30–50,000 men and women.
2. J. France, *Hattin*, Oxford, 2015; Tibble (2018) pp. 321–39; Tyerman (2006), pp. 368, 389, 514 and 637. There were also up to 30,000 western soldiers on the Fifth Crusade of 1213–1221, as well as many non-combatants. The numbers involved, particularly when sustained across such a lengthy period of time, were staggering.
3. C.J. Tyerman, 'Who went on crusade to the Holy Land?', in B.Z. Kedar (ed.), *The Horns of Hattin*, London, 1992, pp. 13–26.
4. DNA analysis of what passes for the Tibble family tree, for instance, shows a shockingly close correlation between the dates on which my ancestors 'chose' to move to Australia and the opening of penal settlements there.
5. Gerald of Wales, *The Journey through Wales and the Description of Wales*, tr. L. Thorpe, Harmondsworth, 1978, pp. 114, 140 and 204; Gerald of Wales, Gerald of Wales, *Opera*, ed. J.S. Brewer, 8 vols, RS, London, 1861–91, I, pp. 73–76; Tyerman (1988), p. 69.
6. Tibble (2023), p. 75; W.L. Warren, *Henry II*, London, 2000, pp. 509–11; Tyerman (1988) pp. 43 and 55. See also G.W.S. Barrow, *The Anglo-Norman Era in Scottish History: The Ford Lectures delivered in the University of Oxford in Hilary Term 1977*, Oxford, 1980.
7. S.D. Lloyd, *English Society and the Crusade, 1216–1307*, Oxford, 1988, pp. 104–05.
8. Lloyd (1988), pp. 93–94.
9. Lloyd (1988), pp. 94–95.

10. M. Olympios, 'Amanieu son of Bernard, count of Astarac, *Croisé Manqué?* Deconstructing the myth of an eighteenth-century crusader', in S. Edgington and H. Nicholson (eds), *Deeds Done Beyond the Sea, Essays on William of Tyre, Cyprus and the Military Orders presented to Peter Edbury*, 2014, pp. 145–54. True to form, Amanieu does not seem to have died in the course of heroic military service, however: there was a fifteen-year truce in place between Armenia and the Mamluks, which started in 1323.

11. See J. Phillips, *Defenders of the Holy Land: Relations between the Latin East and the West, 1119–1187*, Oxford, 1996, for a detailed examination of some of these embassies.

12. FC, pp. 143–44; AA, pp. 542–43. See R. Ellenblum, *Frankish Rural Settlement in the Latin Kingdom of Jerusalem*, Cambridge, 1998, for this rural colonial settlement.

13. A.V. Murray, *The Crusader Kingdom of Jerusalem: A dynastic history 1099–1125*, Oxford, 2000, pp. 107–10.

14. Ellenblum (1998), pp. 282–84. By 1187 there was a large infrastructure of villages, small towns and agricultural estates; there was a series of fortified farms and manor houses; and there was even investment in new road systems. See A.J. Boas, *Domestic Settings: Sources on domestic architecture and day-to-day activities in the crusader states*, Leiden, 2010, for a gazetteer of Frankish domestic sites in the crusader states; and A.J. Boas, 'Three stages in the evolution of rural settlement in the Kingdom of Jerusalem during the Twelfth Century', in I. Shagrir, R. Ellenblum and J. Riley-Smith (eds), *In Laudem Hierosolymitani: Studies in crusades and medieval culture in honour of Benjamin Z. Kedar*, Aldershot, 2007, for an analysis of the evolution of defensive structures in Frankish settlements.

15. M. Barber, *The Crusader States*, London, 2012, pp. 95 and 218–20. The urban populations were very significant for this period, and particularly so relative to Europe. On a nominal basis of 125 individuals per hectare, the cities of the Latin East were substantial communities: Antioch would have had over 40,000 inhabitants and Edessa about 25,000. Even these figures may be underestimates. D. Pringle, 'Crusader Jerusalem', *Bulletin of the Anglo-Israel Archaeological Society*, 10 (1990–91), p. 106, suggests that the population of the almost indefensible city of Jerusalem could have been as high as 30,000, not including an additional refugee or transient population.

16. Riley-Smith (1978).

17. Tyerman (1988), pp. 26, 69, 98, 158 and 220–21.

18. R.W. Kaeuper, *Holy Warriors: The religious ideology of chivalry*, Philadelphia, PA, 2009, pp. 1–36.

19. For an overview of chivalry, see M. Keen, *Chivalry*, London, 1984, and R.W. Kaeuper, *Medieval Chivalry*, Cambridge, 2016, particularly pp. 155–207. See R.W. Kaeuper, *War, Justice, and Public Order: England and France in the later Middle Ages*, Oxford, 1988, pp. 134–83, for a discussion of violence and royal justice in England and France during this period.

20. Kaeuper (2009), pp. 1–36.

21. R.W. Kaeuper, *Chivalry and Violence in Medieval Europe*, Oxford, 1999, pp. 11–29.

22. Lloyd (1988), p. 99. With a fine eye for trouble, Henry's ban also reflected his view on the political reliability, or otherwise, of the potential participants.

23. Kaeuper (1999), pp. 121–88.

4. Crusader Crime: Prevalence, Poverty and Productivity

1. Joinville, p. 324.
2. Ellenblum (1998), pp. 268–70.
3. Ellenblum (1998), pp. 268–70; S. Tibble, *The Crusader Strategy*, London, 2020, p. 163; J.G. Schenk, 'Nomadic violence in the first Latin Kingdom of Jerusalem and the military orders', *Reading Medieval Studies*, 36 (2010), pp. 39–55. For Frankish domestic architecture and settlements, see: A.J. Boas, *Crusader Archaeology: The material culture of the Latin East*, London, 1999; Boas (2010); D. Pringle, *Secular Buildings in the Crusader Kingdom of Jerusalem: An archaeological gazetteer*, Cambridge, 1997; B. Major, *Medieval Rural Settlements in the Syrian Coastal Region (12th and 13th Centuries)*, Oxford, 2016.
4. Ibn al-Furat, *Ayyubids, Mamluks and Crusaders: Selections from the Tarikh al-Duwal wa'l-Muluk of Ibn al-Furat*, 2 vols, ed. and tr. U. Lyons, M.C. Lyons and J.S.C. Riley-Smith, Cambridge, 1971, II, pp. 54 and 198 n.2.
5. Boas (2010), p. 34.
6. Boas (2010), p. 35.
7. Boas (2010), pp. 107–08, 118 and 333.
8. Boas (2010), pp. 23, 61–62, 204, 273 and 297.
9. Usama, p. 23.
10. T. Dean, *Crime in Medieval Europe 1200–1550*, Harlow, 2001, pp. 2–3, 47–48 and 50–52.
11. Indeed, some governments, in need of regular access to men with weapons training, actively encouraged ownership of arms.
12. Dean (2001), pp. 19–23.
13. Boas (2010), pp. 146–47.
14. WT, II, p. 374.
15. Tibble (2018), pp. 91–93; Barber (2012), pp. 256–57.
16. B.Z. Kedar, 'On the origins of the earliest laws of Frankish Jerusalem: The canons of the Council of Nablus', *Speculum*, 74 (1999), pp. 324–25; Barber (2012), p. 131; Tibble (2018), p. 70.
17. WT, II, pp. 304, 388 and 394; Tyerman (1988), p. 29.
18. S. Pinker, *The Better Angels of Our Nature: Why violence has declined*, London, 2011.
19. Joinville, p. 311.

5. Frontier Justice

1. See, for instance, Philip of Novara, *Le Livre de Forme de Plait*, ed. and tr. P.W. Edbury, Nicosia, 2009, pp. 111–12, 130, 153, 179, 195, 254–55, 265, 283 and 319.
2. M.C. Lyons and D.E.P. Jackson, *Saladin: The politics of the holy war*, Cambridge, 1982, p. 240.
3. IJ, pp. 336–38.
4. It should also be noted, however, that monetary sophistication in the crusader states was generally in advance of the (admittedly low) bar set by economic practice in western Europe at this time.
5. Boas (2010), pp. 88–89 and 254.

6. Boas (2010), p. 178 n.51; Lyons and Jackson (1982), p. 342.
7. Dean (2001), pp. 120–24.
8. Philip of Novara (2009), pp. 278–80.
9. Philip of Novara (2009), pp. 278–80. Legally, *Force aparant* was a term which covered many violent crimes, but particularly those that involved theft. If the crime was denied by the accused, it, like other offences, could lead to trial by combat; but in practice, such combat appears to have been rare. Philip of Novara (2009), pp. 309–11 and 309 n. 297. *Cop aparant,* on the other hand, was a term more commonly used for cases of assault and particularly those involving wounding. See also A.M. Bishop, 'Criminal law and the development of the assizes of the crusader Kingdom of Jerusalem in the twelfth century', PhD thesis, University of Toronto, 2011, pp. 94–96.
10. N. Coureas, 'Animals and the law: A comparison involving three thirteenth-century legal texts from the Latin East', in S. Edgington and H. Nicholson (eds), *Deeds Done Beyond the Sea, Essays on William of Tyre, Cyprus and the Military Orders presented to Peter Edbury*, Abingdon, 2014, p. 139.
11. Coureas (2014), pp. 140 and 142.
12. Coureas (2014), p. 138.

6. *Deus Vult:* Trial by Combat

1. Dean (2001), pp. 5–6. See also, for instance, Kaeuper (1988), pp. 154–56, for judicial mutilation and legal developments in England.
2. Dean (2001), pp. 10–11.
3. Dean (2001), p. 12.
4. Conversation with Peter Edbury.
5. See, for instance, the case of the murder trial of James Artude in P.W. Edbury, 'The *Assises de Jérusalem* and legal practice: The political crisis in Cyprus in the early fourteenth century', in J. Devard and B. Ribémont (eds), *Autour des Assises de Jérusalem*, Paris, 2018. Muslim neighbours of the crusaders, such as Usama, clearly thought the process was eccentric and barbaric, but also fascinating. See A.M. Bishop, 'Usama ibn Munqidh and crusader law in the twelfth century', *Crusades*, 12 (2013), pp. 53–65.
6. Philip of Novara (2009), pp. 214–15.
7. Philip of Novara (2009), p. 222. Note that 'sixty' was not an arbitrary number: it was also the age at which knights were no longer expected to serve their lords by active service on campaign.
8. Philip of Novara (2009), p. 215.
9. Philip of Novara (2009), p. 215; John of Ibelin, *Le Livre des Assises*, ed. P.W. Edbury, Leiden, 2003, pp. 240–41.
10. Philip of Novara (2009), p. 221.
11. Philip of Novara (2009), pp. 218 and 221.
12. Philip of Novara (2009), p. 224.
13. Philip of Novara (2009), pp. 236–37 and 237 n.122.
14. Philip of Novara (2009), pp. 270 and 270 n.212.
15. Philip of Novara (2009), p. 293.
16. Philip of Novara (2009), pp. 293–95 and 295 n.272.

17. Usama, p. 151.
18. The land was held directly from the king, as Nablus was part of the royal domain.
19. Bishop (2013), pp. 56–61; Bishop (2011), pp. 134–44; Usamah Ibn-Munqidh, *An Arab-Syrian Gentleman and Warrior in the Period of the Crusades: Memoirs of Usāmah Ibn-Munqidh*, tr. P.K. Hitti, Princeton, NJ, 1929, pp. 167–68; Usama, pp. 151–53.
20. The text makes far more sense when one appreciates that it was written in a particular style of the period – the *adab*. This was a literary form designed to give good instruction to Muslims as to how they should behave. Bishop (2013), pp. 56–61; Usamah Ibn-Munqidh (1929), pp. 167–68.
21. Bishop (2013), p. 57; Usamah Ibn-Munqidh (1929), p. 168.
22. Bishop (2013), pp. 56–61; Usamah Ibn-Munqidh (1929), pp. 167–68. See also Edbury (2018) and Bishop (2011), pp. 174–75, for the shocking case of the knight, a certain James Artude, who murdered his wife and faced justice by combat.

7. Women and Justice

1. Dean (2001), pp. 3 and 23.
2. Dean (2001), pp. 73–74 and 78.
3. Dean (2001), p. 77; A. Finch, ' Women and violence in the later Middle Ages: The evidence of the officiality of Cerisy', *Continuity and Change*, 7 (1992); A. Finch, 'The nature of violence in the Middle Ages: An alternative perspective', *Historical Research*, 70 (1997); T. Dean, 'Domestic violence in medieval Bologna', *Renaissance Studies*, 18:4 (2004), pp. 527–43.
4. Dean (2001), p. 78.
5. H. Skoda, *Medieval Violence: Physical brutality in northern France, 1270–1330*, Oxford, 2013, p. 225.
6. Skoda (2013), pp. 193–231.
7. Skoda (2013), pp. 217–18, 222–23 and 226.
8. Skoda (2013), pp. 219 and 227. See S.M. Butler, *The Language of Abuse: Marital violence in later medieval England*, Leiden, 2007, pp. 136–64, for English case studies.
9. Edbury (2018); Bishop (2011), pp. 174–75.
10. Kaeuper (1999), pp. 225–30.
11. Kaeuper (2016), p. 326; Kaeuper (1999), p. 228.
12. Kaeuper (1999), pp. 228–29.
13. Kaeuper (1999), pp. 228–29.
14. H. Nicholson, 'Knights and lovers: The military orders in the romantic literature of the thirteenth century', in M.C. Barber (ed.), *The Military Orders*, vol. 1, *Fighting for the Faith and Caring for the Sick*, Aldershot, 1994, pp. 340–45.
15. Nicholson (1994), pp. 340–45.
16. Kaeuper (1999).
17. See, for example, Y. Friedman, *Encounter between Enemies: Captivity and ransom in the Latin Kingdom of Jerusalem*, Leiden, 2002.
18. During the Covid lockdown, I started writing a chapter on sexual violence, but the isolation of that time exacerbated the horror and I had to stop. Too pervasive and too grim.

8. Police and Thieves

1. J. Riley-Smith, *The Feudal Nobility and the Kingdom of Jerusalem 1174–1277*, London, 1973, pp. 86–87; J.L. La Monte, *Feudal Monarchy in the Latin Kingdom of Jerusalem, 1099–1291*, Cambridge, MA, 1932, pp. 106 and 135–36.
2. Skoda (2013), pp. 40–41. In Joinville, the translator Caroline Smith defines a bailli thus: 'The primary representative of the French king in a region, or bailliage, a bailli was appointed by the Crown and reported directly to the royal administration on its judicial and financial affairs; his responsibilities included oversight of the *prévôt* and other officials.' However, the title broadly indicates 'king's representative' and it can mean different things, according to context or seniority. Here, for instance, it really means 'chief of police'; but later on, in Chapter 14, the term is used to mean something far grander – almost like a procurator or regent.
3. Joinville, pp. 175 and 366 n.6. For the widespread military presence of 'sergeants' in the Latin Kingdom of Jerusalem, see P.W. Edbury, *John of Ibelin and the Kingdom of Jerusalem*, Woodbridge, 1997.
4. Joinville, p. 175.
5. Joinville, p. 175.
6. For the charming Beauquesne, see Skoda (2013), pp. 45–48 and 225–26.
7. Kemal ed-Din, 'La chronique d'Alep', in *Recueil des historiens des croisades, Historiens orientaux*, vol. 3, Paris, 1872, pp. 585–6.
8. In Joinville, the translator Caroline Smith explains Assassins thus: 'The Nizaris, members of an Isma'ili sect (Isma'ilism is a branch of Shi'ite Islam) were known as *Hasishiyya* (Arabic), or "Assassins" to Latin Christians. They had radical social and political aims as well as religious views deemed heretical by other Muslims. Murder was a favoured tactic against their opponents, both Muslim and Christian, and it is from them that the term "assassin" entered western languages. Their leader was a mysterious figure known as the Old Man of the Mountain.'
9. Kemal ed-Din (1872), pp. 615–16.
10. Kemal ed-Din (1872), pp. 630–31.

9. Criminal Competitors: Muslim Neighbours

1. Usama, pp. 258–59.
2. The Byzantine army, the other main player that might be described as (semi-) professional, campaigned in the region, of course, but only as an occasional visitor.
3. B. Hamilton, 'The crusades and north-east Africa', in S. John (ed.), *Crusading and Warfare in the Middle Ages*, Farnham, 2014, pp. 171–72.
4. Usama, pp. 24–26; J.L. Bacharach, 'African military slaves in the medieval Middle East: The cases of Iraq (869–955) and Egypt (868–1171)', *International Journal of Middle East Studies*, 13 (1981); Tyerman (2006), p. 160.
5. D. Nicolle, *Crusader Warfare*, vol. II, *Muslims, Mongols and the Struggle against the Crusades*, London, 2007, pp. 40–41; Y. Lev, 'Regime, army and society in medieval Egypt, 9th–12th centuries', in Y. Lev (ed.), *War and Society in the Eastern Mediterranean, 7th–15th Centuries*, Leiden, 1997, pp. 115–52; S.B. Dadoyan, *The Fatimid Armenians: Cultural and political interaction in the Near East*, Leiden, 1997, pp. 116–18.
6. Usama, pp. 18–23; W.J. Hamblin, 'The Fatimid army during the early crusades', PhD thesis, University of Michigan, 1985, pp. 62–63.

7. Nicolle (2007), p. 116; Hamblin (1985), pp. 57–61.
8. N. Morton, 'Encountering the Turks: The first crusaders' foreknowledge of their enemy; some preliminary findings', in S. John (ed.), *Crusading and Warfare in the Middle Ages*, Farnham, 2014; N. Morton, *Encountering Islam on the First Crusade*, Cambridge, 2016, pp. 111–82; D. Nicolle, *Saracen Faris 1050–1250 AD*, London, 1994, pp. 5–8.
9. J. Keegan, *A History of Warfare*, London, 1993, pp. 179–217.
10. D. Cook (ed. and tr.), *Baybars' Successors: Ibn al-Furāt on Qalāwūn and al-Ashraf*, Farnham, 2020, p. 88.
11. Cook (2020), pp. 70–71.
12. M. Dengler (ed.), *The Book of Charlatans – Jamal al-Din 'Abd al-Rahim al-Jawbari*, tr. H. Davies, New York, 2020, pp. xiii–xvii. Al-Jawbari wrote the text at some point between 1222 and 1232.
13. Dengler (2020), pp. 65 and 456.
14. Dengler (2020), p. 407.
15. Dengler (2020), p. 411.
16. Cook (2020), pp. 189–90.
17. *Chronicles of Qalāwūn and his Son al-Ashraf Khalīl*, tr. D. Cook, Abingdon, 2020, p. 140. See Tibble (1989), pp. 12, 84–85, 156, 158–59, 165 and 167 for the Sueth condominium.
18. R. Irwin, '"Futuwwa": Chivalry and gangsterism in medieval Cairo', in G. Necipoglu, D. Behrens-Abouseif and A. Contadini (eds), *Muqarnas*, vol. 21, *Essays in Honor of J.M. Rogers*, Leiden, 2004, pp. 161–70; Nicolle (1994).
19. Usama, pp. 157–58.
20. Usama, pp. 157–58; R. Irwin, 'Usamah ibn Munqidh: An Arab-Syrian at the time of the crusades reconsidered', in J. France and W.G. Zajac (eds), *The Crusades and Their Sources*, Abingdon, 1998, p. 77.
21. Usama, pp. 129–30.

10. Gamblers

1. M. Barber and K. Bate (tr.), *The Templars*, Manchester Medieval Sources, Manchester, 2002, p. 223; E. Lapina, 'Gambling and gaming in the Holy Land: Chess, dice and other games in the sources of the crusades', *Crusades*, 12 (2013), p. 128; Bernard of Clairvaux, *In Praise of the New Knighthood*, tr. M.C. Greenia, Piscataway, NJ, 2000, p. 46.
2. Boas (1999), pp. 164–66.
3. Boas (1999), pp. 164–66; G.E. Kirk, 'Nine Men's Morris – Morelles – Muhlespiel in Palestine', *Journal of the Palestine Oriental Society* (1938), pp. 229–32.
4. Boas (1999), pp. 164–66.
5. A.J. Boas, *Archaeology of the Military Orders: A survey of the urban centres, rural settlement and castles of the military orders in the Latin East (c.1120–1291)*, London, 2006, pp. 203–04.
6. H. Nicholson, *The Everyday Life of the Templars: The Knights Templar at home*, Stroud, 2017, p. 33; Rule, pp. 89–90.
7. Boas (2006), p. 203.
8. Lapina (2013), pp. 121–32.
9. Lapina (2013), p. 121.

10. Lapina (2013), pp. 121–23; Boas (2006), p. 204; A.J. Boas, 'Domestic life in the Latin East', in A.J. Boas (ed.), *The Crusader World*, Abingdon, 2016, p. 561.
11. Lapina (2013), p. 124.
12. P. Jackson, 'The crisis in the Holy Land in 1260', *English Historical Review*, 95:376 (1980), pp. 481–513.
13. Philip of Novara (2009), pp. 321–22 and 321 n.324; Tibble (1989), pp. 173–75.
14. TTT, pp. 35–36.
15. R.N.R. Mikulski, H. Schutkowski, M.J. Smith, C. Doumet-Serhal and P.D. Mitchell, 'Weapon injuries in the crusader mass graves from a 13th century attack on the port city of Sidon (Lebanon)', *PLoS ONE*, 16:8 (2021), e0256517.
16. Lapina (2013), p. 124; WT, II, p. 80.
17. Lapina (2013), pp. 121–32; WT, II, p. 95.
18. Lapina (2013), p. 125; J. Folda, *Crusader Manuscript Illumination at Saint-Jean d'Acre: 1275–1291*, Princeton, NJ, 1976, pp. 32–35 and plate 13.
19. Lapina (2013), pp. 130–32.
20. WT, II, pp. 137–39.
21. Lapina (2013), p. 130; N. Housley, *Fighting For the Cross: Crusading to the Holy Land*, London, 2008, p. 174; Joinville, p. 245.
22. Joinville, p. 321.
23. Joinville, pp. 248–49.
24. Joinville, p. 258.
25. *The Chronicle of Amadi,* tr. N. Coureas and P.W. Edbury, Nicosia, 2015, p. 197.
26. Lapina (2013), pp. 125–27; Raymond d'Aguilers, *Historia Francorum Qui Ceperunt Iherusalem*, tr. J.H. and H.H. Hill, Philadelphia, PA, 1968, p. 62.
27. Joinville, p. 181.
28. Joinville, p. 181.

11. Drinking, Bars and Bar Brawls

1. Skoda (2013), pp. 88–118.
2. C&C, pp. 146–47. James was referencing Proverbs 26:11, which was in turn quoted in 2 Peter 2:22.
3. C&C, pp. 146–47.
4. C&C, pp. 146–47.
5. C&C, p. 147.
6. Boas (2010), pp. 140–41.
7. Joinville, p. 270.
8. *Pilgrimage to Jerusalem and the Holy Land, 1187–1291,* tr. D. Pringle, Crusade Texts in Translation 23, Farnham, 2012, p. 82: 'The wine of the Convent, if it be not good enough to strengthen the sick brethren, should be improved upon'; King, E.J., *The Rule Statutes and Customs of the Hospitallers 1099–1310*, London, 1934, p. 42.
9. Boas (2010), pp. 140–41.
10. Ibn al-Furat (1971), II, p. 108.
11. S.D. Goitein, *A Mediterranean Society*, vol. 4, *Daily Life*, Berkeley, CA, 1983, p. 261; Boas (2010), p. 141.
12. WT, II, p. 74.
13. WT, II, p. 75.

14. WT, II, p. 75; Tibble (1989), pp. 37–39, 44 and 46–47.
15. Skoda (2013), p. 46.
16. Skoda (2013), p. 46.
17. Skoda (2013), p. 97.
18. Skoda (2013), p. 100.
19. Skoda (2013), pp. 100–01.
20. Skoda (2013), pp. 106–07.
21. Skoda (2013), p. 89.
22. Skoda (2013), pp. 111–12.
23. C&C, pp. 146–47. James, ostentatiously erudite as ever, was quoting Juvenal Satire VI.
24. Usama, p. 148.
25. OD, pp. 64–65.
26. OD, pp. 40–45.
27. OD, pp. 42–43.
28. OD, pp. 42–43.
29. S.A. Epstein, *Purity Lost: Transgressing boundaries in the eastern Mediterranean, 1000–1400*, Baltimore, MD, 2006, p. 24 n.53 and p. 25. The Mongols still had an eclectic and unorthodox relationship to religion in the first half of the thirteenth century. It is likely that those encountered by Julian and Carpini were not Muslims.
30. Usama, p. 131.
31. Usama, p. 131.
32. WC, p. 138.
33. WC, p. 163.
34. WC, pp. 164–65 and 167.
35. WC, pp. 167–68.

12. Gangsters – and Prisoners of War

1. D. Ayalon, 'Discharges from service, banishments and imprisonments in Mamluk society', in D. Ayalon, *The Mamluk Military Society: Collected studies*, V, London, 1979, pp. 40–45.
2. Ayalon (1979), p. 40.
3. Ayalon (1979), pp. 41–43.
4. TTT, p. 40.
5. TTT, p. 40.
6. J. Loiseau, 'Frankish captives in Mamlūk Cairo, 1291–1350', *Al-Masāq*, 23:1 (2011), p. 40.
7. Loiseau (2011), p. 38. For the use of looted Frankish architectural features in Mamluk Cairo, see K.R. Mathews, 'Mamluks and crusaders: Architectural appropriation and cultural encounter in Mamluk monuments', in S. Lambert and H. Nicholson (eds), *Languages of Love and Hate: Conflict, communication, and identity in the medieval Mediterranean*, Turnhout, 2012, pp. 177–200.
8. Loiseau (2011), pp. 37–38 and 43–45.
9. Loiseau (2011), pp. 43–45; Tyerman (1988), p. 251. For a wonderful examination of this story, see R. MacLellan, 'An Egyptian Jew in King Edward's court:

Jewish conversion, Edward II, and Roger de Stanegrave', *Crusades*, 19 (2021), pp. 143–53.

10. Loiseau (2011), pp. 39–42.
11. A.J. Forey, 'The military orders and the ransoming of captives from Islam (twelfth to early fourteenth centuries)', *Studia Monastica*, 33 (1991), p. 279.
12. Loiseau (2011), p. 43.
13. Loiseau (2011), pp. 37–52; MacLellan (2021).
14. H.E. Mayer, 'Two crusaders out of luck', *Crusades*, 11 (2012), p. 160.
15. Mayer (2012), pp. 161–62.
16. Mayer (2012), p. 162.
17. Mayer (2012), pp. 162–63.
18. Mayer (2012), p. 163.
19. Mayer (2012), p. 163.
20. Mayer (2012), pp. 163–4.
21. Mayer (2012), pp. 163–65.
22. Mayer (2012), p. 164.
23. Mayer (2012), pp. 164–65.
24. Mayer (2012), pp. 165–68.
25. Mayer (2012), p. 169.
26. Mayer (2012), pp. 169–70.
27. Mayer (2012), p. 170.
28. Mayer (2012), pp. 169–70.
29. Mayer (2012), p. 171.
30. Mayer (2012), p. 171.
31. Mayer (2012), p. 171.
32. Loiseau (2011), pp. 43–44.
33. Loiseau (2011), pp. 43–44.
34. Loiseau (2011), p. 44; Cook (2020), p. 76.
35. Loiseau (2011), p. 44.
36. For the drinking habits of medieval Cairo, see P.B. Lewicka, *Food and Foodways of Medieval Cairenes: Aspects of life in an Islamic metropolis of the eastern Mediterranean*, Leiden, 2011, pp. 483–550.
37. Loiseau (2011), p. 46.
38. Loiseau (2011), p. 46.
39. Loiseau (2011), p. 45.
40. Mayer (2012), pp. 164–65; Loiseau (2011), p. 47.
41. Loiseau (2011), pp. 45–46. There were also other opportunities to gather Frankish military prisoners, of course, albeit in smaller numbers than in previous decades – there were continuing skirmishes with the Mamluks, and piracy remained a rich source of slaves.
42. Loiseau (2011), pp. 47–48 and 51–52.
43. Irwin (2004), p. 161.
44. S. Vryonis, 'Byzantine circus factions and Islamic futuwwa organisations', in S. Vryonis (ed.), *Byzantium: Its internal history and relations with the Muslim world – Collected studies*, London, 1971, p. 55.
45. Vryonis (1971), pp. 46–59.
46. Irwin (2004), pp. 161 and 164.
47. Irwin (2004), p. 164.

48. Irwin (2004), p. 165.
49. Irwin (2004), p. 163.
50. Irwin (2004), p. 163.
51. Irwin (2004), p. 164.
52. Irwin (2004), p. 168.

13. A Surfeit of Blood?

1. Philip of Novara (2009), pp. 218–19.
2. Philip of Novara (2009), pp. 219–20 and 219 n.72.
3. Philip of Novara (2009), p. 313.
4. Dean (2001), pp. 1–2.
5. Dean (2001), pp. 1–2.
6. Dean (2001), p. 14. The Imperiale family were Genoese patricians.
7. Zengi was atabeg of Mosul from 1127 to 1146.
8. Usama, pp. 71–72.
9. Usama, pp. 71–72.
10. It is worth pointing out that there were also areas behind the frontiers where fighting rarely took place. It is certainly true, for instance, that some of the coastal regions of the Kingdom of Jerusalem and county of Tripoli were less troubled by warfare in many decades in the twelfth or thirteenth centuries than during most other periods of the medieval era. Even in these areas, however, a disproportionate part of the population was militarised and armed – garrisons, mercenaries, crusaders and soldiers from local feudal contingents were there in abundance. And that was in addition, of course, to the normal level of criminality to be found in the large, impersonal cities of the region.
11. TTT, pp. 101–02; Jacoby (2005), pp. 84–86.

14. Murder in the Cathedral

1. F.V. Tricht, 'Who murdered Archbishop William of Rouen (1217)? – The valley of Philippi under Latin rule (1204–c.1224)', *Jahrbuch der Österreichischen Byzantinistik*, 70 (2020), pp. 305–34.
2. Tricht (2020), pp. 318–19.
3. Tricht (2020). See also F.V. Tricht, 'The duchy of Philippopolis (1204–c.1236/7): A Latin border principality in a Byzantine (Greek/Bulgarian) milieu', *Crusades*, 21 (2022), pp. 100–05.
4. B. Hamilton, *The Latin Church in the Crusader States: The secular Church*, London, 1980, pp. 249–52.
5. CS, p. 141; *The Chronicle of Amadi* (2015), p. 201; P.-V. Claverie, 'Stephen of Mezel bishop of Famagusta and his age (1244–1259)', in M. Walsh, T. Kiss and N. Coureas (eds), *Crusader to Venetian Famagusta: 'The Harbour of all the Sea and Realm'*, Budapest, 2014, p. 50.
6. WT, II, pp. 385–86; Phillips (1996), pp. 208–13; S. Runciman, 'The visit of King Amalric I to Constantinople in 1171', in B.Z. Kedar, H.E. Mayer and R.C. Smail, *Outremer: Studies in the history of the crusading Kingdom of Jerusalem presented to Joshua Prawer*, Jerusalem, 1982, pp. 153–58.
7. Tibble (2020), pp. 176–220.

8. WT, II, p. 377.
9. WT, II, p. 377.
10. WT, II, pp. 377–78.
11. *The Syriac Chronicle of Michael Rabo (The Great)*, tr. M. Moosa, Teaneck, NJ, 2014, p. 698; *The Chronicle of Michael the Great, Patriarch of the Syrians*, tr. R. Bedrosian, Long Branch, NJ, 2013, p. 195; WT, II, p. 378.
12. WT, II, p. 385.
13. WT, II, p. 385.
14. WT, II, p. 385.
15. Hamilton (1980), pp. 116–17 and 132–33. It should be noted that it was normal for travellers to share rooms at this time. The presence of the two men in one room would have been no indication of a sexual relationship.

15. Murderous Monks

1. The crusades, sometimes characterised as aggressive wars, were, for instance, only justified on the grounds that they were fundamentally defensive actions – that is, wars needed to defend the Christian Middle East from the Muslim invasions that convulsed the region from the seventh century onwards.
2. Rule, p. 144.
3. Rule, p. 144; Upton-Ward (2003), p. 55.
4. A. Luttrell, 'Intrigue, schism, and violence among the hospitallers of Rhodes: 1377–1384', *Speculum*, 41:1 (1966), pp. 30–48.
5. Luttrell (1966), pp. 37–38.
6. Luttrell (1966), p. 38.
7. Luttrell (1966), pp. 38–39.
8. Luttrell (1966), p. 39.
9. Luttrell (1966), p. 39.
10. Luttrell (1966), p. 40.

16. Murder and Power

1. WT, II, p. 401.
2. WT, II, p. 401.
3. WT, II, p. 402; Barber (2012), pp. 264–65.
4. Tripoli was an important and heavily fortified coastal city in modern Lebanon, held by the Fatimid Egyptians.
5. K.J. Lewis, *The Counts of Tripoli and Lebanon in the Twelfth Century: Sons of Saint-Gilles*, London, 2017, pp. 34–36.
6. Lewis (2017), pp. 45–46.
7. *Genoa and the Twelfth-century Crusades*, tr. M. Hall and J. Phillips, Crusade Texts in Translation 24, Farnham, 2013, pp. 123–24; AA, pp. 786–87 n.22.
8. AA, pp. 786–87; Qal, p. 89.
9. FC, p. 195.
10. *Colbert-Fontainebleau-Continuation*, para 357, in P.W. Edbury and M. Gaggero (eds), *The* Chronique d'Ernoul *and the* Colbert-Fontainebleau Continuation *of William of Tyre*, 2 vols, Leiden, 2023, II, p. 407.
11. Hillenbrand (1990), pp. 135–36 and 136 n.54.

12. Qal, p. 247.
13. Qal, pp. 253–54.
14. Joinville, pp. 231–33.
15. Joinville, pp. 231–33.
16. Joinville, pp. 231–33.
17. TTT, p. 122; R. Irwin, *The Middle East in the Middle Ages: The early Mamluk sultanate 1250–1382*, London, 1986, pp. 81–82; P.M. Holt, *The Age of the Crusades: The Near East from the eleventh century to 1517*, London, 1986, pp. 105–06.
18. BD, pp. 144–45.

17. Ploughshares into Swords

1. The Cave de Sueth was also known as Ain al-Habis, or Habis Jaldak. WT, II, pp. 470–71; D. Nicolle, 'Ain al Habis: The Cave de Sueth', *Archéologie medievale*, 18 (1988), pp. 113–40; Ellenblum (1998), pp. 141–42; Tibble (1989), p.165; Tibble (2018), pp. 85–87; D. Pringle, *The Churches of the Crusader Kingdom of Jerusalem: A corpus*, vol. 1, Cambridge, 1993, p. 26.
2. For the Byzantine army at this time, see G. Theotokis, *Byzantine Military Tactics in Syria and Mesopotamia in the Tenth Century: A comparative study*, Edinburgh, 2018. For an overview of banditry in the Holy Land, see Tibble (2020), pp. 141–75, and Schenk (2010).
3. *Pilgrimage to Jerusalem and the Holy Land* (2012), pp. 316–17.
4. For the conversion rates of local populations to Islam over time, see Ellenblum (2014), pp. 61–80.
5. C. MacEvitt, *The Crusades and the Christian World of the East: Rough tolerance*, Philadelphia, PA, 2008, pp. 9 and 25; G. Dedeyan, 'Le rôle politique et militaire des Arméniens dans les états croisés pendant la premiere partie du XIIe siècle', in H.E. Mayer (ed.), *Die Kreuzfahrerstaaten als multikulturelle Gesellschaft*, München, 1997, pp. 153–63; N. Hodgson, 'Conflict and cohabitation: Marriage and diplomacy between Latins and Cilician Armenians, c.1097–1253', in C. Kostick (ed.), *The Crusades and the Near East: Cultural histories*, Abingdon, 2011, pp. 83–106; Tibble (2018), pp. 76–81.
6. Matthew of Edessa in WC, pp. 188–89.
7. A.-M. Eddé, *Saladin*, tr. J.M. Todd, London, 2011, pp. 50–52; Tibble (2018), pp. 76–81. There was a major exodus of the Egyptian Armenian community from the early 1170s onwards, as Saladin took over from their erstwhile Fatimid employers: most of them went to the crusader states to the north. In November 1172, even the Armenian patriarch in Egypt relocated to Jerusalem.
8. Barber (2012), p. 43.
9. WT, II, pp. 458–59; Tibble (2018), p. 82.
10. R. Rohricht (ed.), *Regesta Regni Hierosolymitani 1097–1291*, Innsbruck, 1893, nos. 100, 299, 332, 335 and 423; MacEvitt (2008), p. 154; Riley-Smith (1973), p. 10; Tibble (2018), pp. 82–87.
11. Rohricht (1893), nos. 612, 630, 647 and 649. Nearby, in the county of Tripoli, we find a lord 'David the Syrian' in control of a cave fortress and associated lands in the Lebanese mountains in the 1130s and 1140s, presumably commanding a native Christian garrison and the local militia: Rohricht (1893), no. 212.

12. Y. Harari, 'The military role of the Frankish Turcopoles: A reassessment', *Mediterranean Historical Review*, 12:1 (1997), pp. 75–116; Tibble (2018), pp. 117–24.

18. Stand and Deliver: Pilgrims and Travellers

1. JP, p. 100.
2. JP, p. 100.
3. JP, p. 100.
4. JP, pp. 100–01.
5. JP, p. 101.
6. J. Riley-Smith, *The Crusades: A history*, third edition, London, 2014, p. 110; see A. Mallett, *Popular Muslim Reactions to the Franks in the Levant, 1097–1291*, Farnham, 2014, particularly pp. 75–102.
7. JP, p. 126.
8. JP, p. 145.
9. JP, p. 148.
10. JP, pp. 149–50.
11. JP, p. 155.
12. JP, p. 158.
13. JP, p. 160.
14. S.B. Edgington, *Baldwin I of Jerusalem, 1100–1118*, Abingdon, 2019, pp. 139–41.
15. AA, pp. 662–63.
16. AA, pp. 664–65; FC, pp. 175–76.
17. AA, pp. 664–67.
18. C&C, pp. 163–65; H. Kennedy, *Crusader Castles*, Cambridge, 1994, pp. 56–57 and 124–25.

19. Brigands and Bandits

1. WT, II, p. 201; *The Syriac Chronicle* (2014), p. 684.
2. WT, II, p. 201; *The Syriac Chronicle* (2014), p. 678.
3. Barber (2012), p. 179.
4. Barber (2012), p. 195; WT, II, p. 201.
5. Qal, p. 128.
6. Usama, pp. 98–99.
7. Usama, pp. 53–56.
8. Usama, pp. 53–56.
9. Usama, pp. 53–56.
10. Villehardouin, in Joinville, p. 82.
11. Usama, p. 141.
12. Usama, pp. 141–42.
13. Usama, pp. 142–43.
14. Bishop (2013), pp. 61–63.
15. Usama, pp. 152–53.
16. Hillenbrand (1990), pp. 35–36.

17. D. Talmon-Heller, 'The cited tales of the wondrous doings of the Shaykhs of the Holy Land by Diya' al-Din Abu 'Abd Allah Muhammad b. 'Abd al-Wahid al-Maqdisi (569/1173–643/1245): Text, translation and commentary', *Crusades*, 1 (2003), pp. 111–54.
18. Talmon-Heller (2003), pp. 130–31.
19. Talmon-Heller (2003), p. 134.
20. Talmon-Heller (2003), p. 149.
21. JP, pp. 310–11.

20. Bedouin Bandits

1. Schenk (2010), pp. 39–55.
2. Schenk (2010), pp. 39–55.
3. Schenk (2010); Ellenblum (1998), pp. 268–70.
4. Schenk (2010); Tibble (2018), pp. 313–15; Eddé (2011), pp. 437–41.
5. Schenk (2010), p. 42.
6. Joinville, p. 208.
7. Joinville, pp. 208–09. John is confused about who was Muslim or non-Muslim and, for instance, who might be Shi'ite, as opposed to Sunni.
8. Usama, pp. 18–23.
9. Usama, pp. 18–23.
10. Usama, p. 22.
11. Usama, pp. 34–35; *The Chronicle of Michael the Great* (2013), p. 180.
12. Usama, pp. 34–35.
13. Usama, p. 35.
14. WT, II, pp. 251–52.
15. Usama, p. 36.
16. WT, II, pp. 252–53.
17. WT, II, pp. 252–53; H. Nicholson, 'Before William of Tyre: European reports on the military orders' deeds in the East, 1150–1185', in H. Nicholson (ed.), *The Military Orders*, vol. 2, *Welfare and Warfare*, Aldershot, 1998, pp. 114–16.
18. Usama, p. 36.
19. Usama, p. 37.
20. BD, pp. 37 and 147–48.
21. BD, p. 37.
22. BD, p. 148.
23. BD, p. 147.
24. BD, pp. 147 and 184.
25. BD, pp. 155 and 184.
26. Qal, p. 130.
27. Qal, p. 130.
28. Qal, pp. 130–31.
29. Qal, pp. 130–31.
30. Qal, p. 131.
31. AA, pp. 834–37.
32. CS, p. 88.
33. CS, p. 115.

34. CS, p. 115.
35. WT, II, p. 234.
36. Usama, p. 258.

21. The Ghost-Lordships

1. Schenk (2010).
2. WT, II, p. 39.
3. WT, II, pp. 102–03.
4. Pringle (1993–2009), I, p. 26; D. Nicolle, *Crusader Castles in the Holy Land 1097–1192*, London, 2004, pp. 16–19; Nicolle (1988), pp. 113–40; Tibble (2018), pp. 85–86.
5. WT, II, pp. 103–05; Schenk (2010), pp. 43–44.
6. WT, II, p. 437.
7. WT, II, p. 437.
8. WT, II, pp. 437–38; Schenk (2010), p. 44.
9. Usama, pp. 76–77; Bishop (2013), p. 63.
10. Usama, pp. 83–84.
11. Usama, p. 84.
12. Usama, pp. 84–85.
13. Usama, p. 165.
14. Usama, p. 166.
15. Usama, p. 165.
16. Usama, p. 166.
17. Usama, p. 167.
18. Usama, pp. 167–68.

22. Outlaws of the Sea

1. The motto is attributed to the pirate captain Bartholomew Roberts, as reported in Charles Johnson, *A General History of the Pyrates*, 1724 (1972 edition).
2. For the situation in the western Mediterranean, see the fascinating case study in R.I. Burns, 'Piracy as an Islamic-Christian interface in the thirteenth century', *Viator*, 11 (1980), pp. 165–178.
3. S. Rose, 'Islam versus Christendom: The naval dimension, 1000–1600', *Journal of Military History*, 63:3 (1999), p. 573.

23. The Pirate Saint

1. Edgington (2019), pp. 136–37.
2. For the story of Godric, see: AA, pp. 646–49; Reginald of Durham, *The Life and Miracles of Saint Godric, Hermit of Finchale*, ed. and tr. M. Coombe, Oxford, 2022, pp. 42–111; Reginald of Durham, *Libellus de Vita et Miraculis S. Godrici Heremitae de Finchale*, ed. J. Stevenson, Surtees Society, Durham, 1847, pp. 33–34 and 52–58; V.M. Tudor, 'Reginald of Durham and St Godric of Finchale: A study of a twelfth-century hagiographer and his major subject', PhD thesis, Reading University, 1979, especially pp. 215–37 and 376–77; V.M. Tudor,

'Reginald of Durham and Saint Godric of Finchale: Learning and religion on a personal level', *Studies in Church History*, 17 (1981), pp. 37–48; G.G. Coulton, *Social Life in Britain from the Conquest to the Reformation*, Cambridge, 1919, pp. 415–20; Tyerman (1988), pp. 23–28.

3. Tyerman (1988), pp. 24–25.
4. For Godric's early life, see Reginald of Durham (2022), pp. 42–49.
5. Reginald of Durham (2022), pp. 46–47.
6. Or 'Hanapol'. For a discussion of the place name, see Reginald of Durham (2022), p. 48 n.39.
7. Reginald of Durham (2022), pp. 48–51.
8. He may also have had trading links with Brittany. Reginald of Durham (2022), p. 56 n.61.
9. Reginald of Durham (2022), pp. 56–61. For Godric's other maritime skills, see Reginald of Durham (2022), pp. 232–37.
10. Reginald of Durham (2022), pp. 60–65.
11. Reginald of Durham (2022), pp. 64–71. For the second trip to Jerusalem, see Reginald of Durham (2022), pp. 102–11.
12. Note that some sources suggest a far less plausible figure of 700: it is unlikely that there were that many knights in the entire kingdom at this time. AA, pp. 640–41; M. Brett, 'The battles of Ramla (1099–1105)', in V. Vermeulen and D. De Smet (eds), *Egypt and Syria in the Fatimid, Ayyubid and Mamluk Eras, Proceedings of the 1st, 2nd and 3rd Colloquium: Orientalia Lovaniensia Analecta 72*, Louvain, 1995, pp. 24–25; FC, pp. 167–69; Tibble (2018), pp. 242–43.
13. Guibert of Nogent, *Gesta Dei per Francos*, tr. R. Levine, Woodbridge, 1997, pp. 148–49; AA, pp. 644–45 and p. 645 n.21.
14. AA, pp. 640–41.
15. AA, pp. 640–43.
16. FC, p. 169; AA, pp. 642–45; WT, I, pp. 445–46; William of Malmesbury, *Gesta Regum Anglorum: The history of the English kings*, vol. 1, ed. and tr. R.A.B. Mynors, completed by R.M. Thomson and M. Winterbottom, Oxford, 1998, pp. 466–67.
17. Barber (2012), p. 70.
18. AA, pp. 646–49 and 800–01; FC, pp. 167–71; Edgington (2019), pp. 137 and 148 n.29; J.H. Pryor, 'From dromon to galea: Mediterranean bireme galleys AD 500–1300', in J. Morrison (ed.), *The Age of the Galley*, London, 1995, pp. 101–16.
19. As with so much medieval history, it is hard to be absolutely certain about the details. Understandably, not all academics are convinced that Saint Godric the English ship's captain and Godric the English pirate, both operating in the eastern Mediterranean at around this time, are the same person. Tyerman (1988), pp. 23–28 is doubtful. Margaret Coombe is also dubious – see Reginald of Durham (2022), p. 102 n.186 and pp. ix–xxvi. She correctly points out that Godric is said to have undertaken at least part of his second journey to Jerusalem on foot (though presumably he took passage across the Mediterranean), and that the chronology presented by the aged hermit is uncertain.
20. J. Sarnowsky, 'The military orders and their navies', in J. Upton-Ward (ed.), *The Military Orders* vol. IV, *On Land and by Sea*, London, 2008, p. 41.
21. Sarnowsky (2008), pp. 42–43.
22. Sarnowsky (2008), pp. 48 and 52–56.

23. P. Lehr, *Pirates*, London, 2019, p. 16; J. Heers, *Barbary Corsairs: Warfare in the Mediterranean, 1480–1580*, London, 2003, pp. 28–30.

24. Crusader Pirates

1. Qal, p. 108.
2. Qal, p. 108.
3. Qal, p. 108.
4. AA, pp. 760–61.
5. AA, pp. 766–67.
6. Qal, pp. 121–22.
7. Qal, p. 125.
8. AA, pp. 848–49.
9. AA, pp. 848–49.
10. AA, pp. 850–51.
11. AA, pp. 850–51.
12. Usama, pp. 93–95. The port of Jubail was also known as Gibelet. William may alternatively have had connections with the Frankish manor at Al-Jib. He was probably a burgess rather than a knight, and possibly a Frank rather than of Genoese extraction, if only because Usama (who knew these distinctions) did not specifically define him as such. But his background is very uncertain. For this, and the legal implications of this anecdote in the context of Roman law, see T. Karlovic, 'On the role of Roman law in the crusader states: Allocation of risk and the ransom of captives', in T.K. Nielsen and K.V. Jensen (eds), *Legacies of the Crusades, Proceedings of the Ninth Conference of the Society for the Study of the Crusades and the Latin East, Odense, 27 June – 1 July 2016*, Turnhout, 2021, pp. 95–114.
13. Usama, p. 94.
14. Usama, pp. 94–95.
15. Legally, of course, the important distinction lay in the status of the one woman whom Usama had already bought but not paid for (and who was thus at Usama's risk), compared to that of the thirty-seven others whom he had not bought (and who were thus still at William's risk). Caveat emptor!
    Karlovic (2021), pp. 98–99.
16. Usama, p. 191.
17. Usama, pp. 191–93; Usamah Ibn-Munqidh (1929), pp. 210–12.

25. Muslim Corsairs

1. Tibble (2020), pp. 28–65. For galleys in a hot climate, access to fresh water for their crews was the single most important logistical prerequisite.
2. Tibble (2020), pp. 224–25 and 254–58.
3. JP, p. 112.
4. JP, pp. 112–13.
5. JP, p. 113.
6. JP, p. 113.
7. JP, p. 113.
8. JP, p. 154.
9. Edbury and Gaggero (2023), I, pp. 305–06 and 386–87; II, pp. 213–14.

10. IA, III, p. 29.
11. IA, III, p. 29.
12. IA, III, p. 29.

26. Vikings on Crusade

1. This was Sigurd Jorsalafari, or Jerusalemfarer, king of Norway, reigned 1103–1130. R.W. Unger, 'The northern crusaders: The logistics of English and other northern crusader fleets', in J.H. Pryor (ed.), *Logistics of Warfare in the Age of the Crusades*, Aldershot, 2006, pp. 251–74; Snorri Sturluson, *Heimskringla: History of the kings of Norway*, tr. L.M. Hollander, Austin, TX, 1964, pp. 688–99; Theodoricus Monachus, *Historia de antiquitate regum Norwagiensium*, tr. D. and I. McDougall, Exeter, 2006, pp. 52–53.
2. Snorri Sturluson (1964), p. 689.
3. Unger (2006), p. 252.
4. Unger (2006), p. 252.
5. Tibble (2020), pp. 28–65.
6. AA, pp. 798–801.
7. AA, pp. 800–01.
8. FC, p. 199.
9. AA, pp. 804–05.
10. Qal, pp. 106–07.
11. FC, p. 200.
12. FC, p. 200.
13. FC, p. 199.
14. AA, pp. 804–05; Qal, p. 107.
15. Snorri mistakenly says 1110. Snorri Sturluson (1964), p. 696.
16. Unger (2006), p. 255; J. France, *Victory in the East: A military history of the First Crusade*, Cambridge, 1994, pp. 215–16; Tyerman (1988), pp. 19–20.
17. A.R. Lewis, 'Northern European sea power and the Straits of Gibraltar, 1031–1350 AD', in W.C. Jordan, B. McNab and T.F. Ruiz (eds), *Order and Innovation in the Middle Ages: Essays in Honor of Joseph R. Strayer*, Princeton, NJ, 1976, pp. 139–64.
18. Unger (2006), pp. 260–61 and 266.
19. Rose (1999), pp. 573–74.
20. Unger (2006); AA, pp. 158–61, 230–33 and 476–79; France (1994), p. 217.
21. AA, pp. 158–61, 230–33 and 476–79.
22. AA, pp. 158–61, 230–33 and 476–79.
23. AA, pp. 476–79.
24. AA, pp. 230–33.
25. AA, pp. 232–33.
26. AA, pp. 478–79.
27. AA, pp. 366–67; J.H. Pryor, 'A view from a masthead: The First Crusade from the sea', *Crusades*, 7 (2008), pp. 106–10.
28. Lehr (2019), pp. 34–35; *Orkneyinga Saga: The history of the earls of Orkney*, tr. H. Pálsson and P. Edwards, London, 1978, pp. 155–60.
29. Joinville, p. 267.

27. The Pirate Prince and the First Sea Lords

1. WT, II, p. 277.
2. WT, II, p. 253.
3. WT, II, p. 254.
4. WT, II, pp. 254 and 276; *The Chronicle of Michael the Great* (2013), p. 181.
5. WT, II, p. 254.
6. Matthew of Edessa (1993), p. 272.
7. Or possibly 1161. *The Chronicle of Michael the Great* (2013), p. 186. Cyprus, being on attractive but dangerous shipping lanes, continued to be a target for pirates. In 1302, for instance, Greek pirates raided Cyprus and carried off Guy of Ibelin and other members of his family from his country residence at Episcopia. The prisoners were later freed once ransoms had been paid. *The Chronicle of Amadi* (2015), pp. 232–33.
8. Barber (2012), pp. 214–15 and 267–68; C. Hillenbrand, 'The imprisonment of Reynald of Châtillon', in C.F. Robinson (ed.), *Texts, Documents and Artifacts: Islamic studies in honour of D.S. Richards*, Leiden, 2003, pp. 79–102.
9. A. Mallett, 'A trip down the Red Sea with Reynald of Châtillon', *Journal of the Royal Asiatic Society*, Third Series, 18:2 (2008), pp. 141–53.
10. M. Milwright, 'Reynald of Châtillon and the Red Sea expedition of 1182–3', in N. Christie and M. Yazigi (eds), *Noble Ideals and Bloody Realities: Warfare in the Middle Ages*, Leiden, 2006, pp. 236–38.
11. Mallett (2008), pp. 141–53; Milwright (2006), p. 238.
12. Milwright (2006), p. 238.
13. Milwright (2006), pp. 238–39; Lyons and Jackson (1982), pp. 185–88.
14. Mallett (2008), pp. 146–50.
15. Mallett (2008), pp. 146–50.
16. Mallett (2008), pp. 142–43.
17. WT, II, pp. 288–89.
18. WT, II, pp. 291–92.
19. WT, II, p. 292.
20. WT, II, p. 292; Barber (2012), p. 215.
21. WT, II, pp. 220–21.
22. WT, II, pp. 221–22.
23. WT, II, pp. 221–22.
24. WT, II, p. 222.
25. WT, II, p. 223.
26. WT, II, p. 223.
27. WT, II, p. 223.
28. WT, II, pp. 218, 220 and 223.
29. IA, II, pp. 130–31.
30. *The Chronicle of Michael the Great* (2013), p. 184. Ibn al-Athir and Michael the Syrian believed (almost certainly incorrectly) that Gerard's revolt took place in 1161.
31. *The Chronicle of Michael the Great* (2013), p. 184.
32. H.E. Mayer (ed.), *Die Urkunden der Lateinischen Könige von Jerusalem*, 4 vols, Altfranzösische Texte erstellt von Jean Richard, Monumenta Germaniae Historica, Hanover, 2010, vol. I, pp. 462–64.

33. Philip of Novara (2009), pp. 254 and 261–65; John of Ibelin (2003), pp. 307–08; Barber (2012), p. 236; *The Chronicle of Michael the Great* (2013), p. 184.
34. *The Chronicle of Michael the Great* (2013), p. 184.
35. Gerard seems to have died c.1171.

Bibliography

Primary sources

Albert of Aachen, *Historia Ierosolimitana*, ed. and tr. S.B. Edgington, Oxford, 2007

Ambroise, *The History of the Holy War*, ed. and tr. M. Ailes and M. Barber, Woodbridge, 2003

Baha al-Din Ibn Shaddad, *The Rare and Excellent History of Saladin*, tr. D.S. Richards, Crusade Texts in Translation 7, Aldershot, 2001

Barber, M. and K. Bate (eds), *The Templars*, Manchester Medieval Sources, Manchester, 2002

Bernard of Clairvaux, *In Praise of the New Knighthood*, tr. M.C. Greenia, Piscataway, NJ, 2000

Bird, J., E. Peters and J.M. Powell (ed. and tr.), *Crusade and Christendom: Annotated documents in translation from Innocent III to the fall of Acre, 1187–1291*, Philadelphia, PA, 2013

The Chronicle of Amadi, tr. N. Coureas and P.W. Edbury, Nicosia, 2015

The Chronicle of Michael the Great, Patriarch of the Syrians, tr. R. Bedrosian, Long Branch, NJ, 2013

Chronicles of Qalāwūn and his Son al-Ashraf Khalīl, tr. D. Cook, Abingdon, 2020

Cook, D. (ed. and tr.), *Baybars' Successors: Ibn al-Furāt on Qalāwūn and al-Ashraf*, Farnham, 2020

Coulton, G.G., *Social Life in Britain from the Conquest to the Reformation*, Cambridge, 1919

Crawford, P. (ed.), *The 'Templar of Tyre': Part III of the 'Deeds of the Cypriots'*, Crusade Texts in Translation 6, Aldershot, 2016

Crusader Syria in the Thirteenth Century: The Rothelin Continuation of the history of William of Tyre with part of the Eracles or Acre text, tr. J. Shirley, Aldershot, 1999

Dengler, M. (ed.), *The Book of Charlatans – Jamal al-Din 'Abd al-Rahim al-Jawbari*, tr. H. Davies, New York, 2020

BIBLIOGRAPHY

Edbury, P.W. and M. Gaggero (eds), *The* Chronique d'Ernoul *and the* Colbert-Fontainebleau Continuation *of William of Tyre*, 2 vols, Leiden, 2023

Fink, H. (ed.), *Fulcher of Chartres, A History of the Expedition to Jerusalem, 1095–1127*, tr. F. Ryan, Knoxville, TN, 1969

'The First and Second Crusades from an anonymous Syriac chronicle', tr. A.S. Tritton and H.A.R. Gibb, *Journal of the Royal Asiatic Society of Great Britain and Ireland*, 1 (1933), pp. 69–110

Genoa and the Twelfth-century Crusades, tr. M. Hall and J. Phillips, Crusade Texts in Translation 24, Farnham, 2013

Gerald of Wales, *Opera*, ed. J.S. Brewer, 8 vols, RS, London, 1861–91

— *The Journey through Wales and the Description of Wales*, tr. L. Thorpe, Harmondsworth, 1978

Guibert of Nogent, *Gesta Dei per Francos*, tr. R. Levine, Woodbridge, 1997

Hillenbrand, C. (ed. and tr.), *A Muslim Principality in Crusader Times: The early Artuqid state*, Leiden, 1990

Ibn al-Athir, *The Chronicle of Ibn al-Athīr for the Crusading Period from al-Kāmil fī'l-ta'rīkh*, parts 1, 2 and 3, tr. D.S. Richards, Crusade Texts in Translation 13, 15 and 17, Aldershot, 2006, 2007, 2008

Ibn al-Furat, *Ayyubids, Mamluks and Crusaders: Selections from the Tarikh al-Duwal wa'l-Muluk of Ibn al-Furat*, 2 vols, ed. and tr. U. Lyons, M.C. Lyons and J.S.C. Riley-Smith, Cambridge, 1971

Ibn al-Qalanisi, *The Damascus Chronicle of the Crusades*, tr. H.A.R. Gibb, London, 1932

Ibn Fadlan, *Ibn Fadlan's Journey to Russia: A tenth-century traveler from Baghdad to the Volga River*, tr. R.N. Frye, Princeton, NJ, 2005

John of Ibelin, *Le Livre des Assises*, ed. P.W. Edbury, Leiden, 2003

Joinville and Villehardouin: Chronicles of the crusades, tr. C. Smith, London, 2008

Kemal ed-Din, 'La chronique d'Alep', in *Recueil des historiens des croisades, Historiens orientaux*, vol. 3, Paris, 1872, pp. 571–690

King, E.J., *The Rule Statutes and Customs of the Hospitallers 1099–1310*, London, 1934

Matthew of Edessa, *Armenia and the Crusades, Tenth to the Twelfth Centuries: The Chronicle of Matthew of Edessa*, tr. A. Dostourian, Lanham, MD, 1993

Mayer, H.E. (ed.), *Die Urkunden der Lateinischen Könige von Jerusalem*, 4 vols, Altfranzösische Texte erstellt von Jean Richard, Monumenta Germaniae Historica, Hanover, 2010, vol. I

Odo of Deuil, *De profectione Ludovici VII in Orientem*, ed. and tr. V.G. Berry, New York, 1948

Orkneyinga Saga: The history of the earls of Orkney, tr. H. Pálsson and P. Edwards, London, 1978

Philip of Novara, *Le Livre de Forme de Plait*, ed. and tr. P.W. Edbury, Nicosia, 2009

Pilgrimage to Jerusalem and the Holy Land, 1187–1291, tr. D. Pringle, Crusade Texts in Translation 23, Farnham, 2012

Raymond d'Aguilers, *Historia Francorum Qui Ceperunt Iherusalem*, tr. J.H. and H.H. Hill, Philadelphia, PA, 1968

Reginald of Durham, *The Life and Miracles of Saint Godric, Hermit of Finchale*, ed. and tr. M. Coombe, Oxford, 2022

BIBLIOGRAPHY

— *Libellus de Vita et Miraculis S. Godrici Heremitae de Finchale*, ed. J. Stevenson, Surtees Society, Durham, 1847

Roger of Howden, *The Annals of Roger de Hoveden*, vol. II, tr. H. Riley, 1853

— *Chronica*, vol. III, ed. W. Stubbs, RS 51, London, 1870

Rohricht, R. (ed.), *Regesta Regni Hierosolymitani 1097–1291*, Innsbruck, 1893

The Rule of the Templars: The French text of the rule of the Order of the Knights Templar, tr. J.M. Upton-Ward, Woodbridge, 1992

Snorri Sturluson, *Heimskringla: History of the kings of Norway*, tr. L.M. Hollander, Austin, TX, 1964

The Syriac Chronicle of Michael Rabo (The Great), tr. M. Moosa, Teaneck, NJ, 2014

Theodoricus Monachus, *Historia de antiquitate regum Norwagiensium*, tr. D. and I. McDougall, Exeter, 2006

The Travels of Ibn Jubayr, tr. R.J.C. Broadhurst, London, 1952

Upton-Ward, J.M. (ed. and tr.), *The Catalan Rule of the Templars: A critical edition and English translation from Barcelona, Archivo De La Corona De Aragón, Cartes Reales, MS. 3344*, Woodbridge, 2003

Usama Ibn-Munqidh, *The Book of Contemplation*, tr. P.M. Cobb, London, 2008

Usamah Ibn-Munqidh, *An Arab-Syrian Gentleman and Warrior in the Period of the Crusades: Memoirs of Usāmah Ibn-Munqidh*, tr. P.K. Hitti, Princeton, NJ, 1929

Walter the Chancellor's the Antiochene Wars, tr. T.S. Asbridge and S.B. Edgington, Crusade Texts in Translation 4, Aldershot, 1999

Wilkinson, J. (ed. and tr.), *Jerusalem Pilgrimage, 1099–1185*, Hakluyt Society, series II, 167, London, 1988

William of Malmesbury, *Gesta Regum Anglorum: The history of the English kings*, vol. 1, ed. and tr. R.A.B. Mynors, completed by R.M. Thomson and M. Winterbottom, Oxford, 1998

William of Tyre, *A History of Deeds Done beyond the Sea*, tr. E.A. Babcock and A.C. Krey, 2 vols, Records of Civilization, Sources and Studies 35, New York, 1943

Secondary sources

Ayalon, D., 'Discharges from service, banishments and imprisonments in Mamluk society', in D. Ayalon, *The Mamluk Military Society: Collected studies*, V, London, 1979, pp. 40–45

Bacharach, J.L., 'African military slaves in the medieval Middle East: The cases of Iraq (869–955) and Egypt (868–1171)', *International Journal of Middle East Studies*, 13 (1981), pp. 471–95

Barber, M., *The Crusader States*, London, 2012

Barrow, G.W.S., *The Anglo-Norman Era in Scottish History: The Ford Lectures delivered in the University of Oxford in Hilary Term 1977*, Oxford, 1980

Beihammer, A.D., *Byzantium and the Emergence of Muslim-Turkish Anatolia, ca. 1040–1130*, Abingdon, 2017

Binysh, B., 'Give me three good reasons for a Muslim to end a crusade: Saladin and the Third Crusade', in T.K. Nielsen and K.V. Jensen (eds), *Legacies of the Crusades, Proceedings of the Ninth Conference of the Society for the Study of the Crusades and the Latin East, Odense, 27 June – 1 July 2016*, Turnhout, 2021, pp. 73–93

Bishop, A.M., 'Criminal law and the development of the assizes of the crusader Kingdom of Jerusalem in the twelfth century', PhD thesis, University of Toronto, 2011

— 'Usama ibn Munqidh and crusader law in the twelfth century', *Crusades*, 12 (2013), pp. 53–65

Boas, A.J., *Crusader Archaeology: The material culture of the Latin East*, London, 1999

— *Archaeology of the Military Orders: A survey of the urban centres, rural settlement and castles of the military orders in the Latin East (c.1120–1291)*, London, 2006

— 'Three stages in the evolution of rural settlement in the Kingdom of Jerusalem during the Twelfth Century', in I. Shagrir, R. Ellenblum and J. Riley-Smith (eds), *In Laudem Hierosolymitani: Studies in crusades and medieval culture in honour of Benjamin Z. Kedar*, Aldershot, 2007, pp. 77–92

— *Domestic Settings: Sources on domestic architecture and day-to-day activities in the crusader states*, Leiden, 2010

— 'Domestic life in the Latin East', in A.J. Boas (ed.), *The Crusader World*, Abingdon, 2016, pp. 544–67

Boulton, D'A.J.D., *The Knights of the Crown: The monarchical orders of knighthood in later medieval Europe, 1325–1520*, New York, 1987

Brett, M., 'The battles of Ramla (1099–1105)', in V. Vermeulen and D. De Smet (eds), *Egypt and Syria in the Fatimid, Ayyubid and Mamluk Eras, Proceedings of the 1st, 2nd and 3rd Colloquium: Orientalia Lovaniensia Analecta 72*, Louvain, 1995, pp. 17–37

— 'The Near East on the eve of the crusades', in J. Stuckey (ed.), *The Eastern Mediterranean Frontier of Latin Christendom*, Farnham, 2014, pp. 285–302

Burns, R.I., 'Piracy as an Islamic-Christian interface in the thirteenth century', *Viator*, 11 (1980), pp. 165–178

Butler, S.M., *The Language of Abuse: Marital violence in later medieval England*, Leiden, 2007

Claverie, P.-V., 'Stephen of Mezel bishop of Famagusta and his age (1244–1259)', in M. Walsh, T. Kiss and N. Coureas (eds), *Crusader to Venetian Famagusta: 'The Harbour of all the Sea and Realm'*, Budapest, 2014, pp. 41–52

Cobb, P.M., *Usama ibn Munqidh: Warrior poet of the age of crusades*, Oxford, 2005

— *The Race for Paradise: An Islamic history of the crusades*, Oxford, 2014

Coureas, N., 'Animals and the law: A comparison involving three thirteenth-century legal texts from the Latin East', in S. Edgington and H. Nicholson (eds), *Deeds Done Beyond the Sea, Essays on William of Tyre, Cyprus and the Military Orders presented to Peter Edbury*, Abingdon, 2014, pp. 135–44

Dadoyan, S.B., *The Fatimid Armenians: Cultural and political interaction in the Near East*, Leiden, 1997

Dean, T., *Crime in Medieval Europe 1200–1550*, Harlow, 2001

— 'Domestic violence in medieval Bologna', *Renaissance Studies*, 18:4 (2004), pp. 527–43

Dedeyan, G., 'Le rôle politique et militaire des Arméniens dans les états croisés pendant la premiere partie du XIIe siècle', in H.E. Mayer (ed.), *Die Kreuzfahrerstaaten als multikulturelle Gesellschaft*, München, 1997, pp. 153–63

Edbury, P.W., *John of Ibelin and the Kingdom of Jerusalem*, Woodbridge, 1997

— 'The *Assises de Jérusalem* and legal practice: The political crisis in Cyprus in the early fourteenth century', in J. Devard and B. Ribémont (eds), *Autour des Assises de Jérusalem*, Paris, 2018, pp. 143–58

Eddé, A.-M., *Saladin*, tr. J.M. Todd, London, 2011

Edgington, S.B., *Baldwin I of Jerusalem, 1100–1118*, Abingdon, 2019

El-Azhari, T., *Zengi and the Muslim Response to the Crusades: The politics of jihad*, Abingdon, 2016

Ellenblum, R., *Frankish Rural Settlement in the Latin Kingdom of Jerusalem*, Cambridge, 1998

— *The Collapse of the Eastern Mediterranean: Climate change and the decline of the east 950–1072*, Cambridge, 2012

— 'Demography, geography and the accelerated Islamisation of the eastern Mediterranean', in I. Katznelson and M. Rubin (eds), *Religious Conversion: History, Experience and Meaning*, Farnham, 2014, pp. 61–80

Epstein, S.A., *Purity Lost: Transgressing boundaries in the eastern Mediterranean, 1000–1400*, Baltimore, MD, 2006

Finch, A. ' Women and violence in the later Middle Ages: The evidence of the officiality of Cerisy', *Continuity and Change*, 7 (1992)

— 'The nature of violence in the Middle Ages: An alternative perspective', *Historical Research*, 70 (1997), pp. 243–68

Folda, J., *Crusader Manuscript Illumination at Saint-Jean d'Acre: 1275–1291*, Princeton, NJ, 1976

Forey, A.J., 'The military orders and the ransoming of captives from Islam (twelfth to early fourteenth centuries)', *Studia Monastica*, 33 (1991), pp. 259–79

— 'Desertions and transfers from military orders (twelfth to early fourteenth centuries)', *Traditio*, 60 (2005), pp. 143–200

France, J., *Victory in the East: A military history of the First Crusade*, Cambridge, 1994

— 'Surrender and capitulation in the Middle East in the age of the crusades', in J. France (ed.), *Warfare, Crusade and Conquest in the Middle Ages*, Farnham, 2014, pp. 73–84

— *Hattin*, Oxford, 2015

Friedman, Y., *Encounter between Enemies: Captivity and ransom in the Latin Kingdom of Jerusalem*, Leiden, 2002

— 'Peacemaking: perceptions and practices in the medieval Latin east', in C. Kostick (ed.), *The Crusades and the Near East: Cultural histories*, Abingdon, 2011, pp. 229–57

Goitein, S.D., *A Mediterranean Society*, vol. 4, *Daily Life*, Berkeley, CA, 1983

Hamblin, W.J., 'The Fatimid army during the early crusades', PhD thesis, University of Michigan, 1985

Hamilton, B., *The Latin Church in the Crusader States: The Secular Church*, London, 1980

— 'The crusades and north-east Africa', in S. John (ed.), *Crusading and Warfare in the Middle Ages*, Farnham, 2014, pp. 167–79

Harari, Y., 'The military role of the Frankish Turcopoles: A reassessment', *Mediterranean Historical Review*, 12:1 (1997), pp. 75–116

Heather, P., *The Fall of the Roman Empire*, London, 2005

— *Empires and Barbarians*, London, 2009

Heers, J., *Barbary Corsairs: Warfare in the Mediterranean, 1480–1580*, London, 2003

Hillenbrand, C., 'The career of Najm al-Din Il-Ghazi', *Der Islam*, 58 (1981), pp. 250–92

— *The Crusades: Islamic perspectives*, Edinburgh, 1999

— ' "Abominable acts": The career of Zengi', in J. Phillips and M. Hoch (eds), *The Second Crusade: Scope and Consequences*, Manchester, 2001, pp. 111–32

— 'The imprisonment of Reynald of Châtillon', in C.F. Robinson (ed.), *Texts, Documents and Artifacts: Islamic studies in honour of D.S. Richards*, Leiden, 2003

Hodgson, N., 'Conflict and cohabitation: Marriage and diplomacy between Latins and Cilician Armenians, c.1097–1253', in C. Kostick (ed.), *The Crusades and the Near East: Cultural histories*, Abingdon, 2011, pp. 83–106

Holt, P.M., *The Age of the Crusades: The Near East from the eleventh century to 1517*, London, 1986

Housley, N., *Fighting For the Cross: Crusading to the Holy Land*, London, 2008

Irwin, R., *The Middle East in the Middle Ages: The early Mamluk sultanate 1250–1382*, London, 1986

— 'Usamah ibn Munqidh: An Arab-Syrian at the time of the crusades reconsidered', in J. France and W.G. Zajac (eds), *The Crusades and Their Sources*, Abingdon, 1998, pp. 71–88

— '"Futuwwa": Chivalry and gangsterism in medieval Cairo', in G. Necipoglu, D. Behrens-Abouseif and A. Contadini (eds), *Muqarnas*, vol. 21, *Essays in Honor of J.M. Rogers*, Leiden, 2004, pp. 161–70

Jackson, P., 'The crisis in the Holy Land in 1260', *English Historical Review*, 95:376 (1980), pp. 481–513

Jacoby, D., 'Aspects of everyday life in Frankish Acre', in *Crusades*, 4 (2005), pp. 73–105

Kaeuper, R.W., *War, Justice, and Public Order: England and France in the later Middle Ages*, Oxford, 1988

— *Chivalry and Violence in Medieval Europe*, Oxford, 1999

— *Holy Warriors: The religious ideology of chivalry*, Philadelphia, PA, 2009

— *Medieval Chivalry*, Cambridge, 2016

Karlovic, T., 'On the role of Roman law in the crusader states: Allocation of risk and the ransom of captives', in T.K. Nielsen and K.V. Jensen (eds), *Legacies of the Crusades, Proceedings of the Ninth Conference of the Society for the Study of the Crusades and the Latin East, Odense, 27 June – 1 July 2016*, Turnhout, 2021, pp. 95–114

Kedar, B.Z., 'On the origins of the earliest laws of Frankish Jerusalem: The canons of the Council of Nablus', *Speculum*, 74 (1999), pp. 310–35

Keegan, J., *A History of Warfare*, London, 1993

Keen, M., *Chivalry*, London, 1984

Kennedy, H., *Crusader Castles*, Cambridge, 1994

Kirk, G.E., 'Nine Men's Morris – Morelles – Muhlespiel in Palestine', *Journal of the Palestine Oriental Society* (1938), pp. 229–32

Kohler, M., *Alliances and Treaties between Frankish and Muslim rulers in the Middle East: Cross-cultural diplomacy in the period of the crusades*, tr. P.M. Holt, revised by K. Hirschler, Leiden, 2013

La Monte, J.L., *Feudal Monarchy in the Latin Kingdom of Jerusalem, 1099–1291*, Cambridge, MA, 1932

Lapina, E., 'Gambling and gaming in the Holy Land: Chess, dice and other games in the sources of the crusades', *Crusades*, 12 (2013), pp. 121–32

Lehr, P., *Pirates*, London, 2019

Lev, Y., 'Regime, army and society in medieval Egypt, 9th–12th centuries', in Y. Lev (ed.), *War and Society in the Eastern Mediterranean, 7th–15th Centuries*, Leiden, 1997, pp. 115–52

BIBLIOGRAPHY

Lewicka, P.B., *Food and Foodways of Medieval Cairenes: Aspects of life in an Islamic metropolis of the eastern Mediterranean*, Leiden, 2011

Lewis, A.R., 'Northern European sea power and the Straits of Gibraltar, 1031–1350 AD', in W.C. Jordan, B. McNab and T.F. Ruiz (eds), *Order and Innovation in the Middle Ages: Essays in Honor of Joseph R. Strayer*, Princeton, NJ, 1976, pp. 139–64

Lewis, K.J., *The Counts of Tripoli and Lebanon in the Twelfth Century: Sons of Saint-Gilles*, London, 2017

Lloyd, S.D., *English Society and the Crusade, 1216–1307*, Oxford, 1988

Loiseau, J., 'Frankish captives in Mamlūk Cairo, 1291–1350', *Al-Masāq*, 23:1 (2011), pp. 37–52

Luttrell, A., 'Intrigue, schism, and violence among the hospitallers of Rhodes: 1377–1384', *Speculum*, 41:1 (1966), pp. 30–48

Lyons, M.C. and D.E.P. Jackson, *Saladin: The politics of the holy war*, Cambridge, 1982

MacEvitt, C., *The Crusades and the Christian World of the East: Rough tolerance*, Philadelphia, PA, 2008

MacLellan, R., 'An Egyptian Jew in King Edward's court: Jewish conversion, Edward II, and Roger de Stanegrave', *Crusades*, 19 (2021), pp. 143–53

Major, B., *Medieval Rural Settlements in the Syrian Coastal Region (12th and 13th Centuries)*, Oxford, 2016

Mallett, A., 'A trip down the Red Sea with Reynald of Châtillon', *Journal of the Royal Asiatic Society*, Third Series, 18:2 (2008), pp. 141–53

— *Popular Muslim Reactions to the Franks in the Levant, 1097–1291*, Farnham, 2014

Mathews, K.R., 'Mamluks and crusaders: Architectural appropriation and cultural encounter in Mamluk monuments', in S. Lambert and H. Nicholson (eds), *Languages of Love and Hate: Conflict, communication, and identity in the medieval Mediterranean*, Turnhout, 2012, pp. 177–200

Mayer, H.E., 'Two crusaders out of luck', *Crusades*, 11 (2012), pp. 159–71

Mikulski, R.N.R., Schutkowski, H., Smith, M.J., Doumet-Serhal, C., Mitchell, P.D., 'Weapon injuries in the crusader mass graves from a 13th century attack on the port city of Sidon (Lebanon)', *PLoS ONE*, 16:8 (2021), e0256517 https://doi.org/10.1371/journal.pone.0256517

Milwright, M., 'Reynald of Châtillon and the Red Sea expedition of 1182–3', in N. Christie and M. Yazigi (eds), *Noble Ideals and Bloody Realities: Warfare in the Middle Ages*, Leiden, 2006, pp. 235–59

Mitchell, P.D., *Medicine in the Crusades: Warfare, wounds and the medieval surgeon*, Cambridge, 2004

— 'The torture of military captives in the crusades to the medieval Middle East', in N. Christie and M. Yazigi (eds), *Noble Ideals and Bloody Realities: Warfare in the Middle Ages*, Leiden, 2006, pp. 97–118

— 'Violence and the crusades: Warfare, injuries and torture in the medieval Middle East', in C. Knüsel and M. Smith (eds), *A History of Human Conflict: Osteology and traumatized bodies from earliest prehistory to the present*, New York, 2013, pp. 251–62

Morton, N., 'Encountering the Turks: The first crusaders' foreknowledge of their enemy; some preliminary findings', in S. John (ed.), *Crusading and Warfare in the Middle Ages*, Farnham, 2014, pp. 47–68

— *Encountering Islam on the First Crusade*, Cambridge, 2016

— *The Field of Blood*, New York, 2018

BIBLIOGRAPHY

Murray, A.V., *The Crusader Kingdom of Jerusalem: A dynastic history 1099–1125*, Oxford, 2000

Nicholson, H., 'Knights and lovers: The military orders in the romantic literature of the thirteenth century', in M.C. Barber (ed.), *The Military Orders*, vol. 1, *Fighting for the Faith and Caring for the Sick*, Aldershot, 1994, pp. 340–45

— 'Before William of Tyre: European reports on the military orders' deeds in the East, 1150–1185', in H. Nicholson (ed.), *The Military Orders*, vol. 2, *Welfare and Warfare*, Aldershot, 1998, pp. 111–18

— *The Everyday Life of the Templars: The Knights Templar at home*, Stroud, 2017

Nicolle, D., 'Ain al Habis: The Cave de Sueth', *Archéologie medievale*, 18 (1988), pp. 113–40

— *Saracen Faris 1050–1250 AD*, London, 1994

— *Crusader Castles in the Holy Land 1097–1192*, London, 2004

— *Crusader Warfare*, vol. II, *Muslims, Mongols and the Struggle against the Crusades*, London, 2007

Oldfield, P., 'The use and abuse of pilgrims in northern Italy', in K. Hurlock and P. Oldfield (eds), *Crusading and Pilgrimage in the Norman World*, Woodbridge, 2015, pp. 139–56

Olympios, M., 'Amanieu son of Bernard, count of Astarac, *Croisé Manqué?* Deconstructing the myth of an eighteenth-century crusader', in S. Edgington and H. Nicholson (eds), *Deeds Done Beyond the Sea, Essays on William of Tyre, Cyprus and the Military Orders presented to Peter Edbury*, 2014, pp. 145–54

Peacock, A.C.S., *The Great Seljuk Empire*, Edinburgh, 2015

Phillips, J., *Defenders of the Holy Land: Relations between the Latin East and the West, 1119–1187*, Oxford, 1996

— *The Life and Legend of the Sultan Saladin*, London, 2019

Pinker, S., *The Better Angels of Our Nature: Why violence has declined*, London, 2011

Pringle, D., 'Crusader Jerusalem', *Bulletin of the Anglo-Israel Archaeological Society*, 10 (1990–91), pp. 105–13

— *The Churches of the Crusader Kingdom of Jerusalem: A corpus*, 4 vols, Cambridge, 1993–2009

— 'Templar Castles on the Road to the Jordan', in *The Military Orders*, vol. 1, *Fighting for the Faith and Caring for the Sick*, ed. M. Barber, Aldershot, 1994, pp. 148–66

— *Secular Buildings in the Crusader Kingdom of Jerusalem: An archaeological gazetteer*, Cambridge, 1997

— 'Templar Castles Between Jaffa and Jerusalem', in *The Military Orders*, vol. 2, *Welfare and Warfare*, ed. H. Nicholson, Aldershot, 1998, pp. 89–109

Pryor, J.H., 'From dromon to galea: Mediterranean bireme galleys AD 500–1300', in J. Morrison (ed.), *The Age of the Galley*, London, 1995, pp. 101–16

— 'A view from a masthead: The First Crusade from the sea', *Crusades*, 7 (2008), pp. 87–151

Riley-Smith, J., *The Feudal Nobility and the Kingdom of Jerusalem 1174–1277*, London, 1973

— 'Peace never established: The case of the Kingdom of Jerusalem', *Transactions of the Royal Historical Society*, 1978, pp. 87–102

— *The Crusades: A history*, third edition, London, 2014

— 'An army on pilgrimage', in S.B. Edgington and L. Garcia-Guijarro (eds), *Jerusalem the Golden: The origins and impact of the First Crusade*, Turnhout, 2014, pp. 103–06

BIBLIOGRAPHY

Rose, S., 'Islam versus Christendom: The naval dimension, 1000–1600', *Journal of Military History*, 63:3 (1999), pp. 561–78

Runciman, S., 'The visit of King Amalric I to Constantinople in 1171', in B.Z. Kedar, H.E. Mayer and R.C. Smail, *Outremer: Studies in the history of the crusading Kingdom of Jerusalem presented to Joshua Prawer*, Jerusalem, 1982, pp. 153–58

Sarnowsky, J. 'The military orders and their navies', in J. Upton-Ward (ed.), *The Military Orders* vol. IV, *On Land and by Sea*, London, 2008, pp. 41–56

Schenk, J.G., 'Nomadic violence in the first Latin Kingdom of Jerusalem and the military orders', *Reading Medieval Studies*, 36 (2010), pp. 39–55

Skoda, H., *Medieval Violence: Physical brutality in northern France, 1270–1330*, Oxford, 2013

Talmon-Heller, D., 'The cited tales of the wondrous doings of the Shaykhs of the Holy Land by Diya' al-Din Abu 'Abd Allah Muhammad b. 'Abd al-Wahid al-Maqdisi (569/1173–643/1245): Text, translation and commentary', *Crusades*, 1 (2003), pp. 111–54

Talmon-Heller, D. and B.Z. Kedar, 'Did Muslim survivors of the 1099 massacre of Jerusalem settle in Damascus? The true origins of the al-Salihiyya suburb', *Al-Masaq*, 17:2 (2005), pp. 165–69

Theotokis, G., *Byzantine Military Tactics in Syria and Mesopotamia in the Tenth Century: A comparative study*, Edinburgh, 2018

Tibble, S., *Monarchy and Lordships in the Latin Kingdom of Jerusalem, 1099–1291*, Oxford, 1989

— *The Crusader Armies*, London, 2018

— *The Crusader Strategy*, London, 2020

— *Templars: The knights who made Britain*, London, 2023

Tricht, F.V., 'Who murdered Archbishop William of Rouen (1217)? – The valley of Philippi under Latin rule (1204–c.1224)', *Jahrbuch der Österreichischen Byzantinistik*, 70 (2020), pp. 305–34

—, 'The duchy of Philippopolis (1204–c. 1236/7): A Latin border principality in a Byzantine (Greek/Bulgarian) milieu', *Crusades*, 21 (2022), pp. 91–120

Tudor, V.M., 'Reginald of Durham and St Godric of Finchale: A study of a twelfth-century hagiographer and his major subject', PhD thesis, Reading University, 1979

— 'Reginald of Durham and Saint Godric of Finchale: Learning and religion on a personal level', *Studies in Church History*, 17 (1981), pp. 37–48

Tyerman, C.J., *England and the Crusades*, Chicago, IL, 1988

— 'Who went on crusade to the Holy Land?', in B.Z. Kedar (ed.), *The Horns of Hattin*, London, 1992, pp. 13–26

— *God's War: A new history of the crusades*, London, 2006

Unger, R.W., 'The northern crusaders: The logistics of English and other northern crusader fleets', in J.H. Pryor (ed.), *Logistics of Warfare in the Age of the Crusades*, Aldershot, 2006, pp. 251–74

Vryonis, S. Jr., 'Byzantine circus factions and Islamic futuwwa organisations', in S. Vryonis (ed.), *Byzantium: Its internal history and relations with the Muslim world – Collected studies*, London, 1971, pp. 46–59

Warren, W.L., *Henry II*, London, 2000

Widell, M., 'Historical evidence for climate instability and environmental catastrophes in northern Syria and the Jazira: The chronicle of Michael the Syrian', *Environment and History*, 13 (2007), pp. 47–70

Index

INDEX

INDEX

INDEX